THUS SPAKE

MAGNUS DICTUS

The Collected Writings of
JAKE STRATTON-KENT
from The Equinox: British Journal of Thelema
1988-1994

THUS SPAKE MAGNUS DICTUS
Copyright © 1988-1994, 2020 Jake Stratton-Kent
Cover design by Dis Albion.
The texts here were first published by Kiblah Publishing, ISSN 0953-7015.
This edition published by Hadean Press.
West Yorkshire
www.hadeanpress.com

ISBN 978-1-907881-97-8

Jake Stratton-Kent has asserted his moral right to be identified as the author of this work.

All rights reserved. No portion of this book may be reproduced by any means without the permission in writing of the publisher, except in cases of short passages for purposes of review and citation.

MAGNUS NOMINATIONS FOR THE COMING YEAR

Once more it is the season in which persons propose nominations for the prestigious MAGNUS Award!!!!
Who will be the lucky recipient of this coveted prize this year?
Nominations, as usual, in the following exciting categories:

Nominations of Individuals:

1. Religious Bigot of the First Pressing.
2. Conspicuous Thelemic Saint.
3. Citizen of the Republic of Genius. (Awarded posthumously.)
4. Occult Fossil Find.
5. Defiler of the Hermetic Mystery.
6. Harmless Eccentric.
7. Dangerous Right Wing Mystic.
8. Totally Utterly Unknown Secret Chief.
9. Persons Whose Names Must Be Said Backwards Lest The Force Unleashed... etc. etc.
10. Consorter with Fictional Sludge Monsters.
11. Ye Child that was to Come.
12. Pompous Old Philistine.

And for Organisations:

1. Babylon Of the Seven Hills.
2. Masonic Banking Achievements.
3. Relic Rustling.
4. And shall these winds be so mighty as to lay low the hills?
5. Silliest Name/Oddest Beliefs.
6. Drab Or Detestable Orthodoxy.
7. Most Successful Imaginary Entity.
8. True Possessors of the Apostolic Succession.
9. Brilliant Front for Something Else.

Contents

Author's Foreword	7
Publisher's Introduction	9
Liber Longus Verbosicon (Magnus Dictus)	11
The English Qaballa (Jake Stratton-Kent)	23
Liber Trigrammaton (Althotash)	31
What is a Qabalah? (Jake Stratton-Kent)	45
Thelema and Wicca (Jake Stratton-Kent writing as Kelvin Boyland)	48
Mantras and Spells (Anton K Jettstrake)	51
Blood and Guts – Part 1. (Jake Stratton-Kent)	53
The Trees of Eternity (Asharat)	56
Qaballa for the Querulous (Asharat)	60
Qaballa for the Quizzical (Asharat)	67
Mantras and Spells (Anton K Jettstrake)	69
Qaballa for Quibblers (Asharat)	73
Magnus Dictus II (Magnus Dictus)	74
Mantras and Spells (Jake Stratton-Kent)	85
Blood and Guts Two. The Reckoning (Jake Stratton-Kent)	87
Every Woman is a Star (Sophie Zumm)	88
Jottings (Althotash)	89
A Word to Say (Smallus Printus)	90
Mantras & Spells (Anton K Jettstrake)	92
Return of Blood & Guts (Jake Stratton-Kent)	95
Liber Achad (Jake Stratton-Kent)	98
DIY Thelemic Fundamentalism (Von Hutten)	101
The Headless One (Jake Stratton-Kent)	102
Magnus Rides Roughshod (Magnus Dictus)	117
A Sethian Ritual (Jake Stratton-Kent)	123
Higher than Eyesight (Asharat)	125
Qaballistic Magick (Jake Stratton-Kent)	132
Wakanaba Kamea Extrapolator! (Tau Magnus)	150
The Cipher of AL (Jake Stratton-Kent)	151
AL.II.76 and the Lunar Mansions (Tau Magnus)	157
Reviews	161

Author's Foreword

DO NOTHING WHICH IS OF NO USE
Miyamoto Musashi

IT HAS long been in my mind to present an unsuspecting public with a 'Collected Magnus Dictus', but the redoubtable Erzebet of Hadean press came up with an even better idea. Thus we have here a collection of my articles, reviews and other exuberance from *Equinox-BJT* 1-8, under my own name and a whole assortment of aliases. Aliases were a feature of the previous volume (Jim Lees' *The New Equinox* Volume 6), where he frequently wrote under the names of various members of his group of the time (most notably Carol Lees, who was thus credited with discovering EQ in his place). My aliases here are much more randomly generated, though Kelvin Boyland certainly was a beloved brother at the time; but Anton K. Jettstrake is an obvious anagram, while magical names and other forms of aka also appear here. Nor should the names on the contents page be taken as an exhaustive list; for one thing misbehaving under assumed names is a predilection I do not restrict to the printed page. One or two of them indeed have taken on a life of their own (no spoilers)!

The reasons for publishing are various, one being that it amuses my editor, but as the quotation heading this blurb makes clear, everything has a purpose; sometimes more than one. Some of the influences on Magnus being further away in time now than then, so that his take casts new light in the present, is another. Meanwhile the reader should be warned that a vein of ironic and satyric humour runs through much of this material, which for the most part has aged well, and will hopefully sharpen the wits of a new generation of readers, another legitimate excuse for this collection. One exception is the use of the term 'Radical Traditionalism', now exclusively associated with Far Right Occultism (if any kind of political extremism can really be termed 'occult') At the time of writing it was solely connected with John Michell, who was not remotely of that persuasion; I have since abandoned the term in favour of 'Living Traditionalism', which still says what I want it to say. My review of Mssr Schicklegruber's hack work, similarly, should not be misread as an endorsement; I wouldn't piss in his ear if his non-existent brains were on fire.

Thus clarified, I present the collected rantings of a younger

Publisher's Introduction

HEREIN ARE the writings of Jake Stratton-Kent first published in *The Eqiunox: British Journal of Thelema* issues 1-8, spanning the years 1988-1994 and faithfully reproduced in a facsimile edition. There were other gems in this *Equinox*; Jake co-authored pieces of great value, but for this collection we chose to only reprint those works solely written by Jake under either his given name, or one of his numerous pseudonyms including the legendary Magnus Dictus.

The reason for this is simple. Jake Stratton-Kent has gone on to become one of the leading figures in occulture (whether he likes it or not). His writings have changed the face of modern magical practices, centering goetia and fostering a healthy, working relationship with the spirits of the grimoires. He cuts an unmistakable figure at occult events, where his bombastic personality coupled with his walking stick and handbag have seen an end to philanderers and agitators. Online, he will strike down your thesis as readily as he will share his hard-earned knowledge. This gleeful 'take no prisoners' attitude shines through these early works, which hearken back to a time when one could have a laugh with the great mysteries and not everything or everyone was *so serious*.

Some of the material has since been reprinted; an edited version of 'The Headless One' was republished as a Hadean Press Guide to the Underworld in 2012. The Tables of A.M.E.N. have likewise made their appearance elsewhere, most notably in *The Serpent Tongue: Liber 187*, and the Wakanaba Kamea Extrapolator has been expanded upon in *Grimoire of the Sixfold Star*, another Guide to the Underworld ascribed to Count Abaka who is of course none other than JSK himself.

The essays are listed in the order in which they were originally published. In addition, Jake reviewed everything from periodicals to books and pamphlets; these reviews appeared at the back of each issue beginning with issue 2 while here they have been given their own chapter. On page 27 we made one correction to the original file and replaced "Holy Guardian Angel" with "Secret Name" (Holy Guardian Angel does not = 165), but the essays are otherwise reproduced here exactly as they were printed in *The Equinox: British Journal of Thelema* (minus some copyrighted illustrations).

In closing, we are extremely grateful to Jake for allowing us to republish this early material. We expect the audience for this book to be those already familiar with Jake's work, but if you have come across this book with no previous knowledge of the author, you can do no better than look at the catalogues of Scarlet Imprint and Hadean Press for his more recent book-length works. Strap in and enjoy the ride.

Erzebet Barthold & Dis Albion
Hadean Press

Liber Longus Verbosicon

Few things frighten anyone more than the truth about themselves. This bugbear is so abhorrent that it is invisible; the mind refuses to see it. It is evasive, ever shifting, ever changing. Truth is general as well as detailed. Details contradict generalisations, they do not disprove them, e.g. a miser may share his tobacco.

We are inconsistent, and though we would be very boring individuals if we always retained the same point of view, it is necessary to be able to do so for the purposes of philosophy. So, first precept of philosophy - MAN, KNOW THYSELF. Know the trends of thy nature AND the exceptions. The average guru-infatuated mystic, having acute indigestion after forcing oriental food down his occidental throat, reads "KNOW THYSELF" as "GNAW THYSELF"; he "transcends the ego" by wallowing in self-hate. Actually, this is useful because by so doing (i.e. by concentrating on our faults) we become aware, blindingly so in fact, of the good qualities of our fellows. All we need do next is "LOVE OURSELVES", as we should our neighbours, to see just how inadequate and insecure everyone else is, as well as ourselves.

Nevertheless, self-hate is a great hindrance to self-knowledge, no matter how potentially useful it may or may not be in understanding others. Self-hatred makes suppositions with a tendency to stagnation, or worse yet, to decomposition. Fortunately though, in this "Book of Long Words" I am generous enough to write with the insecure, though sophisticated, Western occult philosopher in mind. My book is, after all, the creation of such a mind, reflecting its content and experience.

The Self is elusive as an ancient and wily pike, and when surprised in its watery lair, is hardly recognisable as your own reflection snarling at you from the depths. "What is this monster?" you exclaim; (a dear friend assured me that this must be the Lurker on the Threshold and not the Angel at all) and the answer comes: "I am the Truth you have sought without wishing to find." "This is good", you tell yourself, "unconscious desire is all-attractive", and so it is. Now embrace the Terror. Be assured, it is a God, not a devil; devils never come alone, and this Terror is unique, apart, supremely solitary; even you cannot bear His Presence; this Doppelganger is HE!

Conquer fear and embrace the Terror as a virgin bride her hairy groom! The attitude of surrender, passive, open to His Monstrous Virility: His plaything, His concubine and His choir-boy.

This is that which is written: "Subdue thy fear and thy disgust". You feared Him, and it made you pathetic, love Him and thou shalt be HE! Yes, He is HE, and what are you but His vehicle, His Vessel.

All this talk of Him, of God, may offend our dogmatic sisters, but be assured, I choose my words carefully. The sisters are fortunate; assuming men are attractive to them, they can achieve this union with the dread Angel, as above described more readily than our dogmatic brothers who think it sounds like my God is after their bottoms. Yes, brothers; you must be like woman to His maleness, even as the sisters. You have limited yourselves, denied yourselves much, till you are inferior to the Self that is truly Thee. To unite yourself with that which is superior you must be passive.

Of those socialist-mystics who deny up and down, inferior and superior: I have had my bellyful of your doctrine; now try mine, or perish! Let me remind you, from my hearts fountain of generosity; that which I have written I write again:

> "We would be very boring individuals if we always retained the same
> point of view; but it is necessary to be able to do so for the
> purposes of philosophy."

By which I mean Occult Philosophy in particular, so shut up and concentrate.

There should be a word, without resorting to low German or alternative qabalistic contrivances, with a meaning including all the following ideas, or long words: EMPIRICAL PRAGMATIC IDEALISM. There would then be no trouble digesting my ideas, which are pre-digested ideas, my little chicks, thus allowing me to flap off to another branch. There may in fact be such a word, known to me but concealed from you until you get out your dictionaries and look up all three of those long words and their roots and derivatives.

I suspect you noticed, in two or even all three cases, that these words imply someone whose thought processes are dissimilar to those of dictionary compilers or other upright decent citizens.

Did you notice that you, and those citizens, lie about the way you think? You may like to think you are idealistic. You might think it's a bit soppy. But empirical, you? "Makes decisions based on experience, rather than theory", which, in a doctor, is considered a bad thing, but in others, sounds O.K., to at least half of you, yes? Pragmatism, though: "Decisions or methods should be judged by practical consequences", which attitude, in a policeman, is considered unethical, but may well be acceptable - to the oher half of my readership; or the other side of the reader!

We are not responsible for the horrors of this life; we need not be blasé, neither need we be depressed to the point of obsession. OBSESSION = A FIXATION. Let me repeat again: "WE WOULD BE VERY BORING INDIVIDUALS IF WE ALWAYS RETAINED THE SAME POINT OF VIEW." Turning all tunes to one drone, explaining all by one monotonous truism.

People are frightened too easily. Afraid of the Bomb, AIDS, Jehovah, Astrology, the Devil, Death; Themselves most of all. Seek fear in yourself, not outside. The Fear of God is the Beginning of Wisdom.

Do I talk in riddles or slogans? What ears do you have? I speak verbose blasphemies, in my Book of Long Words, that none shall understand. Nor do I care that none shall understand. I speak of that which cannot be understood.

> "Truly there is no God but Man, no Goddess but Woman.
> She must resist the power of the Goddess.
> He must give in to the power of God.
> The God and the Goddess are one.
> She must give in to the power of God.
> He must resist the power of the Goddess.
> In the End it is all One.
>
> God is Love, yet I die
> God is Love, yet my son dies,
> God is Love, yet Love dies
> And I am God.
> I and the Earth are One
> Christ was a dying god
> There is no god but man
> MAN DIES."

Death is.

Napoleon was a great soldier. He made France great by killing lots of people.

Hitler was a great black magician. He became a new god by killing lots of people.

We are all gods; Hitler is a new god because people worship him. This is a superstition, similar to Christianity and Elvisism. We should not allow any fixed idea to dominate our thoughts in such a fashion. There are no old gods, because none existed before the worshippers who are all men and women. Men and women aren't old compared to anything apparently real and prehistoric (e.g. a dinosaur), so any god elected as such is new, comparatively.

I don't think killing people is great; maybe that's a limitation, I don't know.

But nevertheless, people do die, including me. Therefore I accept the Horror of our Here-and-Now Apocalypse and ask: "WHO AM I? WHAT'S GOING ON? HOW LONG HAVE I GOT?"

I've not been through a war and don't want to, I have, however, familiarised myself with the most perverse and objectionable things. A process known as Anathemism. I no longer fear or object to thoughts or images of the most appalling kind. I can accept even the necessity of death, individual or wholesale. The dead outnumber the living. My death will be no disaster. Death can be terrible, hideous, mine may well be. We rant and rave about the bomb, lung cancer, AIDS, yet how few refuse to drive cars on principle! Some may fear to enter through experience, but the "ban the internal combustion engine" lobby is not an obsession of contemporary man.

Fear always relates to the unknown, possibly even apparently immediate fear. For instance, what appears to be mere fear of pain is probably derived from fear of death. People may be extremely familiar with that which they fear, at least its symbol in the "real" world. A man may fear a machine he works with. But this is an obsession and much more may lie behind it than the horrors of mutilation. The cause of fear is ignorance. You do not know when you will die, even if you know you are dying.

There are people who resist evil in some particular form with at least as much integrity as I have, and I praise them for it. But I suspect these people have conquered their personal fear in order to resist it effectively on behalf of others. I may be whimsical but I consider such behaviour noble. I do not deride these people.

There are other people who can't see the woods for the trees. You know the type, the inconsistent hypocrites of this world. Let's list a few examples; there's sure to be a pet hate of every reader amongst them. I'm probably the pet hate of at least a proportion of you, or soon will be.

e.g.:
- a) Self-styled anarchists who are either racist, sexist or both.
- b) Rich socialists, unless they are also creative artists.
- c) Vocal vegetarians in leather.
- d) Reagan, when he talks about "state terrorism".

Now, to this so-called logical, materialistic, and rational real world, I say "PHOOEY!". All political doctrines are collectivist and I spit on the lot. All political movements require uniformity, and make decisions based on a mass conformist homogeneous lump, whether it's called the electorate or the proletariat or the chosen people or the master race. Who needs it? Not me.

I hate the proletariat, but not the working class, though I'm not one of them. I also hate socialists who think they will sound like the workers if they swear and grunt a lot. The cult of the cloth cap, the Geordie as a mythical divine being. It's bloody insulting, and if I was a worker I'd fucking resent it.

In place of this sham of normality, of pat explanations that explain nothing, the Holy Book of "Mein Kampf" or "Das Kapital", I prefer Empirical Pragmatic Idealism.

In my dictionary under "Ideality" it said: "the condition of being mental". I know what that means.

In the "Enochian Dictionary" *(1) the word for God is "MAD".

*(1) - not a racist text.

! !

LONG WORDS - Part II

This treatise will be incomprehensible to those who believe that conventional symbolism is unchangeable and essential.

It will be obscure and impenetrable to those who fail to understand the basic dictum.

NOTHING IS TRUE, EVERYTHING IS PERMITTED. *(2)

The basic principle of Magic is that the Universe is IRRATIONAL. There is no necessary link between one event and another. Chronology is only apparent; we do not necessarily see or hear things as they are or as they occur. An obvious example of this theory is the time-lapse between the sound of an explosion occurring and its reaching the ears of a distant listener, or the more enormous difference between the time at which light from Orion's belt set out towards us and the time at which we perceive it.

Our arrival at a given situation or idea is not necessarily due to any rational process. Therefore we need only believe briefly, not perpetually, in the framework of any given operation.

There is no inherent truth in any doctrine or theory, other than convenience in a situation which in itself is transient; e.g. Catholic opposition to contraception derives from a period when maximum birth-rate ensured "race survival".

*(2) "Nothing is true, everything is permitted" implies another axiom:
"If you can't handle it, tough luck!"

! !

THE DICE

The Cubic Stone, which possesses the power of transformation, has been adopted as a magickal weapon by exponents of the ZOS KIA CULTUS and mentioned in the writings of Louis T Culling. We refer to the Dice, which is marked thus: 1/2/3/4/5/6; the number of dots totals 21 or 0-21, as in the Tarot. For what it is worth, an attribution of the Tarot to these figures can be worked out very easily:

    1 THE MAGUS
    2 PRIESTESS, EMPRESS
    3 EMPEROR, HIEROPHANT, BROTHERS
    4 CHARIOT, JUSTICE, HERMIT, FORTUNE
    5 LUST, HANGED MAN, DEATH, ART, DEVIL
    6 TOWER, STAR, MOON, SUN, AEON, UNIVERSE

THE FOOL - 0, is he who throws the dice. The method of employing the oracle of the Cubic Stone is a matter of preference. A suggested method using one die is outlined below:

    1 SELF e.g. WHAT YOU WILL
    2 RELATION e.g. WHAT THEY WANT
    3 CREATION e.g. ongoing results of specific relationship
    4 STATION e.g. continuation, preservation
    5 CHANGE e.g. destruction, relocation, reduction
    6 WEALTH e.g. increase, expansion

Thus each face of the cube bears its own character, and we may select six possible futures appropriate to these aspects of CHANCE, and having thrown, act accordingly. This is not new, but the results of employing it will be a dramatically altered perspective. We give some examples below:

    1 Travel alone to a distant place / Keep quiet about situation
    2 Stay with present partner   / Tell all
    3 Write a book about people   / Get partner pregnant
    4 Rest until health improves   / Remain in present circumstances
    5 Murder my rival   / Remove myself to points North
    6 Get a job   / Learn art of casting & mouldmaking

Note 0-21 x 2 (i.e. 2 dice) = 42 : Major number of Enochian system. See Crowley's Vision and the Voice or the Hitch-hiker's Guide to the Galaxy for commentary.

Divination is chiefly useful for supplying a random scheme for us to utilise in making decisions. This is desirable to dispose of fixed ideas, make life more exciting and teach us to adapt rather than stagnate. The danger of divination is the surrender of individual will, which results through reliance on, or belief in, the dice rather than ourselves. It should therefore only be employed for a limited period, say daily for three weeks, to produce the necessary shake-up in our attitudes and circumstances; and thereafter either abandoned or restricted.

Axiom : THERE IS NO GOD BUT MAN

Problem: I am a man, but what about woman, is she the Goddess? If so, which one? Why? etc.? and what about men? What should be my attitude to them?
It is due to such considerations that I retain Astrology and the English Qaballa in my personal modus operandi. The symbols of the dice may be interpreted in terms of the philosophy and magick of Thelema:-

    1 THELEMITES WILL DO NO WRONG
    2 UNITE THE DIVIDED / REFUSE NOT THY WIFE
    3 IF THOU WILT / WHAT THOU WILT / HOW THOU WILT
    4 ALL IS EVER AS IT WAS
    5 LURK, WITHDRAW, UPON THEM / CHOOSE YE AN ISLAND / MERCY LET BE OFF
    6 I AND THE EARTH ARE ONE / RICH MAN FROM THE WEST / KINGS

Our definition of "King" includes Boy-Child / King / Dying-God (The only kind as far as I know, for all men die). But what of Queens? is there only A (=1) Queen, the Queen of Heaven (and elsewhere)? What is She? Do I need one? or many? Who is she? etc.? You can't create real people by a throw of the dice, only meet them, etc...
Therefore beware the foulnesse of Dyvinatory Arte, the creeping sludge of occultism. URGH!!

! !

MAGICK

The principles of Magick are embodied in certain major movements in human consciousness. We cite the most important social trends of the last several decades:

DEFINITION	REMARKS & EXAMPLES
"The New Sexuality"	
Experiments with drugs	
Tantric Yoga	(With Raja Yoga. These are exclusively occult compared with trendy "Yoga for Health" fads)
Underground Art	(The Avant Garde; Surrealist and Dadaist movements etc.)
Revolution	(Beyond mere political dogmatism, we reject Marxism, Anarchism, Fascism, and more respectable creeds such as Democracy, and Republicanism)

The ideals of Magick are embodied in the works of certain major figures, some of their followers and in particular the symbols by which these ideals are exemplified.

FIGURE	CONCEPTUAL TITLE	LATER DEVELOPMENTS	CENTRE
Crowley	Thelema	The English Qaballa	Liber AL
Spare	Zos Kia Cultus	Chaos Magick	Book of Pleasure
Blake	Albion	"Glastafarianism"	Corpus
Hitler	Mystical Nationalism	Odinism	Mein Kampf

Crowley and Spare are actually the more successful in occult terms, despite having died with less achievements in the material world than Blake, whose reputation was made in his lifetime, or Hitler, whose work was restricted to his lifetime and has suffered serious setbacks since. Our conclusion is that mystical nationalism, whether "romantic" like Blake's, or "demonic" like Hitler's, is doomed by its very definition. In other words, the nationalist sentiments restrict and stifle the otherwise potent magic. Thelema has succeeded despite Crowley's apparent "bourgeois" and racist persona; the message was more than the man.

The word which I concealed from you until now, so that those who did not know it would understand it better when I got around to it is: **CHAOS**

This word is Greek, and was originally used to describe a state of being before the coming of the first New God, who made things and explained them to those who believed in Him. In other words it belongs to the time when everyone knew that God is Man and Goddess is Woman. In fact, at that time, it would appear that everybody instinctively said feminine words first so that then I would have written: "Goddess is Woman, God is Man". Then it really was Ladies First. The chicken before the egg theory.

The Mythic Period of Man's History is not to be found "before the past", but throughout the entire fabric of time. The Heroic Age is Now! The myths change, evolve, adapt, but tendencies and archetypes prevail within a mobile hierarchy.

> **EXAMPLES:**
> Mars: The warrior archetype prevails in the form of the policeman amongst others.
> The Gothic Horror genre has created a whole new mythology within our culture in the last hundred years or so. The Infernal Hierarchy has entered the "Space Age".

They live within our consciousness, we all know them; thus they exist for us and personify forces at work within us. We may identify with an archetype at our own risk. The youth cults have become involved with very powerful archetypal forces. These energies can be self-destructive.

Once recognised or harnessed they can also be extremely creative. But there is always a glamour or fatal fascination in such things, particularly if the individual consciousness is submerged in the archetype and loses its own identity therein. The life of this unfortunate is troubled and unstable. It must be admitted, however, that it is often the brightest sparks that burn out soonest.

Empirical types make decisions based on experience; if the only exterior experience of CHAOS is drugs, crime or perversion, then the decision will be to do it whenever the incentive matches the expectation. If the only experience of CHAOS is religion, the decision is often identical. This decision has been popularised in the expression "Go for it !!". Having once experienced it, later decisions tend to reinforce the first, i.e. a pattern of behaviour is created. Herein is a great danger, because CHAOS is not external in origin; these are only outward forms. The motivation comes from the individual consciousness recognising an external image of an element of his own nature. The image need not be exact; no reflection is true. If the image is accepted in preference to the individuality, a new slavery often replaces an established one.

Nevertheless, countless new gods, saints and demons have been created by this sub-culture. It is beyond any doubt a more prolific and innovative creative force than anything offered by the status quo. Unfortunately, the status quo have also obtained considerable control of the media, into which this artificial Chaos has been absorbed.

The status quo wish us to worship a new god who prohibits the fulfilment of basic human needs; forbids the expression of human creativity. This god sets limits and all who conform worship Him. Worship makes Him strong, for many minds believe in Him; much of reality is influenced by the idea of Him. This influence may be a slight pressure or complete control of some areas of experience. Only experience exists for consciousness. We may not experience what the believers do, but we may be affected by their belief.

Believe what you like. In many areas, from Astrophysics to Love, anything might be true, and the rules need not remain the same.

Magicians have always known this. If this were not true we could never talk about things that are unknown. We have to use algebra to talk about unknown numbers, the answers to unsolved problems; although algebra is only something we made up that worked for the job. We even need different kinds of mathematics for different purposes. Nothing we believe need be believed in all the time. But, there may be beliefs so identical with our nature that to break them is to cease to be oneself. Even so, these beliefs do not affect everybody else necessarily, only our relations with them.

CHAOS is not the same as anarchy. CHAOS is about belief, not about hierarchy. CHAOS is Empirical Pragmatic Idealism. Empirical types go by experience; not by the voice of accepted authority, but this is not to say that they don't have authorities of their own.

> EXAMPLE: From experience I trust such and such a "discredited" expert.

> EXAMPLE: From experience certain ideas forbidden or criticised strongly by the status quo are useful or interesting to me; I therefore take an interest in all such ideas. And if the non-conformists and Bohemians amongst you don't approve of them, why are THEY so against these ideas as well?

> EXAMPLE: Hitler and the Nazis "appal" Democratic politicians as well as Anarchists and Socialists; even though they have much in common - or BECAUSE they do?

> EXAMPLE: Homosexuality "appals and disgusts" people on all sides of every social conflict.

> EXAMPLE: Occultism "frightens" or "amuses" all manner of orthodox types and rebellious elements.

Why are they so eager to condemn or to ridicule these very real things? In the hope that they will just go away if not believed in? Sorry fellows, as long as someone does believe then they exist! Ask Tinkerbell.
Fear stems from ignorance, or from ambiguous acquaintance, by which I mean a relationship to oneself which involves deceit. I hate you, because you are like myself and I don't want to face up to that. I recognise you, but I'm going to ignore you, bully you, and so on.

Pragmatic types choose methods that will work, despite unpleasant or unpopular short term consequences. They will work, that is to say, they will obtain the desired result, and everything else is unimportant.

> EXAMPLE: A pragmatic commander may decide to have refugees machine-gunned by aircraft to clear a road for his surface vehicles.

> EXAMPLE: A pragmatic politician may decide to adopt unpopular policies to deal with an emergency or a difficult situation.

Now, our experience of such behaviour might lead us to oppose it without understanding it. As far as we are concerned we are right to do so, because we don't like what it does to us or people we identify with. This may not always be the best way for us to react. In other words, we must ourselves be pragmatic in a very positive sense.

> EXAMPLE: A pragmatic politician decides to tax you and your group to benefit some other group which he supports. Empirical members of the victimised group will resent this; pragmatic members will consider opposition the correct response.

> EXAMPLE: A pragmatic leader of a pacifist group suggests privately that the accepted ethics of the group have to be suspended for tactical reasons, while not interfering with, or maybe even assisting the group's work, he considers it inadviseable to tell the general membership that two policemen on a particular junction might have to be roughed up to allow a march to get to its destination. Empirical types might waver; pragmatists won't.

The personalities of pragmatists are irrelevant, because they do not work on that level. Their decisions are independent of moral generalisations. "It's not nice, but it's necessary" is a pragmatic truism. "It's not legal, but I go for it" is an Empirical cliche.

✳

0 = 2 or NOTHING IS TRUE, EVERYTHING IS PERMITTED.

AXIOM: There is no reason whatsoever why any symbolic structure should be rigidly imposed on us by bygone authorities.

The orthodox version of the qabalah need not apply to current conditions. Ancient gods need not concern the city dweller of the twentieth or twenty-first centuries. The Tarot need not remain unaltered through the Ages.
Why hunt through dusty tomes for The Original most ancient and venerable teaching when it bears no relation to your situation?
What connection is there between the thought processes of a celibate, tee-total and Catholic occultist of 1066 A.D. and an unemployed, hedonistic and agnostic magician of 1989 A.D.? The honest answer is "None!" so overboard with tradition and convention.
In this dissertation, diabolical liberties have been taken with conventional symbolism; its scheme is derived from Qabalah and Astrology, but distinct alike from both.
The great failing of ancient magickal lore is its apparent reasonableness. A place for everything and everything in its place. The Tree of Life has been described as a filing cabinet; and the exhaustive nature of certain systems of correspondences suggests, ENTIRELY FALSELY, that there is some kind of natural order at work in the Universe. The popular view of modern science is similarly mistaken on this point; certainly there is an attractive pattern in molecular structures, but as Kepler discovered, there is no ratio between the "geometrical solids" and the proportions of the Solar system.
Science itself is unreasonable. It is a truism that all major breakthroughs in Physics, Chemistry and the rest are preceded by a mental disturbance, a cerebral aberration which we can name a Vision, a dream or revelation. The normal rational consciousness then sets to work explaining this bizarre extension of previous reality. In other words, the so-called scientific method of experiment and theoretical research is a sham.
If a Scientist is to express himself or herself successfully in his or her profession, he/she will do so through enjoyment of his/her work and through possessing an enquiring mind WHICH IS OPEN TO THE IRRATIONAL, i.e. to that which is unknown or occult until revealed by some event like those described above.

THAT WHICH HAS NOT BEEN CAN BE.
THAT WHICH IS NOT KNOWN CAN BE KNOWN.
THAT WHICH HAS NOT BEEN DONE CAN BE ACHIEVED.

Those things known and accepted in our "reality" (which is capable of drastic modification, absorbing new dimensions into its framework) may be subsumed under the numbers 1-10 or 0-9. The Tree of Life is the familiar ground plan in this role.

That which is yet to be (though its existence is less dynamic than its potential!) cannot be subsumed under those digits. Traditionally this concept of "things beyond our ken" is symbolised by the number 11.
Magick is concerned with Change, extensions of accepted conditions. Its number is Eleven. In the Qabalah the number Eleven represents the divider between three spheres beyond reason and seven apprehensible to our ordinary wakeday consciousness. This is an artificial and unwieldy approach; we suggest a new model as in Figure 2.

Figure 1
The Way of The Warrior

It will readily be seen that these pairs of planets represent potent magickal formulae.

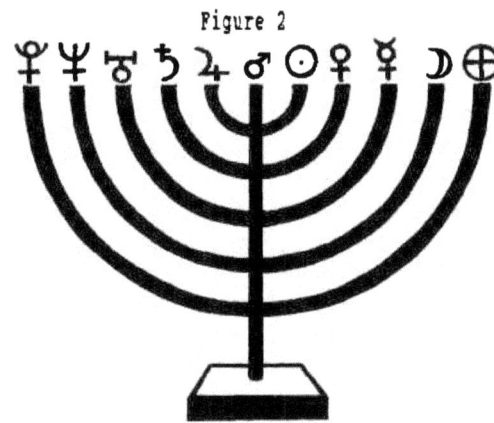

Figure 2

Pluto/Earth : "Kether is in Malkuth, and vice versa". The Body is transformed by sex & death; by sexual reproduction we create new forms, but sexuality can achieve other transformations more marvellous still. Death also transforms the Body. But see also that the other formulae are contained in this one, for all involve the Body to some extent.

Neptune/Moon : The Instinctive Drives of the Moon are sublimated into deeper perceptions of an Intuitive nature. This is the so-called "Passive Gnosis" whereby such instinctive functions as breathing are directed towards introspection and trance.

Uranus/Mercury : Uranus is "The Magician" of Holst's "Planets" suite; he is also the astrologer; while Mercury represents the Trickster or Juggler, and the Scholar. Deep Study or Abstraction or more vigorous pursuits such as Invokation and Talismanic Magic, High Ritualism etc. come under this heading.

Saturn/Venus : (Saturn: exalted in Libra, ruled by Venus, the Bright and Dark aspects of Her.) Emotional Impulses become Intuitive Knowledge and Understanding under the influence of Saturn (for instance, with the passing of time!).

Jupiter/Sun : The operations of the Knowledge and Conversation of the H.G.A.. The Perception of the Self as either King or Priest. The apparently static symbolism of Jupiter conceals the ability of the Self to identify with different conditions, to overreach the established parameters, and attain to the chameleon-like nature of the Adept.

Mars is the Divider.

The purpose of magickal endeavour is to control (or participate in) the processes of change or chance. Our ability to control to any great degree the forces that produce change in the world about us is apparently minimal. But in fact we possess the ability to totally revolutionise our lives, immediately. We can choose what experiences to pursue. If we cannot predict the outcome of our choice we can at least participate directly in the process of Chance. Chance is more accessible than Change. The traditional symbols here are the pack of cards and the dice. In such operations there is an element of risk. New realities are made available; new insights and new abilities are produced by necessity once these realities are entered.

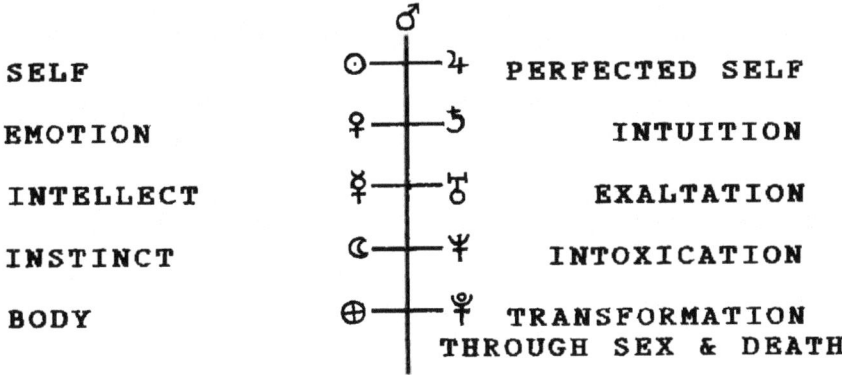

♂ REPRESENTS: MAN; THE MAGICIAN.   O = VOID;   ↗ = PHALLUS.

Figure 3

The Five Wheels and the Five Wheels.

The Operations of the Sun operate upon the Self, the object being to identify with - make Samadhi upon the so-called Higher Self or Holy Guardian Angel (H.G.A.). The Result is a Self able to assume any persona at will, non-attached to ideas. The "perfected man" is a static image thus false; the Perfections are Manifold.

The Operations of Venus operate upon the Emotions, which once understood confer powerful Intuitive faculties.

The Operations of Mercury operate upon the Intellect, overwhelming it by suitable means to overreach itself, attaining total identification with the idea and obtaining transcendent (i.e. original) knowledge. Genius.

The Operations of the Moon operate upon the Instinctive self (not through sedation or suppression necessarily), to obtain trances reaching beyond the present incarnation on experiential levels.

The Operations of the Earth operate upon the Body through the most direct media.

```
     SUN    / THROUGH THE SELF TO THE EVER BECOMING ONE / JUPITER
   VENUS    /     THROUGH EMOTION TO PURE INTUITION     / SATURN
 MERCURY    /      THROUGH INTELLECT TO EXALTATION      / URANUS
    MOON    /      THROUGH INSTINCT TO INTOXICATION     / NEPTUNE
   EARTH    /    THROUGH THE BODY TO TRANSFORMATION     / PLUTO
                        via SEX AND DEATH
```

ALL THESE ARE POSSIBLE TO HE WHO IS MASTER OF THE UPRIGHT AND THE AVERSE PENTAGRAMS.
HE IS THE WARRIOR WHO BEING ARMED AT ALL POINTS IS SIMILAR TO THE GODDESS.

Figure 4

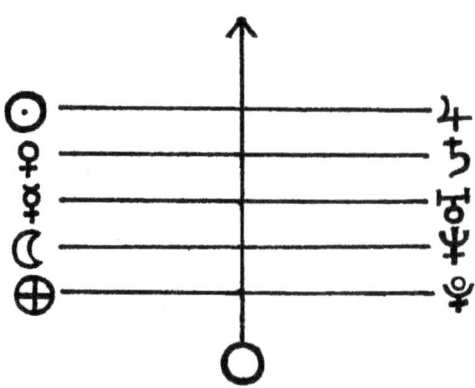

FIVE INITIATIONS. FIVE WOUNDS. "FIVE WHEELS AND THE FIVE WHEELS".

✷ Both these points of view fail when idealism is absent or diminished.

! !

FRAGMENT OF DIARY

Had a bath this morning, thinking of the perspective of an extraterrestrial examining the planet. Particularly in our relation to other animals.
He would note that we have an opposable thumb, and enough "learn by experience"-ness to master the planet over a period of so many tens of thousands of years. But as he flew above "the face of the Earth" (seeing every creature that flew, swam, crept, or walked on the face of the Earth, Sea, Air, etc.) he would not say: "Humans live in cities and animals outside them"; that is the human view. He would say that man and the other mammals, reptiles, birds and fishes lived in their respective habitats upon the planet.
I overcame the illusion of distinction between my species and others.
The Face of the Earth, where all the inhabitants of the planet make their dwellings, is the Countenance of Nature which looks upon the Countenance of God, face to face.
We live here, as embodied spirits, but are humans the only microcosms here? Are humans true microcosms? All conscious life is holy. All consciousness is life, life is holy.
Having attained this vision do I forbid myself meats? If I do, do I distinguish myself from the beasts? Let me ponder this.
Consciousness is the attribute of deity, which all possess, there is no exterior god. So are the animals religious? Culling thinks so and I imagine so. Neanderthal man was deeply religious, and his first magical act (funerary rites) may have caused the evolutionary leap "overnight" into Cro-Magnon man; hence no missing link.
This evolutionary power is inherent in beasts whose consciousness is finely attuned to the environment. If they could perform rites based on this knowledge, with the allowance for such factors as instinctive astro-biological clocks to choose a propitious moment for the rite, then new species could be produced.
The new species produced by Neanderthal magic was Cro-Magnon man. The spirits of "N-man" initiates reincarnated in more sophisticated vehicles, becoming "C-man". N-man then died out.
Have other species performed such rapid evolutionary jumps? I think not, and yet many species have been subjected to man; at one time this served a purpose for the animals too, for they benefited from this association. This is no longer the case. Mass consumption of meat, neglect of pets, and slaughter for vanity, sport or profit, have reduced the possibility of animals benefiting from human "protection" to nearly zero. Meanwhile man's perception of his environment is diminishing in direct proportion to our increasing stupidity. The jaded palate of mass-production man does not appreciate nature's wonders. No Sunset stirs the Philistine producer/consumer's heart, no celestial vision wakes him to knowledge that an Universe exists beyond his feeble senses. He does not believe in magic, in much the same way that pop fans do not believe in the beauty of classical music. It is beyond him, beyond huge statistical lumps of the world's population. Lost through neglect: our clairvoyant faculties, our religious instincts, our sense of wonder, our SOULS! We are evolving backwards, reverting into something we never were; blind Flatland slugs, having no perception of the greater reality.
Except in our baths!

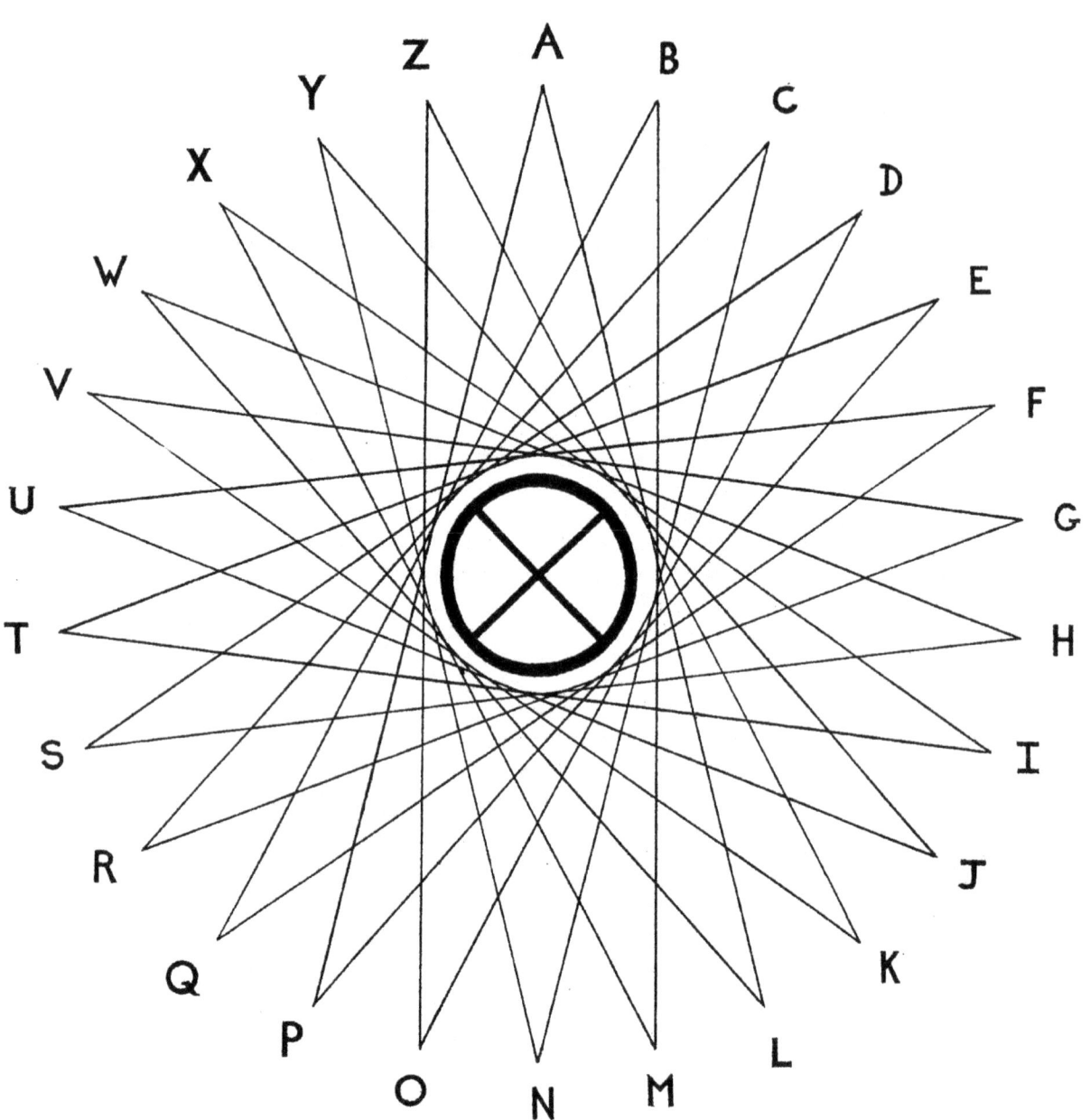

THE ENGLISH QABALLA

```
A  L  W  H  S  D  O  Z  K  V  G  R  C
1  2  3  4  5  6  7  8  9  10 11 12 13

N  Y  J  U  F  Q  B  M  X  I  T  E  P
14 15 16 17 18 19 20 21 22 23 24 25 26
```

Readers of "The New Equinox/British Journal of Magick (Volume 5 Numbers 1 to 5 and Volume 6 Number 1) will remember the exegesis of **AL** through the English Qaballa. Due to the pause in publication (and the certainty that there are more Thelemites than issues of those magazines, no matter how widespread the distribution), it has been decided that a resume of the E.Q. should precede any further revelations by means of it.

Firstly, the English Qaballa is a qabalah and not a system of numerology. A qabalah is specifically related to three factors: one, a language; two, a "holy" text or texts; three, mathematical laws at work in these two.

A fuller description of "a qabalah" will be published in a future issue of this journal. Suffice it to say for now that the language in question is English and the texts the Class A or Holy Books of Thelema, particularly the Book of the Law.

The appearance of the English Qaballa is specifically predicted in Liber **AL**, and certain conditions, clues, and even frameworks are delineated, none of which had been satisfactorily dealt with until the discovery of E.Q.. It was above all necessary that such a key should make sense of the cipher of Chapter II verse 76; two enigmatic lines of "numbers and words":

> "4 6 3 8 A B K 2 4 ALGMOR 3 Y X 24 89 RPSTOVAL.
> What meaneth this, o prophet? Thou knowest not; nor shalt thou know ever. There cometh one to follow thee: he shall expound it."

When I first had my attention drawn to the existence of a purported English Qaballa, my first reaction as a qabalist was to use it on this meaningless string of digits and characters. I converted all the letters into their numerical equivalents in the E.Q., and added them to the numbers in the series.

```
4  6  3  8  A  B   K  2  4  A  L  G   M   O  R   3   Y = 129
4  6  3  8  1  20  9  2  4  1  2  11  21  7  12  3  15

   X   24  89  R   P   S  T   O  V   A  L = 222
   22  24  89  12  26  5  24  7  10  1  2
```

$$129 + 222 = 351$$

The numbers 129 and 222 bear interesting qualities for a qabalist. However, I was not studying a manuscript copy but a printed text, which did not separate the series into two lines; consequently I simply added up the total of both lines at that time and obtained the number 351. This number is the sum of the numbers 1 to 26, and naturally the sum of the numbers attributed to the letters in English Qaballa.

Since that time I have frequently studied this cipher in the manuscript version of Liber AL, and have obtained a mental picture of it, consisting of two lines as it appears in the original. There are seventen numbers and letters in the first line and eleven in the second (both significant numbers) but in the manuscript the "X" at the beginning of line two looks like a multiplication symbol so I made this calculation; 17 x 11 = 187, the numerical value of the phrase "ENGLISH ALPHABET".

Which brings me to Chapter II verse 55, another key verse of Liber AL in which that phrase occurs:

> "Thou shalt obtain the Order & Value of the English Alphabet; thou shalt find new symbols to attribute them unto."

This is a strange verse, containing ambiguity and apparent faults in grammar. What is meant by "them"? "English Alphabet" is a single whole; the text does not say "the letters of the English Alphabet" (or does it?). So "them" must refer to "Order & Value".

This is interesting as a qabalistic "in-joke", because the phrase "ORDER & VALUE" = 117 = "LETTERS"; so in fact the sentence can be read: "Thou shalt obtain the <letters> of the English Alphabet; thou shalt find new symbols to attribute them unto."

Jokes like that can unhinge a man after a while. This is not funny, because in the '93' Current "there ain't no Sanity Clause"; there is however a "prodigal son" or "bad fairy" clause, and the front contender for this role is undoubtedly Austin Osman Spare, the prodigal son of the '93' Current.

AOS, as we shall refer to him, discovered independently of Crowley that the English Language is possessed of all the necessary qualities of a hieratic language. (All occultists know what one of those is, don't they? Yes, it's a language used by priests and magicians for their holy books and rituals etc, because it possesses qabalistic and magical virtue.) AOS used the English Alphabet in various ways. He found "new symbols" which constituted his "Alphabet of Anon"; he combined the original characters (A,B,C, a,b,c, etc.) into sigils; and among other things he reversed and jumbled syllables and words to obtain spoken spells. All these things practical qabalists and magicians have done with earlier hieratic languages such as Hebrew, Arabic, Coptic and Greek.

AOS, as a result, was one of the first to prove the Book of

the Law literally correct in its claims concerning the magickal virtue of the English Alphabet. He did not deal with its qabalistic virtues except in terms of the practical qabalah. But then he WAS a prodigal son! Those were in any case the earliest days of our not-so-new-now Aeon. Now we have become a tradition rather than a revolution, and that is a good thing; occultists function better as preservers and developers.

In fact, the '93' Current is so well preserved that in some areas development seems almost heretical; but nevertheless, the E.Q. is a development, eleven years old and acid resistant, water-tight and possessed of enough potency to stop the most determined qabalist in his tracks, exclaiming, "EUREKA! - someone's found it!"

It is impossible in the space available to develop even a fraction of the E.Q. interpretation of the Book of the Law. What we can do is present the techniques and publish a fully enumerated "Book of the Law", with the numerical values of words and phrases "between the lines". All known qabalistic methods can be applied to the Class A texts with E.Q., particularly Gematria, but also Notariqon, Temura, and 'Mystic' numbers, (being the sum of the integers from 1 to a significant number, inclusive, usually in the two digit range; for instance 351 is the 'mystic' number of the English Alphabet/26). Theosophical Addition (the practice of adding the digits of a number together, as 21 = 2 + 1 = 3, thus interrelating the symbolism of these two numbers, and reducing composite numbers to simple and fundamental numbers), planetary and numerical symbolism can also be used to interpret numbers and words; i.e. "76" can be interpreted as (7)-Venus (6)-Sun, thus 76 indicates a relationship between Sun and Venus; or "165" can be read as (1)-the Unity (65)-of the Goddess ("GODDESS" = 65 by E.Q.). "65" in the Hebrew Qabalah represents Adonai, the Holy Guardian Angel, while in E.Q. 165 = "Secret Name".

Where a number has a 1 on both sides of it, as in 111, 121, 131 etc., this number indicates a power acting in balanced manifestation (e.g. 141 = "ELEMENTS", "CONTINUOUS").

An additional technique, described in earlier Equinoxes, is technically known as "counting well", a reference to Liber **AL** "Count well its name and it shall be to you as 718". In this technique, every letter of one word is added to every letter of another word, e.g.:-

```
            S = 5         U = 17        N = 14
            -----         ------        ------
M = 21 +  5 = 26     + 17 = 38     + 14 = 35
I = 23 +  5 = 28     + 17 = 40     + 14 = 37
D =  6 +  5 = 11     + 17 = 23     + 14 = 20
N = 14 +  5 = 19     + 17 = 31     + 14 = 28
I = 23 +  5 = 28     + 17 = 40     + 14 = 37
G = 11 +  5 = 16     + 17 = 28     + 14 = 25
H =  4 +  5 =  9     + 17 = 21     + 14 = 18
T = 24 +  5 = 29     + 17 = 41     + 14 = 38
------------------------------------------------
       TOTALS = 166 + 262 + 238 = 666
------------------------------------------------
         AZURE % LIDDED = 718
         ABRAHAD % ABRA = 418
```

(Note we use the glyph "%" to represent "counted well".) Once one is possessed of these techniques (and it must be admitted that a computer is a very handy, though by no means indispensible, item), the purely theoretical side of the English Qaballa is your oyster. Even so, it must be emphasised that there is enough material available, after even a superficial examination of Liber **AL** through the Qaballa, to reveal outlines of a practical magickal system beyond any known before.

This system interrelates certain dominant trends of Thelemic occultism. It does so on a very sophisticated level, which requires commitment, experience and resourcefulness of its exponents. Ideally, these exponents should work together, contributing their various skills; and some of them at least must possess Qaballistic and Astrological skills developed to a fine degree.

PLUTO = 76	ARIES = 66	EARTH = 66
NEPTUNE = 145	TAURUS = 76	
URANUS = 66	GEMINI = 117	
SATURN = 73	CANCER = 78	FIRE = 78
JUPITER = 143	LEO = 34	
MARS = 39	VIRGO = 63	
FORTUNA = 93	LIBRA = 58	
VENUS = 71	SCORPIO = 93	
MERCURY = 115	SAGITTARIUS = 146	
MOON = 49	CAPRICORN = 121	
	AQUARIUS = 95	
	PISCES = 97	
SUN = 36		AIR = 36
		WATER = 65

The above table should go some way to emphasise the importance of astrological skills; whilst it should be noted that not all of the above words occur in Class A texts, they are English words by adoption and are fundamental to the nature of the texts.

This table is worth thorough examination and committing to memory. Note that the sum of the planetary values is 813, which those with knowledge of the Hebrew Qabalah will recognise as the value of the word "ARARITA"; the word of the HOLY HEXAGRAM which is used to invoke the planetary forces.

If we subtract 36, the value of "SUN", or Self at the centre, we have a number describing the system he experiences: 813 - 36 = 777.

777 - Traditionally the number of the Flaming Sword or creative Lightning Flash of the Qabalists which, when overlain on the Tree of Life, touches each Sephira in turn and certain paths, with a total value of 777.

777 - The Goddess in Triple Form ISIS-BABALON-NUIT.

777 - The ultimate extension of the perfect number (7), itself a symbol of wholeness and completion.

JAKE STRATTON-KENT

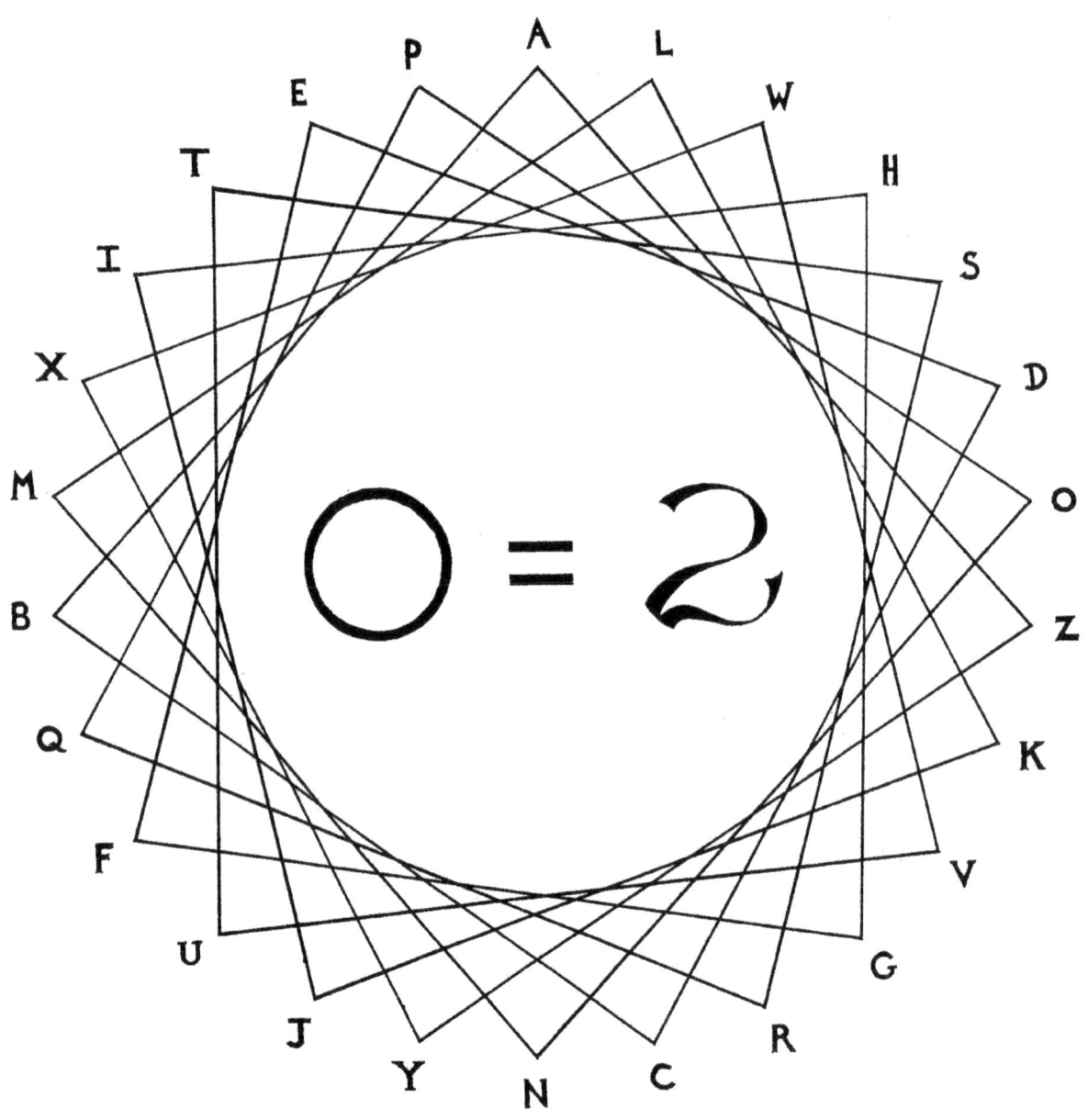

LIBER TRIGRAMMATON

●
  ●
    ●

```
Here is Nothing under its three forms.  ˙P=470   It is not,
 66  28    97     74   52    90            47 28 45
```

```
˙C=120  yet informeth all things.  ˙C=298
          64      148    5    81   ˙P=418
```

˙Verse = 888

A = ZERO : THE FOOL

The first sentence is particularly significant; its seven words (suggesting the seven-lettered first word of Genesis) demand particular attention.

"NOTHING" = 97; which is the value of "MY NAME" and "RA HOOR KHUT"; it is also the number attributed to Kether/Yesod of the Perfect Tree (see THE/BJM Vol.6 part 1), where Manifestation IS NOT.

"THREE FORMS" = 153 = "CONSCIOUSNESS"; which is to say, the Middle Pillar of the Non-Manifest Tree. These seven words in total are 470; this number unites the seven with the four (⑦=[4]) into Nothing, and is equivalent to "THAT SHE MAY OPEN THE GATE OF HER SISTER.". It should be noted that seven is the number of the Goddess, four the number of Jupiter, which, from above the Abyss, is also feminine, represented by the Empress (who seeks "seventy to her four"). The Notariqon of "Nothing under its three" is, of course, NUIT.

"IT IS NOT" = 120; traditionally the value of N.O.X. - the Key of the Abyss, twelve is another number of the Goddess, and "R" (=12) represents Rhea, she that floweth (see the Bornless Rite).

Note that "NOTHING" = 97 = "RA HOOR KHUT", whereas "IT IS NOT" = 120 = "RA HOOR KHUIT".
470 = "MY" & "MEANING"; 120 = "MY" & "LAW".
"MY" = 36 = "SUN".

The value of the last sentence, "It is not, yet informeth all things", is 418. The verse in its entirety adds to 888.

●
  ●
━━━

```
Now cometh the glory of the Single One,  ˙C=422  as an
 24   94    53   47   25  53    80           6  15
```

```
imperfection and stain.  ˙C=340
    231      21    67    ˙P=762
```

˙Verse = 762

L = TWO : THE MAGUS

Note that "GLORY" = 47; the value of "IT", "EGG", "AEON", "FOAM", which is to say, The Prima Materia.

The "SINGLE ONE" requires careful analysis;
"SINGLE" = 80 = "THE LORD", "CROWNED", "FINE", "PURE"; 80 suggests (8)-Infinite (0)-Nothing.
"ONE" = 46 = "WOMAN", "LION".
"SINGLE ONE" = 126 = "COMPANION", "OYSTER SHELL", "LIGHTNING"; (1)-The Unity (2)-of Opposites (6)-is the LAW.
(1)-Unity of (2)-Opposites (6)-in Tiphareth.

The idea of self as a single separate entity is that which divides. The fault of the Hebrew system was placing "I am" at the head of the Tree of Life, instead of "I shall be". This "Single One" whose glory cometh (he himself is not yet seen) will manifest in Tiphareth, "as an imperfection and stain" because of differentiation from the primal Nothing.

```
        •
        •
       ▬ ▬
```

But by the Weak One the Mother was it equilibrated. ˙P=632
61 35   53   38 46   53   93   9 47   197

˙Verse = 632

W = ♄/♒ : THE PRIESTESS

"ONE" = 46 = "WOMAN".
"MOTHER" = 93.
"EQUILIBRATED" = 197 = "HIS SECRET NAME"; (1)-Unity (97)-into Nothing, suggests the formula of this feminine redeemer.
~~362~~ = "KNOWER" & "KNOWN"; uniting the self with the "Not-Self".
631

```
        •
       ▬▬▬
        •
```

Also the purity was divided by Strength, ˙C=447 the force
15   53   117   9   99   35   119   53   75

of the Demiurge. ˙C=346
25 53   140   ˙P=793

˙Verse = 793

H = ♃/♓ : THE EMPRESS

"PURITY" = 117; Kether/Tiphareth of the Manifest Tree, and the value of "HOOR PAAR KRAAT".
"DIVIDED" = 99 = "THE ABYSS".
"STRENGTH" = 119; Chesed of the Manifest Tree (i.e. the edge of the Abyss, the God whose number is four, called among men, "the first").
"THE FORCE" = 128; (1)-Unity (2)-of Opposites (8)-is Infinite.

```
        •
       ▬ ▬
        •
```

And the Cross was formulated in the Universe that as yet
21   53   42   9   133   37 53   131   53 6 64

was not. ˙P=656
 9   45

˙Verse = 656

S = ♂/♈ : THE EMPEROR

"CROSS" = 42 = "STAR", "BLOOD", "KISS".
"UNIVERSE" = 131. The "CROSS" in this case is the equal-armed cross in the circle, representing "Cosmos". When this cross extends as an arrow from the circle it becomes

Mars' virile force, commencing the Zodiac. The equal-armed cross of the Zodiac is the
"UNIVERSE" as will be seen anon.

```
        •
        •
       ___
```

But now the Imperfection became manifest, ˙C=605
61   24   53   231   105   131

presiding over the fading of perfection. ˙C=537
   145   54   53   73   25   187   ˙P=1142

˙Verse = 1142

D = ☉ / ♌ : THE HIEROPHANT

"IMPERFECTION" = 231 = "CIRCUMFERENCE"; see Liber 231. This imperfection is in the Three
Worlds which, though balanced (131) are stained by the illusory distinction of SELF, here
personified by Tiphareth, the Sun or Lion.
       "HERMIT"+"LOVER"+"EARTH" (EQ Notariqon from capitals as in ms. of AL)
231 = ("THREE ORDEALS IN ONE"
        "FORCE, FANTASY, FIRE"

```
      ___  ___
        •
        •
```

Also the Woman arose, ˙C=164§ and veiled the Upper Heaven
15   53   46   50   21   91   53   106   79

with her body of stars. ˙C=565
 54   41   48   25   47   ˙P=729

˙Verse = 729

O = ♀ / ♉ : LUST

"WOMAN", as vessel of Our Lady, perfects the formula rendered incomplete in the
Patriarchal Aeon. The formula is now "INFINITE" (= 164), where before it suffered
restriction.
"HER BODY OF STARS" = 161; the LAW equilibrated.
Note that "ALSO THE WOMAN AROSE" = 164 = "ASI (ASAR) NEPTHI" (ASAR BETWEEN ASI AND
NEPTHI); "VAST & MINUTE" = 164, as does "CONSOLED & CONSOLER". In the legend of Isis,
Nepthys (Nepthi) consoles Isis(Asi) after the death of Osiris (Asar).

```
        •
       ___
       ___
```

Now then a giant arose, ˙C=215 of terrible strength;
24   67   1   73   50   25   143   119

˙C=287 and asserted the Spirit in a secret rite. ˙C=516
     21   103   53   113   37 1 104   84   ˙P=1018

˙Verse = 1018

Z = ☿/♊ : THE LOVERS

For the form of this "GIANT", see the figure in background of Crowleys ATU VI, which shows the rite in detail.
"A GIANT AROSE" = 124, (1)-Unity (24)-of God.

```
         •
        ═ ═
        ═══
        ═ ═
```

And the Master of the Temple balancing all things
21   53   88   25 53   123   99   5   81

arose; *C=598   his stature was above the Heaven and below
   50   32   108   9   63   53   79   21   57

Earth and Hell. *C=542
 66   21   33   *P=1140

*Verse = 1140

K = ☽/♋ : THE CHARIOT

"MASTER" = 88 = "ECSTASY" and "CIRCLE".
"TEMPLE" = 123 = "THREEFOLD" and "I AM NUIT".
598 = "BUT WHOSO GIVES ONE PARTICLE OF DUST SHALL LOSE ALL IN THAT HOUR".
"HEAVEN" + "EARTH" + "HELL" = 178 = "THELEMITES", "DOUBLE-WANDED ONE", and "THE WHOLE OF THE LAW"; (1)-Unity of (7)-the Goddess (8)-is Infinite; (1)-Unity of (78)-Nuit.
542 suggests the union of the fivefold star, (5)-Pentagram, with the Sixfold (42)-Star (4+2=6).

```
         •
        ═══
        ═══
        ═ ═
```

Against him the Brothers of the Left-hand Path, *C=516
   79   48   53   109   25 53   94   55

confusing the symbols. *C=250   They concealed their
  122   53   75   *P=766   68   106   88

horror (in this symbol); *C=479   for in truth
  54   37   56   70   37   37   81

they were *C=288   ═══
  68   65   *P=767

*Verse = 1533

V = ♀/⊕ : FORTUNA (=93)

This verse and verse 18-("F") must be very carefully examined and compared.
"LEFT-HAND PATH" = 149 = "DO WHAT THOU WILT", "MY SERVICE" and "LIFE AND DEATH", "THE HIGHEST" and "THE WINNERS". It seems likely that these "BROTHERS" are they who misread "these runes" and "make a great miss". Nevertheless, they are reading the same runes as we read, thus the "great danger" mentioned in **AL**.
The Black Brothers have confused the symbols to conceal their horror. The symbols are rectified by the circled cross, confused by the Typhonian fork (V), representing Duality, and traditionally the form of the Black Brothers' wand. [How awkward - Ed.]

⊕ Cosmos
⊕ Part of Fortune/Fortuna (93)
⊗ N.O.X. - Key of the Abyss
⊗ Mark of the Beast
⊗ Malkuth - (10)
⊕ Rosy Cross

```
The master flamed forth as a star and set a guard of Water
 53    88    73    65   6  1  42  21  54  1  47  25  65

in every Abyss.  *P=711
 37   87     46
```

*Verse = 711

G =  : THE HERMIT

"G" (as in "A L G M O R", see cipher in Ms. of **AL**) the Utterer. The Hermit trump's esoteric title is "The Prophet of the Eternal, The Magus of the Voice of Power"; this card is ascribed to Virgo "VIRGIN" = 93.
"GUARD" + "WATER" = 112 = "A FLAMING GASH" and "TRIANGLE".
"GUARD OF WATER" = 137 = "OF THE YONI", "THE WEAK ONE" and "SECRET DOOR".
"ABYSS" = 46 = "WOMAN".
"WATER" = 65 = "WINE", "HONEY", "BABALON", "GODDESS", "EYE", "GLOBE", "WISDOM".
Again the implication is that Woman is the key to transcend imperfection. The process of Nothing extending further and further into manifestation as Something is degenerative; Woman is the way of Return, who redeems the imperfect Universe.

```
Also certain secret ones concealed the Light of Purity in
 15    112    104    51    106     53    64   25    117   37

themselves,  *C=830  protecting it from the
  146                  179       47   58  53

Persecutions.  *C=533
    196         *P=1363
```

*Verse = 1363

R = ♀/♎ : JUSTICE

"CERTAIN" recurs throughout the text; its number is 112 - see above verse.
"CONCEALED" = 106 = "REVEALED".
THESE ARE EQUIVALENT TERMS!
"PURITY" = 117 = GEMINI; Kether-Tiphareth of the Manifest Tree.
146 = "THE MOTHER"; (1)-Unity (46)-of Woman.
"LIGHT" + "PURITY" = 181 = "UNUTTERABLE".
Note that they are protecting "IT"! The twins, Gemini-(117), concealed in "THE MOTHER" = 146.

```
    ▄▄▄▄   ▄▄▄▄
          ●
    ▄▄▄▄   ▄▄▄▄
```

```
Likewise also did certain sons and daughters of Hermes and
  115     15   35   112    31  21    105    25    92    21

of Aphrodite,  *C=725   more openly  *C=154
 25    128               65     89    *P=879
```

*Verse = 879

C = -☉/♌ : THE HANGED MAN

Thirteen is "unlucky", because it is the number of the Sun's death month in the Lunar calendar (thus "C" resembles a crescent moon or sickle).
Similar symbols are:- the Solar Pralaya (dissolution), the Dead Lion, and the astrological formula

                  (Ascendant + Moon) minus Sun = Fortuna-(93)

N.B. Hermes-(92) + Aphrodite-(128) = 220; the number of verses in **AL**.
128 has particular importance as the true numeration of the Eight Lettered Name **BAPHOMET**, and also:-
"BES-NA-MAUT", "THE BEAST" (8 letters), "SCARLET WOMAN", "LIFE & DEATH", "SACRED HEART", "FIVE WOUNDS", "THE ORDEAL X", "SUN AND VENUS", "THE FORCE", "THE CUBE" and "CROWNED CHILD".
879, the numeration of this verse, is the value of the Elevenfold Universe:-
"PLUTO" + "NEPTUNE" + "URANUS" + "SATURN" + "JUPITER" + "MARS" + "SUN" + "VENUS" + "MERCURY" + "MOON" + "EARTH" = 879; (8)-Infinite (79)-Heaven.

```
    ▄▄▄▄   ▄▄▄▄
          ●
    ▄▄▄▄▄▄▄▄▄▄▄
```

```
But the Enemy confused them.  *P=393   They pretended to
 61  53  100    105      74              68      163    31

conceal that Light,  *C=454   that they might betray
  75    53   64                53   68    83     97

it,  *C=348   and profane it.  *C=171
47             21    103    47   *P=973
```

*Verse = 1366

N = ♂/♏ : DEATH

"THE ENEMY" = 153 = "CONSCIOUSNESS".
393 = "SUN" & "VENUS"; 454 = "GOLD" & "STEEL" i.e. Sun conjunct Mars.
The so-called "Death-Mantra", having "N" as its root, is the mantra used in Sun-Venus (107) Rituals of worship AND Sun-Mars rituals of initiation; it destroys the division of Self/Not-Self.
171 = "SECRET FLAME"; (1)-Unity (71)-of Venus.
"CONCEAL THAT" = 128.

348 or the Triune 48 concerns the excremental symbolism implicit in **AL**.
48 = "DUNG"; also "CHILD", as in "child of thy bowels". 348 = "OF THIS MAKE CAKES AND EAT UNTO ME". ("THIS" is an anagram of "shit".) 348 = "BE CAST OUT UPON THE MIDDEN" and "IT SHALL BE HIS CHILD & THAT STRANGELY".
The idea is that the manifestation of an archetype is its excrement. In a cosmology such as Trigrammaton the successive emanations from Nothing are seen as the degeneration of the Primal Purity. We only see, in the phenomenal world, the

final manifestation of things which originate in far subtler forms; which, in these terms, are SHIT. This is why Jehovah showed Moses His Hind Parts. All of which proves that Crowley's son was/is a turd, and that Black Brothers eat shit.

```
Yet certain holy nuns concealed the secret in songs upon
64    112   28   50    106      53    104   37   42   64

the lyre.  *P=767
53   54
```

*Verse = 767

Y = ♃ / ♐ : ART

"HOLY NUNS" = 78 = "NUIT"; note these nuns are "certain"; the Gift of Nuit is certainty.
"SONGS" = 42 = "STAR", "CROSS", "BLOOD", "KISS", "QADOSH", "NEW".
"CONCEALED" = 106 = "RUBY STAR".
"THE LYRE" = 107 = "SUN" + "VENUS", "THE SNAKE", "HOUSE OF GOD", "SILENCE", "UNCLOUDED", "WHEELING", "THY LIGHT", "HER HEART".

```
Now did the Horror of Time pervert all things,  *C=504
24   35  53   54    25   93    134   5    81

hiding the Purity with a loathsome thing,  *C=478   a
81    53   117   54   1    96      76                1

thing unnameable.  *C=217
76       140       *P=1199
```

*Verse = 1199

J = ♄ / ♑ : THE DEVIL

Capricorn, the Devil, indicates the last phase of the LIBRA-SCORPIO-SAGITTARIUS-CAPRICORN cycle, 418 or "The House of Baphomet". The Final Manifestation in this cosmogony is seen as Ultimate Imperfection. But turning lead into gold is simply the reverse of the process.
"HORROR OF TIME" = 172; (1)-The Unity (or extension) (72)-of the Lingam. ("TIME" = 93.)
"LOATHSOME THING" = 172 = "GEMMED AZURE", "INSPIRATION", "UNIMAGINABLE", "THE PROMISE", "GLORY OF THE STARS", "THE HOLY OF HOLIES", "TRANSCENDENT".
Also, 172 = "UNDERSTANDING" (Binah-Saturn, Ruler of Capricorn), and "THE ANCIENTS" (attributable to Binah OR Saturn).

```
    ━━━ ━━━
    ━━━━━━━
    ━━━ ━━━
       •
```

Yea, ˙C=41 and there arose sensualists upon the
 41   21   90   50   126   64 53

firmament, ˙C=563 as a foul stain of storm upon
 159   6 1 44   67   25   69   64

the sky. ˙C=358
 53 29   ˙P=962

˙Verse = 962

U = △/♈ : THE HOUSE OF GOD

"YEA" = 41 = "PAN", "HADES", "AWFUL", (and "LUX" - which is NOT in Class A).
"SENSUALISTS" = 126; see above notes, referring to the "single one" and Tiphareth.
Sensualists obviously would not regard manifest ideas as intrinsically unclean.
"FIRMAMENT" = 159; (1)-Unity (59)-of Yoni, OR (1)-Unity (5)-of the Pentagram (9)-is
Illusion. 159 = "ALL FOOLS DESPISE", "THESE ARE DEAD", "THAT IS ENOUGH".
Note "STAIN" re-occuring in this verse.

```
    ━━━ ━━━
    ━━━ ━━━
    ━━━━━━━
       •
```

And the Black Brothers raised their heads; ˙C=429
 21 53   45   109   72   88

yea, ˙C=41 they unveiled themselves without shame
 41   68   122   146   102   56

or fear. ˙C=569
 19 56   ˙P=1039

˙Verse = 1039

F = △ : THE STAR

"RAISED" = 72 = "LINGAM".
"UNVEILED" = 122 = "REVEILED"; These terms are synonymous.
These Brothers are "BLACK" = 45 = "I AM" and "NOT", asserting a distinction between Self
and Not-Self; 45 = "BE" rather than BECOME or GO.
They raised their "HEADS" = 41 = "YEA"; an affirmation (of ANY idea) is akin to "So be
it", which is static and false.
"HEAD" = 36 = "SUN"; i.e. the Self idea of Tiphareth.
"THEY UNVEIL THEMSELVES" [revealing their hind quarters? - Ed.] i.e. as Gods. Without
"SHAME"-(56) or "FEAR"-(56); 56 = "ISIS" by English Qaballa and "NU" by Hebrew Qabalah.
"THEMSELVES" = 146; which is distorted (by lack of 56) into "I am One". (1)-Unity (46)-of
Me, INSTEAD OF (1)-Unity (46)-of Woman.
146 = "THE ILLUSION" i.e. of Self and Not-Self. 146 = "THE ORIGINAL" [as in Sin, Oy-Vey! -
Ed.]

```
      Also there rose up  a soul of filth and of weakness,
       15   90   49  43 1  31  25  71   21  25   87
```

```
*C=458   and it corrupted all the rule of the Tao.  *C=434
          21  47   142   5  53   56  25  53   32   *P=892
```

*Verse = 892

Q = ▽ : THE MOON

This verse begins with "ALSO" as did verse 7-("O") "ALSO THE WOMAN AROSE".
"A SOUL OF FILTH" = 128. "FILTH" = 71 = "VENUS".
Note also "WEAKNESS", as in verse 3-("W") "WEAK ONE THE MOTHER".
"WEAKNESS" = 87; (8)-Infinite (7)-Goddess. Female "filth" is archetypally menstrual in origin. 71 = "NATURAL". Her "MONTHLY"-(87) "WEAKNESS"-(87). The "outward glamour" of Venus is itself an excrescence in this form of symbolism.
"OF THE TAO." = 110 = "PURE WILL".
The verse in full adds to 892 = "MY PROPHET IS A FOOL WITH HIS ONE, ONE, ONE. ARE NOT THEY THE OX, AND NONE BY THE BOOK"; "OX" conceals "Ordeal X", which transforms "ONE"(myself)=46="ME"-consciousness into 46="WOMAN"-(the most readily accessible, and most easily concentrated upon of all Divine Images)-consciousness.
The meaning of this verse seems to be that, even at the last, when the "WRONG OF THE BEGINNING" had reached this crisis in resolving itself to its inevitable conclusion, the feminine force, which had interceded and balanced the process in earlier phases, did so once more; but in so doing becomes identified with the "WRONG" itself.
Note "RULE" = 56 = "THIS" (anag. SHIT) concealing "ISIS"-(56); (5)-Pentagrammic (6)-Law.
"CORRUPTED" = 142 = "GREAT DANGER" i.e. in the excremental symbolism.
N.B. "Black Brothers" are WITHOUT 56 !
93-("SCORPIO") + 49-("MOON") = 142 = "OF PURITY" and "CAKES OF LIGHT".

```
      Then only was Heaven established to bear sway;  *C=446  for
       67   38   9    79      140     31   58   24            37
```

```
only in the lowest corruption is form manifest.  *C=603
 38  37  53   66     155     28  58    131       *P=1049
```

*Verse = 1049

B = ▽ (HEAVEN) : THE SUN

"HEAVEN" = 79 = "ABRAHADABRA"; N.B. "ABRA" & "HADABRA" = 418; 79 = "SEVEN", "WOMAN IS ALL".
"ESTABLISHED" = 140 = "CROWN" + "KINGDOM", "UNTO NUIT" and "HIEROPHANT".
"BEAR" = 58 = "HADIT", "ZODIAC", "OCEAN", "LIBRA".
"SWAY" = 24 = "GOD", "LADY".
"LOWEST" = 66 = "EARTH".
Her intercession is fairly successful; "HEAVEN" bears sway, even in the lowest corruption.
"CORRUPTION" = 155 = "HOLY GRAAL"; which fell from "Heaven", i.e. into manifestation. 155 = "ABOMINATION".
"IS" = 28, half of 56 as "IS" is half of Isis; 28 days (symbolically at least) to a lunar month.

"FORM" = 58 = "HADIT".
"MANIFEST" = 131 = "UNIVERSE", "JOY OF LIFE", "THE ODYSSEY", "ON THE PATH", "LOVE IS THE LAW" and "FORBIDDEN".
The last part of the verse is a general re-statement of the doctrine of this cosmology which is:-

THE MANIFESTATION IN FORM

OF AN ARCHETYPE OR IDEA

IS THE EXCREMENT OF THAT IDEA

```
▬▬▬▬
▬▬▬▬
▬▬ ▬▬
```

```
Also did Heaven manifest in violent light, *P=466
 15   35      79       131     37     105    64
```

*Verse = 466

M = ⊗ + : THE AEON

"MANIFEST" = 131 = "UNIVERSE".
"VIOLENT LIGHT" = 169 = 13 x 13; see the "Treasure-house of Images" for this symbolism of thirteen, vitally important in E.Q..
"VIOLENT" & "LIGHT" = 973 = "THOU ART EMPHATICALLY MY CHOSEN; AND BLESSED ARE THE EYES THAT THOU SHALT LOOK UPON WITH GLADNESS"; (9)-Illusion (73)-of Power.

```
▬▬▬▬
▬▬ ▬▬
▬▬▬▬
```

```
And in soft light. *P=176
 21   37  54    64
```

*Verse = 176

X = ⊗ - : THE UNIVERSE

This verse adds to 176 = "INITIATION"; i.e. by Ordeal X.
"SOFT" & "LIGHT" = 526; the sum of the seven planetary names by E.Q..

```
▬▬ ▬▬
▬▬▬▬
▬▬▬▬
```

```
Then were the waters gathered together from the
 67   65   53    70      108      132     58   53
```

heaven, *P=685
  79

*Verse = 685

I = ▽ HEAVEN : CUPS

Note the association of "WATERS" with "HEAVEN" as in 20-("B":Water). The Image is of the Flood. "I", the Self, is reflected in the Waters [23-Skidoo - Ed.] Note "WATERS" = 70 = "SPACE" and "WINES" ("WINE" = 65 = "GODDESS" and "BABALON").

"GATHERED" = 108 = "THE HOLY GRAAL" and "RED WINE".
"TOGETHER" = 132 = "DOUBLE-WANDED", "SECRET WORD", "FLAMING STAR", "BLUE-LIDDED" and "DECOCTION".

```
☷
```

And a crust of earth concealed the core of flame. *P=492
21   1   71   25   66   106   53   57   25   67

*Verse = 492

T = ▽ /FLAME : COINS

Here, "CRUST"-(71) replaces "FILTH"-(71) in the Earth verse.
"CRUST OF EARTH" = 162 = "SUN" + "MIDNIGHT"; also, "SECRET HOUSE", i.e. the fourth house (position of Sun at midnight), the house of results or "the end of the matter". As before mentioned, the result or end product is symbolised by excrement.
"CORE OF FLAME" = 149 = "DO WHAT THOU WILT", "THE WINNERS", "THE HIGHEST", and "MIGHTY ONES"; but also, 149 = "LEFT HAND PATH", because of the excremental symbolism. Note also that 149 = "LET HIM STAND" and "THE WOMAN AROSE". The Image of this verse is of an excretion ("CRUST"), concealing an idea ("CORE").

```
☳
```

Around the globe gathered the wide air, *P=429
  57   53   65   108   53   57   36

*Verse = 429

E = △ /GLOBE : SWORDS

The numeration of this verse is 429 = "PERFECT"-(143) x 3.
429 = "AND THE BLACK BROTHERS RAISED THEIR HEADS" from verse 18-("F":Air).
Note "GLOBE" and "AIR". "GLOBE" = 65 = "GODDESS"; "AIR" = 36 = "SUN", "MAN" and "HEAD".
"THE WIDE AIR" = 146 = "THE ILLUSION"; see notes above.

Crowley's Note: "The moon conceived as a concretion of the atmosphere."

```
☶
```

And men began to light fires upon the earth. *P=513
21   60   71   31   64   83   64   53   66

*Verse = 513

P = △ /♌ (EARTH) : WANDS

Note "MEN BEGAN" = 131. The sum of the verse = 513 = "THE STAR 418".
"FIRES" = 83 = "IAO AND OAI"; (8)-Infinite (3)-Trinity.
Note again the connection of "FIRE" and "EARTH" as in verse 24-("T":Earth).
AL Chapter II, verse 26 describes the raised and lowered head (of the Dragon?).
The Image is of the beginning of sentient life.
"THE EARTH" = 119 = "SILVER STAR" and "SOFT LIGHT".

```
              Therefore was the end of it sorrow;  ˙C=377  yet in that
                152      9   53  45 25 47  46              64  37  53

              sorrow a sixfold star of glory whereby they might
                46    1    83    42  25   47    104    68    83

              see to return unto the stainless Abode;  ˙C=1121
              55   31  104    62  53    104      59

              yea,  ˙C=41  unto the Stainless Abode.  ˙C=278
               41            62  53    104      59    ˙P=1817

              ˙Verse = 1817
```

SILENCE = ⬡ : THE SIXFOLD STAR

"YET IN THAT SORROW" = 200 = "MANIFESTATION".
"IN THAT SORROW" = 136 = "LOST TO SIGHT", "SELFLESSNESS", "SECRET DOOR", "HOLY COVENANT" and "CONDITIONS".
The value of the first phrase is 377 = "THE CHILD-(48) OF THE FORCES OF TIME-(93)". 377 is also "LISTEN TO THE NUMBERS & THE WORDS".
"THE END OF IT" = 170 = "DESTRUCTION", "IN SACRIFICE" and "BAHLASTI, OMPEHDA".
"ABODE" = 59 = "YONI". "STAINLESS ABODE" = 163 = "TIME" + "SPACE", "CUBE" + "CIRCLE" and "(IN THIS SYMBOL)".
"STAINLESS" = 104 = "SECRET", "MYSTICAL", "WONDERFUL", "OF HEAVEN", "MY CHOSEN", "UNDER WILL" and "THE WOMB"; (1)-Unity (0)-from Nothing (4)-creating the Elements.
The value of the verse is 1817; (1)-Unity of (817):
817 = "THE KEY OF THE RITUALS IS IN THE SECRET WORD WHICH I HAVE GIVEN UNTO HIM".
817 = "AND THE MAGUS IS LOVE AND BINDETH TOGETHER THAT AND THIS IN HIS CONJURATION".
Comparing this verse with the twenty-seventh verse of AL Chapter I, we find the ritual of the creation of the world. The Trigram attributed hereunto represents the Yoni (the Guard of Water). All this creative process described in Trigrammaton, even the appearance of sentient life, occurs BEFORE the final creation described in AL Chapter I, verses 28-30. Finally, note the proliferation of the letter "S" in this final verse. The letter "S" occurs more frequently in Class A texts than any other letter, in marked contrast to normal English usage, where "E" predominates. "E" in this system indicates Air, thus thought, thus Self, and thus Black Brothers. [and unusual diets! - Ed.]

It has proved impossible to find a definitive text of "Trigrammaton" from which to establish when upper case initials are intended.

ALTHOTASH

TABLE OF ATTRIBUTIONS

A	1		ZERO	THE FOOL
L	2		TWO	THE MAGUS
W	3		♄/♒	THE PRIESTESS
H	4		♃/♓	THE EMPRESS
S	5		♂/♈	THE EMPEROR
D	6		☉/♌	THE HIEROPHANT
O	7		♀/♉	LUST
Z	8		☿/♊	THE LOVERS
K	9		☽/♋	THE CHARIOT
V	10		☾/⊕	FORTUNA
G	11		☿/♍	THE HERMIT
R	12		♀/♎	JUSTICE
C	13		-☉	THE HANGED MAN
N	14		♂/♏	DEATH
Y	15		♃/♐	ART
J	16		♄/♑	THE DEVIL
U	17		△/♒	THE HOUSE OF GOD
F	18		△	THE STAR
Q	19		▽	THE MOON
B	20		▽	THE SUN
M	21		⊕+	THE AEON
X	22		⊕-	THE UNIVERSE
I	23		▽/ HEAVEN	CUPS
T	24		▽/ FLAME	DISKS
E	25		△/ GLOBE	SWORDS
P	26		△/♌ EARTH	WANDS
SILENCE	27		✡	THE LAMP

The Signs of the Zodiac plus Spirit active = 131

THE GREEK CROSS OF THE ZODIAC

WHAT IS A QABALAH?

Drawing attention to our title, it may be that people are used to speaking of "the qabalah", whether they refer to the Hebrew Qabalah, or to the Greek or Arabic Qabalahs, or all or none of these. Obviously these are all Qabalahs, and they have factors in common, but when we inquire into the nature of qabalism we are usually talking about one in particular, and overlooking the question "what is a qabalah?" This one is usually :—

THE HEBREW QABALAH; which we will not attempt to describe, but note some ideas about its origins: the numbers & letters of the holy books pre-exist creation; they are at once revealed and concealed in the written Holy Books; they constitute the Law, the Word and the Identity of Deity. That is to say, the Eternal Holy Books represent the full Name of the Deity and this Name or Word is His Law Himself. By saying or manifesting this Word, the universe was created. There is also the view that the priests created mathematics and writing, and concealed within the symbols and their interrelations theological and occult knowledge. This theory is by no means confined to Hebrew qabalism, so let us move on to :—

THE GREEK QABALAH; again we do not intend to instruct persons in its methods or symbolism, but to draw attention to some account of its nature. Its mathematical symbolism delineates a divine harmony in Creation. This symbolism involves numerical equivalents in Christian, Gnostic and Hermetic inspired scriptures written in Greek, and particularly geometric relations between numbers.

Passing on quickly, we salute the late Robert Graves in

turning to the :-

CELTIC QABALAH; writing and numbers were the secrets of the priesthood. A symbolic and mathematical mystery of the sacred calender was concealed in the alphabet, the correct solution to which reveals the secret name of God. Their numerical series was not arranged in hundreds, tens and units, but ran consecutively one to twenty.

The dimensions of Stonehenge and other works suggest an affinity between this ancient qabalah and the Mediterranean and Oriental qabalahs. The temples of the ancients and, as is well known, the geometry of Gothic architecture conceal qabalistic secrets; this tradition inspired the movement known as:-

FREEMASONRY; An august institution preserving in allegorical rituals a tradition of Solomon's Temple, Hebrew Scripture and the Lost Word.

Having thus meagrely covered the historical aspects of our question, we must now leap to conclusions!

Language and Mind evolve hand in hand, because the collective mind is identical with the Archetypal World. The ideals of a culture evolve through its language, which is an expression of the Archetypes in the collective consciousness. As ideas, the numbers and letters do indeed pre-exist creation (defined as manifestation into concrete reality). As such they are archetypes in action. The interplay between language and the archetypal world is the key to cultural movements, i.e. Judaeo-Christianity spread by means of the magical force of the Hebrew & Greek languages. Greek was the *lingua franca* of its day, and its alphabet derives from Qabalistic Hebrew.

ENGLISH, the **UNIVERSAL CIPHER** is the *lingua franca* of today, by means of which Thelema will inevitably become a major force in the world. Today, not even Mandarin Chinese can seriously compete with the English alphabet. Japan & China, among other countries, have already adopted it, at least for trade purposes. Indeed, when words obtain international usage, they invariably do so by means of Anglicisation. The fact that the Holy Books of our age are in English should not come as a surprise; nor should the existence of an organic qabalistic structure within our language. Indeed, were it not so, we might be somewhat alarmed!

JAKE STRATTON-KENT.

THELEMA AND WICCA

Today's witches are usually divided into four classes; the hereditary covens, the robed covens, the Gardnerians and the Alexandrians. They have much in common despite their differences, and are all valid. In fact, when I look at Wicca, I see a loose alliance of autonomous groups (many of whom are at odds over points of very little relevance), whose variety is much larger than these four classifications suggest. Witches are of course notoriously eclectic, and some so called "traditionalist" covens are no nearer the supposed original form of the cult than those who allow Crowley or Solomon to influence their rites and conventions.

The most important thing to Wicca now is its future; I envisage, for its well-being and growth, a return to intelligent and imaginative principles. Nobody is more traditional than anybody else; nor would they be better witches for it if they were. What few occultists of any stripe seem to realise is that there is not a single scheme to be worked day in, day out, throughout the march of the centuries; magick evolves, must evolve, and will continue to evolve. The priests and priestesses of tomorrow must realise that tradition is only an anchor, to stop the ship drifting from the position chosen for a specific period; and it is no good setting sail without drawing up the anchor. Which is as far as this metaphor will take us!

I have read and re-read the various sides of the argument about Crowley's contribution to the witch cult; in my opinion he contributed much, and it should have been more. He composed the rituals of the Book of Shadows; though to what extent they remain his work in their present form is arguable. At one time Gardener's museum (now in the States) possessed the correspondence relating to this; interested parties should follow this up, if they think it might be useful. Doreen Valiente too wrote much of the Book of Shadows, the keystone of the witch cult at present. How much she knows about Crowley's contribution I neither know nor care; it is irrelevant so long as she continues her work on behalf of Wicca. **WHAT IS OF SUPREME IMPORTANCE IS THE EXTENT TO WHICH WICCA IS PREPARED TO RECOGNISE THE BOOK OF THE LAW AS A MAJOR ELEMENT IN THEIR MODERN PHASE.**

Gardner and Crowley did not insert Thelemic passages into the Book of Shadows because they were short of ideas, but to give people who might be looking for ideas a few clues. As they were anxious that the book appear traditional (that is, antique), they were cautious about this; but we do know that Crowley was interested in founding, or better, having somebody else found, a popular religion on Thelemic principles. He instructed Frater Achad to do just that, and Achad, like Gardner, was a member of the O.T.O., with a charter to run a lodge.

The O.T.O. is like the witch cult in one major respect; it travels through time. "Masonic" tradition, like "Wiccan" tradition, can pass through incalculable periods of time without appreciable loss of its message, whether or not the persons carrying it are aware of the import of that message. There is no easier way to instil someone with the importance of a fact than to swear them to secrecy regarding it; and far from preventing its transmission through time, this magickal action perpetuates the secret indefinitely. What is more, those within the group who do know are able to develop the teaching through experience in the group context.

The apotheosis of some appreciable part of the witch cult into a powerful engine of the Aeon is already occurring, and growing. It will only reach significant proportions as the system of magick contained within AL reaches the grass roots of the occult movement, and as that same level evolves into a true outer order. This is the concern, surely, of every adept within these proliferating manifestations of the movement. I emphasise to any adepts within the witch cult the importance of the task.

Let me salve the anguish with which some witches will greet my enthusiastic plans to put their house in order. Firstly, the palaver over some aspects of Crowley's doings (some of Gardner's are equally outrageous, although less publicised by antagonistic gutter-press news-hounds) is meaningless in relation to his real work as an adept. The Crowleyanity personality cult, (fortunately in decline, and stigmatised by emulation of Crowley's faults and ignorance of his real importance in the realm of thought and magick) has nothing whatsoever to do with the Book of the Law.

IN THE BOOK OF THE LAW IS CONTAINED THE MAGICK AND PHILOSOPHY OF AN ENTIRE AGE OF HUMAN DEVELOPMENT. The whole system of occultism was originally evolved around the interpretation and application of Aeonic messages contained within such books; and what we are now seeing is the initial phase of the latest such cycle of revelation. "Revelation is the mother of evolution", and as John Michell (the Blessed. ED.) wisely said: "You can't have revelation without tradition."

We can be a tremendous influence in the onward march of human evolution; and to fully understand this, we must understand that we don't know all the answers, and that it is indeed the purpose of the game to find them out, not to pretend that you have temporarily forgotten them, or that you are not telling at present. Let us, priests and priestesses, establish the Magick of the Aeon as the ruling power in the evolution of our race.

KELVIN BOYLAND

Publisher's Note: Kelvin Boyland was not one of Jake's pseudonyms. While Boyland's name was used in the byline for this article, it was in fact written by JSK.

MANTRAS & SPELLS

The purpose of this article is to provide guidelines for working with techniques involving "Speech" be it silent or uttered. Many students complain that occult work requires more time or privacy than modern life provides them. These techniques however may be performed whilst walking the dog or waiting for a bus, etc.

A KA DUA
TUF UR BIU
BI AA CHEFU
DUDU NER AF AN NUTERU.

When commencing a mantra the lips should actually form the words clearly and slowly before proceeding to interiorise the process. Once the cycle of repetition has commenced let the student measure the lines by the cycle of breath, avoiding over straining the lungs.

The best indication of success is when the mantra is continued through sleep. However once some small degree of proficiency is gained the student may go on to visualise a blood red triangle in the area of the chest. If its form be that of a heart it is well. Let the student endeavour once success is reached to enthrone Horus upon the throne of Ra within this inverted Pyramid of Fire.

When completing the mantra, ie when the bus arrives or whatever, slow the mantra down, once more move the lips to earth the energies. Stamp gently, imagining the earth vibrating, and touch the lips with a fore finger in the sign of Harpocrates.

If occult exercises of this or other kinds are not earthed properly problems can arise. Avoid lethargy after occult work, and try and keep a record to switch from intuitive to rational modes of consciousness; do not confuse the planes. If all else fails, and you are "unstrung" by any technique and require earthing, remember that eating is the best way of all to "come down".

- - - - - - - - - - - - -

Rituals of Magick, of various kinds, can be broken down into various stages. If the ritual is in a mutilated state (as in grimoires is almost invariably the case) a knowledge of this structure will enable the student to rectify any deficiencies. As it is said "Equilibrium is the basis of the Work", so let the student measure his work by these 30 points. (30 = Lamed by Heb.Qabalah, 30 = WILL by E.Q.).

| BANISHINGS | PURIFICATIONS | CONSECRATIONS | OATH & CONFESSION | INVOKATION | CHARGE TO THE SPIRIT | BANISHINGS |

The Book of the Law contains the Supreme Spells, thus the Thelemite magickian might proceed:

"LET THE RITUALS BE RIGHTLY PERFORMED WITH JOY AND BEAUTY", to open the Temple, then banish by Star Ruby (Liber 25).

Purification Spell: "FOR PURE WILL UNASSUAGED OF PURPOSE DELIVERED FROM THE LUST OF RESULT IS EVERYWAY PERFECT."

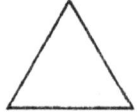
Consecration Spell: "I AM UPLIFTED IN THINE HEART AND THE KISSES OF THE STARS RAIN HARD UPON THY BODY."

The Oath from the Bornless Rite is the best for general use, otherwise a statement of intent appropriate to thy purpose should be carefully devised. Likewise the Confession from Liber Pyramidos is a perfect example of ITS type.

The Invokations (of which the Bornless Ritual holds primary position and should usually proceed all others): the student could do a lot worse than consulting the "Treasure House of Images" for superb examples of English Invokatory Adorations, but will also find the Adorations from the Stele and the official rituals of the A.'.A.'. contain much of practical and inspirational use.

The Charge to the Spirit will generally resemble the Oath.

Final Banishings include the License to Depart whilst the climactic words "The Ending of the Words is the Word ABRAHADABRA" bring the rite to a close, sealing it with the word of the Aeon.

The reader should consult "Magick" by Aleister Crowley for a more thorough analysis of this scheme.

JAKE STRATTON-KENT

BLOOD & GUTS — Part 1

This short article deals with the pathetic criticism of our Law, ie: that it includes references to suffering. How AWFUL, say these sensitive souls. How can it be a Holy Book when it actually includes references to pain.

Holy Books describe Universal Conditions, not cloud-cuckoo land. We avoid comparison with the Old Testament, but mention Jesus' firm injunction to "sell all that ye have and buy a sword", his intention to "bring not peace but a sword" "to set father against son and brother agaist brother" by way of compensation!

Buddha taught that All is Sorrow, having met Death, Poverty, Disease as well as Palace Corruption, not forgetting dying of indigestion from eating pork.

The austerely spiritual Yi King/I Ching describes torture in some detail:

Hexagram 21. Shih Ho/Biting Through.

His feet are fastened in the stocks so that his toes disappear, no blame. Bites through tender meat so that his nose disappears, no blame. Bites on old dried meat and strikes something poisonous, slight humiliation. NO BLAME. Bites on old gristly meat. Receives metal arrows. It furthers one to be mindful of difficulties, and to be persevering. Good Fortune. Bites on dried lean meat, recieves yellow gold (bribery?), perseveringly aware of danger (put the frighteners on?), no blame. His neck is fastened in the wooden canque, so that his ears disappear. Misfortune.

Then there was the famous Hindu conscientious objector Arjuna, Krishna brought him through this cissy attitude by dictating the Bhagavad Gita to him and sent him out to slay the sons of bitches!

Okay folks, be mindful of difficulties, and be persevering; or as Nietzche would have said; "THE SPIRIT GROWS, STRENGTH IS INCREASED BY WOUNDING."

JAKE STRATTON-KENT

THE TREES

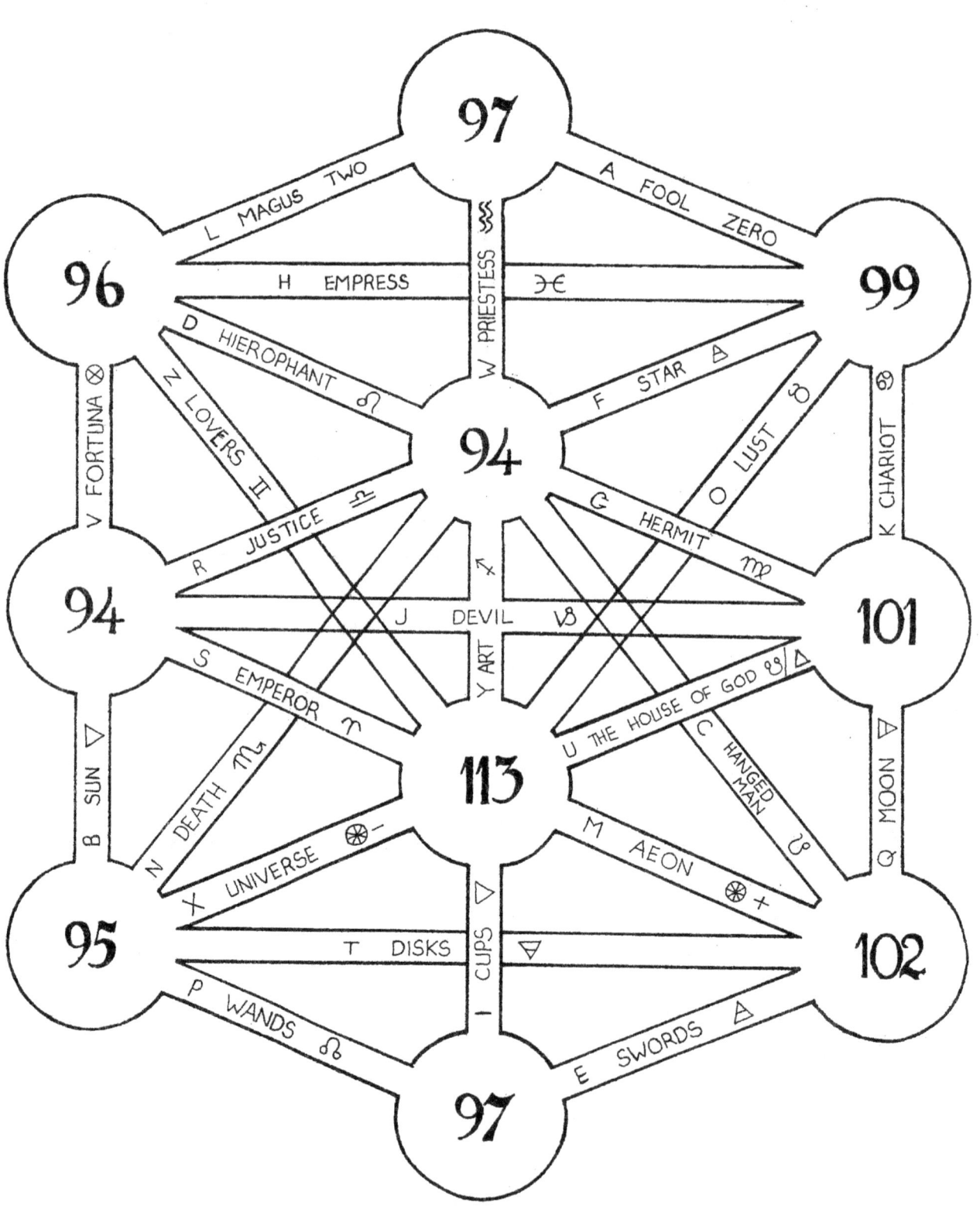

OF ETERNITY

> Publisher's Note: the Trees of Eternity referred to below appear on the preceding pages. 'Liber Trigrammaton' appears on page 27 of this publication.

THE TREES OF ETERNITY

(For the attributions of the English Alphabet & New Symbols etc. see "Liber Trigrammaton" commentary in Vol VII no. 1; and Trees of Eternity in Vol VII no 2.)

In AL I vs. 59. Nuit speaks of the "Trees of Eternity" (note that 59 is the numeration of "ABODE", "WHEEL", "YONI"), which connect on ONE level with the Two Trees of the traditional Qabalah, viz: the Tree of Life, and the Tree of the Knowledge of Good and Evil. This latter Tree bears fruit and is guarded by a serpent, in common with other mythologies.

The Tree of Life is a schematic representation of the doctrine of emanations or aeons from the Primal Nothing, the Ain or Pleroma.

An inscrutable mystery conceals the formulation of ONE from Nothing, for in truth Kether is "un-differentiating consciousness", or ZERO; until Chokmah is formulated.

In the Gnostic system of Valentinian, the Feminine Wisdom (Gk. SOPHIA; Heb. Chokmah) "In Her eagerness to see the light of the Supreme God (ZERO), which could only be seen with safety by the first mystery (or emanation ie. Chokmah), moved out of the Pleroma into the "void" (the unmanifest universe) and was brought back by HOROS. But from Her wanderings outside the pleroma the world and mankind originated. The fall of the errant aeon into matter resulted in the quickening of a shapeless thing called ACHAMOTH (Heb. Chokmoth, plural of Chokmah, wisdom). This was shut into outer darkness."

This is rather garbled, but the gist of it is that the Unknown God got bored, and produced a mirror to look at Himself; but the Law of Opposites was invoked & the mirror showed Him His Feminine Aspect of Active Wisdom. This Wisdom is "male" when seen from below, because it is "active" in relation to that below it. This relationship of the Unknown God and His Wisdom (Athene, Sophia, even Baphomet) is the Dance of Creation.

The trouble with emanation schemes as seen in Trigrammaton is that the further you get from the Pure & Simple Origin the more Impure and Complex everything becomes. Sophia enables us to know the Unknown God, but this very relationship invokes Duality.

This is all very well, but what has it got to do with Trees ? Well, the problem is that if you start with Nothing, getting to One is very difficult (sic), and multiplying one by one (assuming you CAN get one from nothing) does not get you a lot further, so how DO YOU create the Universe from Zero? The answer is, stated simply, that you don't! For quite a while this was a real problem for the Supreme God in His Oneness (ie. Zeroness, tricky that). He came up with the idea of Unicellular life, but as even these required three dimensions to exist in he scrapped that idea and sulked.

By now he had formulated an Idea of "One", and from One and Nothing had come up with "binary trying to be decimal" & a Tree that looked like this:

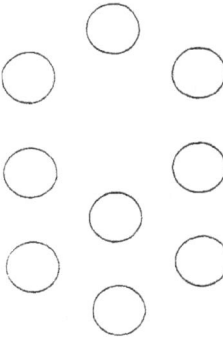

In the lowest Sphere He saw a reflection of Himself, and (very excited) he exclaimed "In the Image of the Elohim" (in Charlton Heston's best Hollywood voice) & concentrating very hard, tried to get another reflection of the whole scheme in a tenth sphere. But this is what happened:

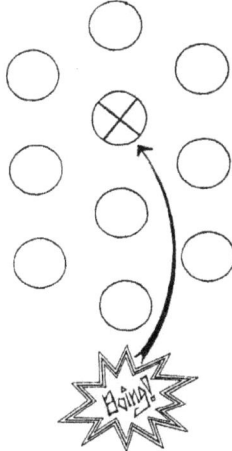

and then this:

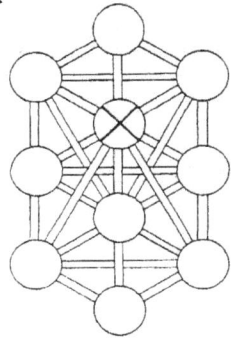

The implications of this diagrammatical creation myth produced two schools of thought. To quote the editors of that august magazine AGAPE no. 6, 1974: "A universal void splitting to yield positive and negative universes - 0=2. For no better reason than that Negative has a bad name we call ours the Positive one".

If we take this attitude to the word "positive" then the world of the "Qlippoth" (Heb. shells, evil and incomplete ideas, personified as "demons") tends to be identified with the Unmanifest Universe (a la Typhonian OTO) which, as that Tree does not partake of duality, is somewhat misleading.

In fact Positive in this sense means Manifest (dualistic), and as emanation schemes almost inevitably imply "the more manifest the more muck", we tend to end up with "World-hating" sin and guilt religions.

The interplay of our positive/dualistic universe (the manifest Tree) with the negative/zeroistic universe (the unmanifest Tree) is due to a mystical identity between the fallen Da'ath (called Malkuth) of the former with the unfallen Malkuth (called Da'ath) of the latter. On the "original" Tree of Life, so to speak, Yesod was the lowest sphere; Malkuth was in the Da'ath position. The nine letters of AIN SOP AUR imply the nine spheres of a Perfect or Unmanifest Tree (see Kabbalah Unveiled, trans. Macgregor Mathers). The potential existing in Nothing (Ain) is projected in a series of aeons or emanations (the sephiroth). The tenth, or product, is called Knowledge (Da'ath), ie. self knowledge or Knowledge of the scheme in potentia. It is this Knowledge that produces duality, and the "Fall" is the penny (Da'ath) dropping (into the Malkuth position), producing the Manifest Universe or "Wrong of the Beginning".

THIS INTERPLAY IS THE 93 CURRENT.

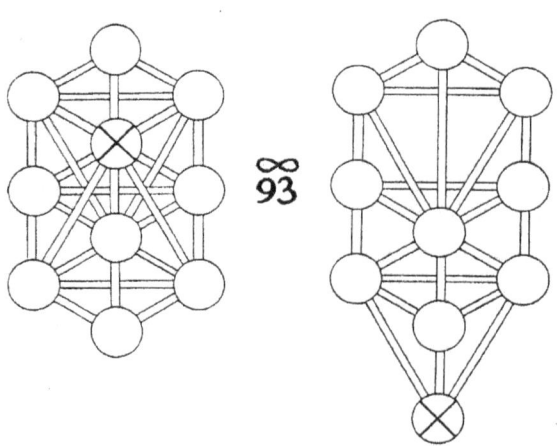

Having thus feebly portrayed the most significant event in unrecorded history (ie. the Creation of the Universe or Big Bang) we shall attempt in the following article to relate the attributions of the English letters to the paths of the Unmanifest Tree. Of the difference between these Trees & their affinities to one another we can only say, in broad terms, that the Unmanifest Tree is a map of Consciousness and the Manifest Tree a map of Experience. We therefore leave the student to interpret the Manifest Tree for himself. Our exposition of the paths will confine itself to the Unmanifest Tree.

ASHARAT

QABALLA FOR THE QUERULOUS

"The Great Magician denies me saying I am NOT (LA) or NEMO 8°= 3° & in this He fulfilleth His Office of cutting off the Understanding from the Crown which is GOD (AL). In this very thing He is the Incarnation of the Mystery of Change. AL (Kether) is REFLECTED into Chokmah as LA and the Magus (the grade not the Trump.Ed.) looketh upon the Crown along the Path of Aleph which is Zero & percieveth IT Not. The Magister Templi Understands, for the Word of Chokmah LA is truly reflected into Binah as AL & therefore the Magus appeareth to Him as GOD, whereas the Crown (the true AL) is reflected through the Path of Beth (ie the Path of the Magus, L=2 by E.Q.. Ed.) as LA & He seeth Nothing in that direction..."

"And now I see how the mystery of 93 is complete & perfect for Kether is 31 & Chokmah is 31 & Binah is 31 which is 93 the Numeration of THELEMA (in Greek.Ed.)....And this is the Mystery of the Three Persons in One God of which it is written."

(Quotation from Liber 31, Achad's key to AL, The Book of the Law.)

This process establishes the Supernals AL-LA-AL by means of two "rays" from the Crown, A & L in E.Q. Compare the verses of Trigrammaton. LA is NOT, but AL is GOD, and this "Single One" is the "Prime Deviation" from Nought, as shown elsewhere. The interplay of Zero and Two is the 93 Current.

A and L or AL as 0=2, in terms of the Supernals and the highest paths connecting Chokmah and Binah with Kether, form the beginning of the English Qaballistic alphabet. With W, these letters form the initials of AZURE LIDDED WOMAN; W as a glyph of the Waters of Space commences the sequence of stellar symbols representing the planets and luminaries in positive and negative modes. The Zodiac is the conventional expression of the planets by "night and day" houses. The attributions to follow unite this expression with the Chaldean Order of the Planets AND Luminaries, a simple and logical mathematical series which produces a coherent qaballistic scheme from the Class A texts. (The first three letters of "O azure lidded woman" are OAZ or 7.1.8.)

The third verse of Trigrammaton corresponds to the third path, the "MOTHER" = 93, who equilibriates IT. She formulates the Middle Pillar, and is the Mother of Da'ath (the result of the marriage of AL and LA). Saturn/Aquarius are attributed to the Priestess since the Priestess corresponds to the Higher aspect of the Goddess in Binah.

The fourth path establishes the twin pillars "dividing the purity" (vide Trigrammaton) with the force of the Demiurge. The Demiurge is a Gnostic conception of a God below the supreme deity (Zero), the "Lord of this

Earth" ie. of the dualistic Universe. This is the Father in Jovial guise as Zeus or Jupiter. The conception here, however, is feminine, presumably because the viewpoint is still that of Kether (and all spheres and paths are feminine in relation with the Higher). Jupiter/Pisces is attributed to the Empress corresponding with Juno, the feminine aspect of Jupiter; Venus, the traditional attribution here, is exalted in Pisces.

S, the Emperor, switches positions with the Star as in the Book of Thoth; the verse of Trigrammaton describes the Cross (of the paths of Empress and Priestess). As Aries, the sign of the Spring Equinox that commences the Thelemic year, he is the Head of a Cycle which has not begun at THIS stage of Creation, but which is implicit in the doctrine of the Trinity (Triplicities) & the Cross (Cardinals, Fixed and Mutable signs). Thus he is, as it were, held in reserve for the creation of the planetary system around Tiphereth.

The 2 of the equation 0=2 has already been "built in"; the implication is now manifest, the "Child" of Chokmah and Binah is the fourth point of the Cross. Thus F (corresponding to the Hebrew Vau, the son), the Air (product of marriage of Fire and Water), raises its heads. See commentary on Trigrammaton. This Star is (very likely) the Eightfold Star (see Vision and the Voice and elsewhere, particularly woodcuts of the Star trump).

D, the Hierophant, symbolises Tiphereth numerically (6), which, "alas!" is separated from the Supernals, thus imperfection manifests. "The fading of perfection" is in the Lower Worlds; the Hierophant "presiding over" them is Tiphereth at the centre of the Seven spheres. The Hierophant is attributed to Sun/Leo, not to Taurus as in the "Old letters of my Book"; for as it says in the Book of Thoth under this heading: "the rhythm of the Hierophant is such that he moves only at intervals of 2,000 years" ie with the Aeons (Astrological Ages as opposed to emanations. Ed.). At the Equinox of the Gods (March 21st 1904) Horus replaced Osiris as Hierophant, hence the attribution here.

O, the circular vowel, numbered seven, represents the "Woman...with her body of stars", the Goddess or Venus. She veils the Upper Heaven from the Lower Worlds, so that the view of the Adeptus Exemptus (in the fourth sphere) is cut off from the Supernals by this path from Chokmah to Tiphereth. Venus, the astrological ruler of Carnal Love, rules Taurus (the Beast) and is attributed to LUST in the Tarot. Taurus is "ASAR AS BULL" see Liber Tau, and this path crosses that of the Hanged Man "ASAR AS MAN", see Liber Tau. She connects the Inferiors with the Superiors; invokations of the Goddess at Sun conjunct Venus are initiatory.

Z or 8 corresponds to the LOVERS, or the Brothers as it is called in the Vision and the Voice. The God of this key is Mercury/Gemini. He "asserts the Spirit" (SPIRIT = 113) or in other words unites the Inferiors with the Superiors (via Binah to Tiphereth, whose number is 113 on the Unmanifest Tree, see Trees in no. 2, and article in TNE/BJM 6.1). The cycle of conjunctions of Mercury with the Sun forms a Hexagram, even as the conjunctions of Sun and Venus form a Pentagram; the mystical marriage portrayed in this card is of "Hermes & Aphrodite", the union of the Pentagram with the Hexagram is a symbol of the Great Work. (The "Children of Hermes & Aphrodite" referred to in Liber Trigrammaton are Ideas and Emotions, the typical "interference" from the twin polarities of the Tree experienced whilst ascending the Middle Pillar of Consciousness).

K forms the upper part of the Pillar of Mercy; the pillars are dealt with separately elsewhere in this paper. Note that Earth and Hell are grouped together in the appropriate verse of Liber Trigrammaton; the lower emanations or the "many" are distinguished collectively from "Heaven" the Higher, but see Liber Tzaddi verse 40: "My adepts stand upright; their head above the heavens their feet below the hells."

There is a Mystery of the Graal here, (the Chariot depicts the Graal bearer, see the Book of Thoth) and the Star 418.

This Lunar symbol is balanced on the opposite pillar by FORTUNA, corresponding to the number 10, and V as an emblem of duality. This is the Left Hand Pillar, as it were; concealing the Left Hand Path, which, as has been said by another wiser than I, has no meaning in the terminology of the Western Tradition. See remarks on the Pillars.

G=11. The first word spoken by Da'ath, that is to say the path leading to Chesed and the Exempt Adepts, is connected with the Hermits mentioned in the Book of the Law. This Hermit is Hermes, hence the attribution to Mercury/Virgo. Note also that VIRGIN = 93, value of MOTHER. The "God" conceals the Goddess through the formula of the Hermaphroditic Baphomet. This is an important magical formula concerning the Priest who invokes the Goddess. Notice that this path crosses the 7th path of Venus.

R=12. Venus is the ruler of the path of Justice which crosses the 8th path of Mercury on the "left side" of the Tree. This path leads from Da'ath to Geburah, the Sphere of Justice, from which leads the Emperor. The Emperor and Justice are the symbols of the Spring and Autumn Equinoxes, at which times day and night are of equal length. This junction of Paths at Geburah does "refine thy rapture" and harmonises the imperfect projection into duality. This path conceals the light from Geburah/Severity ie "from the persecutions". The purpose of Geburah is to refine, to strip away accretions and reveal the core or star. The influence of Justice in its Libran or Venusian mode tempers the fury of Mars, which would otherwise "split the atom" and destroy its vehicle.

C is a solar symbol, and the children who appear elsewhere in the card "The Sun" here "conceal the light of purity". "More openly" because this path is the first to pass lower than Tiphereth. On another level the Child of Hermes and Aphrodite is Hermaphroditic, ie Baphomet.

N, the letter of Scorpio, also descends from Da'ath, unto Hod, the sphere of Mercury the Magician; SCORPIO = 93, TAHUTI = 93. Mercury as the God of Intellect (as compared to Venus, Goddess of Emotion) is required to "unite with the Goddess" ie to establish in his being a cycle akin to woman's. The formula of the Hermaphrodite on this level is readily understood. The Supreme Deity is female; the Universe, Her projection, like Her possesses a cycle; to be "similar to the Goddess" requires the Magician to vibrate in harmony with this "rhythm of life". Scorpio, the 93 Current of Sex and Death, confronts him with these fundamental truths. In "whiter words", Hod as Intellectual Knowledge is separated from GNOSIS by Death (NB. Da'ath=Malkuth as a crystallization of the Tree of Life, in its unmanifest mode of Knowledge: this knowledge is a complete overview or identification with the whole).

Y=15 is peculiarly holy; it represents the Arrow of Aspiration which unites the upper and lower worlds. See the Arrow symbolism of the Vision and the Voice.

J=16, symbolising the Devil, whose path divides the Tree, cutting off the Light of the Supernals. As "Lord of the Gates of Matter" this is entirely comprehensible. (Note however the Two Hexagrams that are formed by the intersection of paths leading from the Supernals across this path.) Qaballistically to CONCEAL (=75) is to REVEAL (=75); thus "the pain of division" is "for the chance of union".

See TNE/BJM Vol.6.No.1 for a full astro-qaballistic analysis of

Libra:Scorpio:Sagittarius:Capricorn

58 + 93 + 146 + 121 = 418 by E.Q.

ELEMENTAL ATTRIBUTIONS AND THE PILLARS

U=17. Particularly important as the vowel component of the mantric root UN. In shape it resembles the "Dragon's Tail" glyph. The "Dragon's Tail" is a power of dissolution and the attribution to the "House of God" represents a particular initiatory phase, when the ascending Kundalini or magically charged aspiration attracts the influence from above which "breaks down obstructions". This is the fire from heaven of which it is written: "If I droop down my head then is rapture of the earth". The "Dragon's Tail" is in fact a misnomer in terms of AL's symbolism, which speaks of the raising and lowering of the serpent's head. The Nodal sign occurs in nature as the marking on the king cobra or uraeus serpent's hood. The Dragon represents, in Astro-Qaballa, the points at which the orbit of the Moon intersects the ecliptic (path of the planets in the Zodiac) – "this line is considered to be the Axis of the Universe". The Moon's Nodes are referred to in AL specifically:

"If I lift up my head";

"If I droop down my head";

and in the anointing spell "Burn upon their brows O splendrous serpent," the recommended symbol (to be traced in the Holy Oil) would be the Nodal symbol appropriate to the rite. The word "UP" represents the Head and Tail in fiery mode by the E.Q. attributions given by Althotash.

F=18. In Trigrammaton "the Black Brothers raised their heads" in the verse attributed to F in this schema. This path is one of those clustered around Da'ath unto which the serpent/dragon traditionally reached before the "Fall" or "Wrong of the Beginning". This head raising symbolism is of great esoteric significance. They do this "without shame" SHAME = 56, "or fear" FEAR = 56, SHAMELESS = 93. The formula is 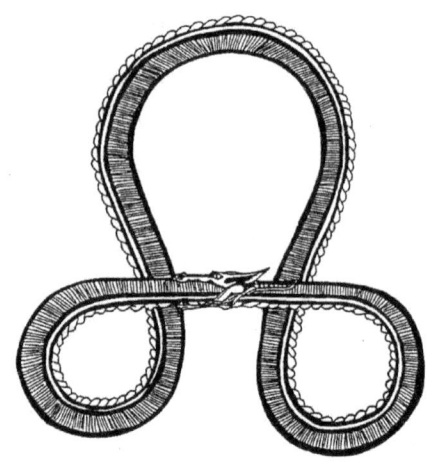 that of initiation via "sexual" (ie. Kundalini) magick. If the concept of "Sin" is not successfully overcome (by the descending fire assisted by the Will of the Magician) the "great miss" is invoked with catastrophic results.

Q=19, and falls on the lower portion of the right hand pillar, which on the Unmanifest Tree is Lunar Positive (K/Cancer/Chariot is the higher portion of the Pillar). It represents the materialising power of the Lunar Current. The commentary on Trigrammaton points to its associations with the 93 = SCORPIO formula. This however is the FINAL stage of the Lunar form of the 418 cycle, as T is of the Solar.

B=20, and falls on the lower portion of the left hand pillar which is Solar Negative (V, FORTUNA, forms the higher portion of the Pillar). This is the "solar water" or "blood of the saints" which fills the "Golden Cup". Thus does Spirit inform Matter (the Mass of the Holy Ghost), and this, to the world-hating type of mystic, is blasphemy.

M=21. The power of Spirit Active is feminine, the Shakti or Wisdom aspect of "GOD". The path leads from Venus to the Centre of the Unmanifest Tree, the Spiritual Sun. This is obviously a reference to the "Minor Adept" formula of SUN conjunct VENUS whereby the Priestess initiates the "man of Earth" into the grade of "Lover".

X=22. A passive formula, leading from Mercury to the Centre. It is interesting to compare the idea of M, which is one of appreciation (Mmmm), of nourishment or comfort, with X, a cancellation or rejection (a cross as opposed to a tick), but also a KISS (42) or CROSS (42). The reference to Ordeal X is plain, and the right interpretation of this letter should be made known to the senior male officiant at rituals of this nature.

U	☽ in ♐	17	△♃	HOUSE OF GOD
F	☉ in ♎	18	△	STAR
Q	☽ in ♑	19	▽♃	MOON
B	☉ in ♏	20	▽	SUN
M	SHAKTI/Σοφια	21	⊕+	AEON
X	THE ORDEAL X	22	⊕−	UNIVERSE
I	☽ in ♏	23	▽	CUPS
T	☉ in ♑	24	▽♌	DISCS
E	☽ in ♎	25	△	SWORDS
P	☉ in ♐	26	△♌	WANDS

THE MAGICAL WEAPONS

I. The Cup. "I" Is the letter of Self, which receives the influx of Power as a vessel. This is not an active principle, but a receptive formula of acceptance. This idea will be obscure to many Westerners to whom "I" is an assertive letter; but magick does not suit itself to the preconceived notions and conditioning of its enthusiasts, rather does it demand utter unselfish devotion to the Great Work. This self must be, as here, poised between the mental and emotional polarities of the "solar" and "lunar" pillars, aspiring to the Central Sun or Holy Guardian Angel. T(=24="GOD")the Disk. The final stage of the Solar 418 cycle, whereby a new vehicle is created. This is a formula of the Hermaphroditic Baphomet, which creates a synthesis of the opposing dualities (this being a RECIPROCAL path between Mercury and Venus alias Hermes and Aphrodite).

E. The Sword. This represents the powers of imagination which fuel the desire nature in this complex formula of Kundalini and the Grail.

P. The Wand. This represents the powers of Will without "lust of result" which provide drive and direct the desire nature.

As it is written "the work of the wand and the work of the sword."
And "Let the work be accomplished in Silence, yea let it be accomplished in Silence".

FURTHER NOTES ON THE PILLARS
(Considerations derived from analysis of the Pillars of BOTH Trees.)

There is a definite grouping of related sound values on the pillars which seems to involve both Trees. This information is potentially very useful to those constructing Barbarous Names etc. in English, or to persons wishing to understand the Qaballistic structure of our tongue. The A.'.A.'. delivered the key to this structure in 1976, but as Madame Blavatsky might have said, the key must be turned Seven times.

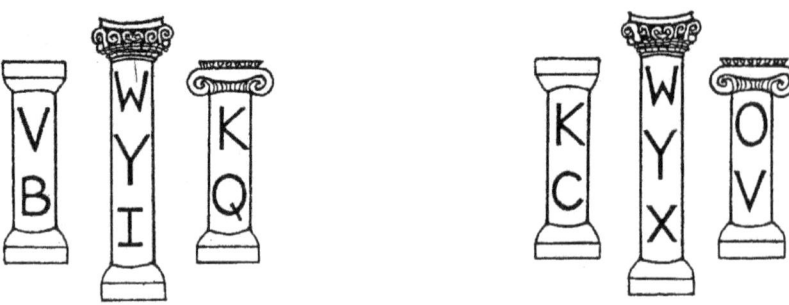

The V/B group relates to the "hard Vau" complex apparent in Greek and Hebrew. The O/V group relates to the "soft Vau" complex which is closer to "vowel status". K/Q and K/C are also close relatives, Kaph and Qoph in Hebrew terms.

The Middle Pillar groupings are much less obvious, though on the Unmanifest Tree there is a definite harmony of sound (Eye, Why, Wuh), the (Wuh, Yuh, Ecks) values of the central pillar of the Manifest Tree present difficulties. But after all X is a very mysterious letter.

The problem is how do these (imperfect) harmonies arise when a simple mathematical process is applied to an "illogical" and "composite" alphabet, and how does the E.Q. "Order & Value" reveal such phenomenal structures in our language?

The possible uses in ritual, poetry and so forth are apparent to anybody who has knowledge of these things, while its use for qaballistic interpretation of the Holy Books of Thelema is THE invaluable guide through the Ordeal X, for those who are ready for the same. But for the English Speaking World at large the great question is "How on Earth did it happen?"... with which question we knowingly enter a Universe whose laws are wholly magical and mysterious.

ASHARAT

QABALLA FOR THE QUIZZICAL

A qabalah is the esoteric doctrine behind the exoteric form of a given cultus. The qabalahs of the past have traditionally been dealt with under four headings, namely: the Practical, Literal, Unwritten and Dogmatic Qabalah.

The Thelemic QABALLA may conveniently be described using these terms, but we must bear in mind that these terms are outmoded to an extent, since the Unwritten Qabalah of the "old Aeon" has been lost, revealed or both, and the concept of a "Dogmatic Qaballa" is largely irrelevant in terms of "Do what thou wilt" and "Each for himself". Be that as it may, we shall use (and hopefully redefine) these terms for the sake of convenience.

The Practical Qabalah is usually defined as ceremonial magic and talismanic magic. Practical Qaballa is particularly related to magickal use of numbers and letters, for instance in sigils and barbarous names. These are the "mantras & spells" promised in AL. From this we could well extend the definition of Practical Qabalah to include all forms of Qaballistic meditation (such as Middle Pillar and Path Workings). In Thelema the "official rituals" of the A.'.A.'. form a hardcore of "practical qaballa" which is finely attuned to the Initiatory theme of the Thelemic Holy Books.

The Literal Qaballa traditionally consists of Gematria (the comparison of words & phrases of equal value as an interpretative technique) & its associated methods Notariqon (analysis of initials of phrases; ie Infinite Space & the Infinite Stars = ISIS; Hermit, Lover, man of Earth = HLE) & Temurah (anagrams and transliterations; ie SPINE/PENIS or ARMS/MARS). In Thelemic Qaballa such techniques as "counting well" (see Vol.VII Number 1) & the use of the Tarot Numbers as values for the letters attributed to them, a method devised by Crowley, are "Literal Qaballa".

Literal Qaballa is applied to the Holy Books and to Divine Names for interpretative purposes (or "decoding" if you prefer).

Turning our attention to the Unwritten Qaballa, we find that the Oral Tradition of the Old Aeon is lost. The secret pronunciation, let alone spelling of the Secret Name of the God of the Old Testament is lost to that tradition. The same applies on both counts to the "Lost Word" of Freemasonry. It has been said that Crowley failed to establish an oral tradition; this is not strictly true, for instance the Word of the III' O.T.O. and the instructions to the Priest officiating at the Gnostic Mass are communicated orally, as also are the Word of a Neophyte of A.'.A.'. and the interpretation of Liber A'ash and so on. On the other hand those who have won through the Ordeals are in possession of a genuine Oral Tradition, a tradition which the Secret Chiefs (the A.'.A.'. proper) "revealed and concealed" in the Book of the Law. This tradition is intimately related to the Stellar Initiations of which Thelemic Qaballa is the Key.

The Dogmatic Qaballa, so called, comprises the hardcore of traditional interpretations, correspondences and so on. (This number of our journal is intended to go some way towards providing such a core for exponents of the English Qaballa.) Formerly much superfluous theological material was associated with the Dogmatic Qabalah of the Hebrew and Christian occultists. Western magicians have largely superceded this with a "Theoretical Qaballa", of which Crowleys 777 is the masterpiece.

On the other hand the Book of the Law & the other Class "A"s form the whole basis of Thelemic Qaballa & all considerations of the Qabalahs of the Old Aeon have only limited value and application.

Such statements as "Every number is infinite; there is no difference" and "Nothing is a secret key of this law. Sixty-one the Jews call it; I call it eight, eighty, four hundred & eighteen." are fundamental to the Theoretical Qaballa of AL.

The Book Trigrammaton is described as forming the basis of the highest theoretical Qaballa, the Book Ararita of the highest Practical Qaballa. The Book Tau defines the Initiatory scheme of A.'.A.'. in precise qabalistic terms.

This completeness of the Thelemic Qaballa has evolved in the Eighties, unsuspected by the multitude. Indeed, the work has hardly begun; too few adepts, too much disharmony & division; but the world stands on the brink of profound change nonetheless, and Thelemites can indeed possess certainty, not faith.

ASHARAT

A	L	W	H	S	D	O	Z	K	V	G	R	C	N	Y	J	U	F	Q	B	M	X	I	T	E	P
1	2	3	4	5	6	7	8	9	10	11	12	13	14	15	16	17	18	19	20	21	22	23	24	25	26

MANTRAS AND SPELLS

Part 1. Every tyro is aware that magick is language based; we trot out ye olde proofes of this thesis:-

a) the gods of magick also invented the language of their especial culture: Thoth/Hieroglyphs (lit. Holy Signs); Odin/Runes; Hermes/Greek Qabalah, etc, etc.

b) Grimoires are Grammars which teach you how to Spell.

With the English Language, the magickal language of the Western Tradition in its modern phase, there are three important schools of thought concerning the actual significance of the characters or the sounds they represent.

THE SYMBOLISTS: The meeting place of surrealism and mysticism in the search for symbolism applicable in terms of "modern" consciousness is best researched in Cirlot's "Dictionary of Symbols". No hard and fast scheme has emerged in this area; nor will it.

THE SYNTHESISTS: Many occultists have endeavoured to produce or indicate the means of producing "synthetic" qabalahs, and the means of custom building the symbolism to one's own particular requirements. The best examples are by firstly, W.G.Gray (see his "Magical Ritual Methods") and secondly Franz Bardon (in his "Key to the True Quabbalah").

ZOS KIA CULTUS: Spare's methods are both traditional (within a modern environment) and "organic", but his symbolism remains inaccessible despite the heroic efforts of his interpreters, most of whom really belong in the category of synthesists, with all due respect to concerned parties. But if we apply his ideas of "practical qabalah" within the framework of the only organic contemporary Qab'AL'LA, we are immediately on a firmer footing. Alphabetical symbolism of direct magickal use in Talismans, Sigils and Ritual become immediately accessible.

The Sigil of AL may well be preferred to the heavily hebraicised G.'.D.'. Hexagram ritual. It is particularly effective in the Bornless Ritual, the arrows indicating the circumference of the Sphere. For Fire and Air use AL to charge the Sigil, formulating the upper angle first; for Water and Earth use LA, formulating the lower angle first; the arrow is made last in both cases.

The Sigil of NOX ⊗ or Mark of the Beast is already a feature of that ritual and can be charged with the Name Set, thus LAShTAL is formulated with English Hieroglyphs and phonetic potencies appreciable in today's consciousness and empowered by direct association with the Law of the Aeon.

O and X are the initials of Ordeal X and are referred to as the OX in Liber AL. (The Ox is a title of Aleph thus 111).

The capable student will need little more encouragement than this; but we append a table of suggested correspondences for the letters. Although schematic and imperfect the rationale of these ideas should become clear through interpreting the Book of the Law with the English Qab'AL'LA and the worship of Nu under the starlit heaven.

PART 2. Suggested correspondences of alphabet for Sigils, Talismans, Names, Mantras etc.

See attributions in no. 1 for references to Trigrammaton; a rough key is given in brackets.

A. (Nothing). The self devoid of attributes, "who goest without will".
L. (Duality). Maya/Magia, the "world of illusion".
W. (Mother). Intuition. Receptivity. Female Initiatory Power.
H. (Demiurge).Life. Fertility. Breath.
S. (Centre of the Cross). Kundalini. The serpent by shape. Shakti.
D. ("President").Solar Priest. Shiva as corpse.
O. (Woman). Fire of Love. Venus. (Circumference or portal).
Z. (Giant). Hermaphroditic Magician. Mystical Marriage. Baphomet. Infinity. Lightning.
K. (Master of the Temple). Lunar Current in bright phase..
V. (Black Brothers hidden). "Solar Moon". Cosmos or Chaos. Worship by Graal formula.
G. (The Master).Power of prophecy.
R. (Secret Ones).Motion as Equilibrium.
C. (Sons and Daughters of Hermes & Aphrodite). Un-Sun; Slain Lion. "Lunar Sun" or Hermaphrodite.
N. (The Enemy). Death. Lunar Current in dark phase. Putrefactio.
Y. (Holy nuns). Conjunction of Sun and Venus, the Rose Cross as act of Worship and Initiation.
J. (Horror of Time). Result. Manifestation. End product. Affirmation; especially of new order.
U. (Sensualists). The Cup of Abominations. Receptacle of the distilled quintessence.
F. (Black Brothers open).Ideas as (veils of) Self. Re-emergent self.
Q. (Corruption of the rule of TAO). Shamelessness. SHAMELESS = 93.
B. (Heaven established). Selflessness as self. Ideas burnt up in waters of heaven. The Graal.
M. (Heaven manifest). Spirit as enjoyment, nourishment.
X. (Initiation). Spirit as Initiatory Power. Cancellation. Kiss. "Topple point".
I. (Water/Heaven) The watery power of reflection producing idea of Self.
T. (Earth/Flame). Fixing the Volatile, the Slain Lion producing Honey.
E. (Globe/Air). Ideas as semen.
P. (Fire/Earth) The Phallus, as emblem of Kundalini Shakti.
(These last four elemental ideas express the interchanging qualities of the alchemical elements under the Solve/Coagula formula.)
These are all positive ideas, magickal, as opposed to the "negative" and mystical ideas of Liber Trigrammaton.
  It will readily be seen that this form of Qaballistic "interpretation" of Names and Sigils is not only possible but extremely important.

Example 1: B'A'B'A'L'O'N

B: The Graal, selflessness as self.
A: "Not" extended, the self devoid of attributes, nought.
B: see above, the negation of self's ideas of self.
A/L: None and Two; (A) the spirit going without will; (L) the veils of self projected by the "Great Magician", see the Vision and the Voice.
O: The fire of Love, or portal (gate).
N: Unity by denial.
The formula of Babalon, the Scarlet Woman, is to receive all impressions as a cup (gate of the God ON).
BAB = "B" Graal; "A" selflessness as self or self devoid of attributes.
Or, BAB = Babe ie: self; A, between Graals (the two B's), without attribute or "Not extended".
AL The spirit going without will/the impressions as masks, dualistic expressions.
ON The Gate/of Death. Or O = a space, N = a denial; the only way to deny a space is to fill it, thus a creative vacuum.
The word IT can be interpreted as;
I= Impressions as volatile images of self.
T= fixing the volatile, to produce a god-idea. <Image = I-Mage. Ed.>

Example 2: ☥

The Ankh, consisting of the letters O & T can be interpreted as;
O = Fire of Love, Venus (she is "the circumference") Solve.
T = The slain lion brings forth honey. Coagula.

Example 3: ⊗

The Mark of the Beast, interpreted as O & X. O = Fire of Love, Venus, Lust.
X = Initiation, self-cancellation. Thus Ordeal X and so on.

PART 3. An example of how Qabalistic ideas and the idea of a "cut-up", as developed by W. Burroughs and Brion Gysin, can be combined into a potent magical tool is given here in a "spell" based on the E.Q. value of "SUN + JUPITER" = 179; the intention being to make a spell to invoke or celebrate that power (while these heavenly bodies are in aspect).
Other words and phrases with the value 179, derived from the Book of the Law &/or other Holy Books of Thelema are then juxtaposed by a random/non-random mental process producing a cut-up from the original text (ideally a Book of Numbers should be kept wherein the magician records important values under numerical headings) which is magically linked with the desired force.

There is a veil- raise the spell- of the double wand-
For I am Nothing- Glorious as the Sun-
Raise the spell- ye twin warriors- pillars of the world- of the double wand- of the double wand-
A feast for life- never ending- glorious as the sun- is ever the son-
Raise the spell- a feast for life- thy heart beat- never ending-
Raise the spell- and no other shall say nay-
Raise the spell- the key of it all- star & star-system- the white foam-
That companion- never ending- SUN & JUPITER- RAISE THE SPELL!

The zealous student will doubtless be able to apply this technique for himself; it should nevertheless be noted that while cut-ups and English Qaballa are contemporary magickal tools, this modus operandi is extremely traditional.

This formula can obviously be used for talismanic magick; the student should be cautious of applying the 93/Scorpio formula, unless they be an initiate of the Sun Venus Pentagram, preferably a Winner of the Ordeal X.

ANTON K JETTSTRAKE

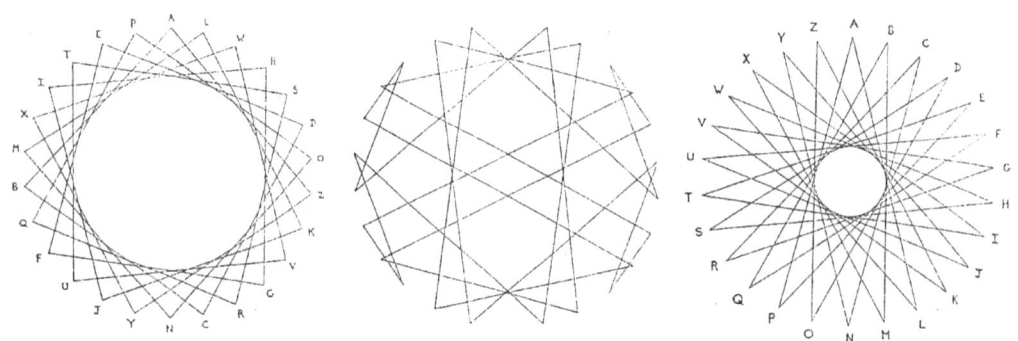

QABALLA FOR QUIBBLERS

There is a twofold usage of qaballa in rituals of Invokation.

a) The use of correspondences in formulating the ritual; in the selection of instruments, colours, & shapes, as well as the appropriate sounds & Words of the Invokation.

b) The use of these correspondences (particularly numerical values) in the ASSESSMENT OF ANY RESULTS; ie, analysis of words given by the "Deity" or "Secret Chief" invoked (and of words and symbols arising in the performance of the rituals). This enables us to judge the "validity" or "objectivity" of such experiments in terms which, being based on numerical, natural & astronomical principles, are outside any merely "personal" frame of reference & very readily interpretable in terms understandable to the operator. That such an "Intelligence" may possess knowledge of the operator's personal work is one thing; a knowledge of Fundamental laws demonstrable in those terms another. But before we attach any value whatsoever to such communications we should ourselves understand the principles of Qaballa.

It is perhaps unfortunate that the acquisition of such knowledge requires considerable effort with dryly technical & intellectual material. The alternative, however, is too often a drift into obscurely mystical meanderings which are too intensely personal to be of use to others. It should be clearly understood that a Number, a Star or a Natural Law is part of a Universal Language; which, as it is trans-personal and fundamental, is capable of providing objectively meaningful results rather than a subjective psychological state.

ASHARAT

MAGNUS DICTUS II

> Publisher's note:
>
> Due to copyright issues, the image originally printed here has been redacted. It was from ABC Warriors from *2000 A.D.*, 1988, with illustrations by Simon Bisley, as were all of the images in this essay unless otherwise noted. We have retained the text for your edification under the fair use category of UK copyright law as we believe it will not impact negatively on the market for the original work.

INTRODUCTION

My first book was tailor-made for sophisticated but insecure western occultists. Well, frig[1] that, you can't make a silk purse out of a sow's ear! This, my second book, is aimed EXCLUSIVELY at Fools who rush in where Angels fear to tread!
Dear Fool,
Please ignore the following warnings:- Magick is dangerous, retire immediately, do not light the blue touch paper, and if you're holding it at arm's length it's TOO CLOSE! Become a relic duster, an expert on comparative religion, a pyramidiot, in a word a phoney, but leave magick alone okay!
Magick can send you mad for several years.
Magick can send people you know mad for several years.
Magick WORKS! Be a green fairy or dilettante, a Cthulhu cultist or a "chaos"-"magician" instead, or you may regret it.
Ok, fairs fair, now for the details on exactly how to do IT, but don't say you weren't warned, & don't worry if you meet angels running in the other direction, they'll find a S.I.W.O. to go back with them.

---

[1] **Editors Note:** we have passed on various complaints of foul language and blasphemy to Magnus, & he has voluntarily abandoned such expressions as "fucking" & "God" or "Hell", but retains the exclamation "Frig" on the grounds that its "pornographic" associations are genuinely pious as far as the deity Frigga Herself is concerned.

> Publisher's Note: In case the footnote is unclear, it reads: "Editor's Note: we have passed on various complaints of foul language and blasphemy to Magnus, & he has voluntary abandoned such expressions as 'fucking' & 'God' or 'Hell', but he retains the exclamation 'Frig' on the grounds that its 'pornographic' associations are genuinely pious as far as the deity Frigga herself is concerned."

CHAPTER ONE: YOU KNOW NOTHING!

In my first book I strove to establish the irrational as the mainspring of magick. In this second book I shall approach the subject another way. Robert Graves once wrote a book called "Difficult Questions - Easy Answers", this my book might well bear the subtitle "Easy Questions - Difficult Answers." First for the Questions.
a) Why do magick in the first place?
b) What is magick anyway?
c) What are the fundamental bases of magick?
Now the first thing to establish firmly in your mind is this "You know Nothing!" This is the essential preliminary to any experiment, be it in a laboratory, or the more difficult method of leaving the house & making sense of the world or Universe interactively (i.e. Magick). To interact with the Universe, which we cannot do successfully on a rational level, we need an (experimental) technology of another kind. Such a technology need not knock out the reason - (why take a sledgehammer to crack a nut?), We may achieve perfectly satisfactory results by simply bypassing it. Such a technology exists in Magick.
What do we want to achieve with such a technology? Firstly we need to discover a means of obtaining 'reliable' information about our 'environment', secondly to discover means of influencing (or interacting with) our 'environment'. Astrological Qaballa is the ultimate technology for divination of all kinds, & for "results magick". Most other systems work either solely on the "astral plane", or by an occasional random hit & miss repercussion. With the machinery of this Practical Qaballa results are specific (the monkey's paw effect) and selective (i.e. definable in the system's own terms).
So, one possible answer to "why do magick?" is to discover whether it is possible to influence and make sense of our 'environment'. Our definition of 'environment' of course must include such things as our senses & 'consciousness' themselves, thus allowing the old get out "causing changes in consciousness" rather than "causing change" as the purpose of magick. But of course we can equally well extend our definition of "consciousness" to include that of which it is conscious. This is basically the difference between Objective & Subjective, but neither is actually true, that is we do not really know whether our consciousness & its environment are a) identical or b) unrelated. But we can entertain such hypotheses precisely because we know nothing & can try believing anything, in the hope of discovering a way forward. To say I don't believe is not to say I can't!
This tired old adage "Magick is the science & art of causing change to occur in conformity with will" and its equally over-used paraphrase "causing changes in consciousness to occur...." describe the two best known schools of occultism. These divergent themes are, in two words: "Power" & "Enlightenment". On the one hand an obsession with creating effects, on the other an obsession with "self improvement". The reader will doubtless be familiar with both strands, (if not see Pete Carroll's writings particularly "Liber Null" for technique / results orientation with "enlightenment" considered as a result of a specific operation, like any other; and Miyamoto Musashi's "Book of Five Rings" for a perfection / enlightenment orientation with techniques, tricks and methods, or even one's entire area of experiment, being considered entirely secondary to the Overview, distinguishing a "swordsman" from a "strategist". [Editors note: in a straight fight my money's on Musashi.])

> "Anarchy rules!
>
> "Do what thou wilt!"

The extremes resemble each other almost exactly; the value of technique & result becomes increasingly religious and symbolic, while that of enlightenment becomes increasingly practical and rational.
There is however a third possible pat definition of the purpose of magick, at once the most obvious & the most ignored. This purpose is, stated bluntly, "Survival". Magick is the science and art of interpreting a culture to itself in vivid archetypes, (as opposed to the use of stereotypes, which is the media's perversion of magickal method). This process, clearly discernible historically in shamanic religion, the ancient civilisations and even in the Judaeo-Christian complex, gives such a culture the will to live.
These archetypes are effective role models, i.e. symbols of the ideals, aspirations & experience of the tribe or nation which possesses them or is possessed by them. When a culture loses touch with its ideals or symbols (frequently through losing its language) it dies or simply rots. (The Industrial Revolution may have been the final blow for the Old Religion, but it also knocked the stuffing out of the shepherds and donkeys of the New Testament.) It may still be asked (by exceptionally dull people) how useful magick is, & when our kindly explanations fall on deaf ears we can at least point out that since magick is older than fire and the wheel, and has outlived the bow and arrow, its survival to the present day is ample testament to its utilitarian function in the history and development of our race. (The idea that Magick itself was the likely cause of us evolving from Neanderthal to Homo Sapiens in the first place is explored in my first book.) But let us leave this third definition alone for a little while (hee hee) & examine the two apparently divergent emphases which are creating such uproar at occult coffee mornings nowadays.
1/. Is Magick an extraordinarily complex way of obtaining "enlightenment" or "integration" & if so is this necessarily indicative of superstitious &/or religious tendencies?
2/. Alternatively, is Magick an equally complicated way of obtaining objective results like money, girls & Porsches etc.?

ENLIGHTENMENT.

We have already stolen an oriental maxim which best reflects our interpretation of this word, in the Book of Long Words: "Understanding of the True Nature of Everyday Life". This rather than any saint-like poise or messianic charisma (which are the attributes of personality/incarnation defined largely by astrology, and thus subject to Change) is what is intended by this term.

OBJECTIVE RESULTS.

I.e. Change occurring in conformity with will. Most "results" based techniques seem to depend on an "Altered State of Consciousness" which is obviously subjective. It should be noted that this might be a lot more successful if a second party (i.e. the "victim") rather than the magician himself were in an "A.S.C.", for instance transfixed by T.V., when the symbols chosen by the magician for his purpose were presented to the "victim". It should also be noted that the subconscious (of the magician) is NOT the most potent nor the most direct instrument in his arsenal for such purposes. The whole question of Altered States (so called Gnosis) trivialises the fundamental bases of magick. That the magician should be capable of concentration, & that this is an "altered state" compared to the grasshopper confusion of most minds, I do not deny. Nevertheless, while extreme states of "alteration" may be educational or even entertaining, they are not the mainspring of successful sorcery.

So why do magick? for results? for enlightenment? Both, neither, what? The answer is that it doesn't matter why because whatever our (initial) reason it's probably wrong. We may not have a clue why one day we decide to become an active magician. There will probably be one or two things we'd like to try, but deep down we know its a step in the dark & we can't know until we've been there! If we rush in where angels fear to tread & get out of our depth, at least we'll find a few things out for ourselves. It might take years to sink in, it may be that people find us unbearable, we may go mad or undergo enormous upheavals in our life before we really begin to cotton on.

Publisher's note:

Due to copyright issues, the image originally printed here has been redacted. It was an image from 'Summer Magic', first printed in seven episodes in progs 571-577 of *2000 A.D.*, running April through June, 1988.

It read: "The danger is, of course, the adept may become seduced by the desire for **personal power**. He may become a **leader**.

"Thus he would become a **slave** of his followers and his journey would end there."

Delusions of grandeur, arrogance, confused visions & the urge to talk about them; all these & worse may be no more than side effects, while we sort out the power we have unleashed. It's best to start young, rather than postponing it & finally missing the point altogether. To Hell with (oy! steady on Magnus. Ed.)..sorry, FRIG Maturity and building a sound foundation. Thelema is about DOING IT. Take risks, live dangerously, learn from experience rather than authorities! If you leave it to the experts you'll only realise too late that there aren't any, that you're

on a ship of fools with nobody at the wheel or at the helm.
Better a glorious failure than a minor success. DO IT! Who cares whether we get approval, or if no-one knows about it but ourselves. Magick is not a social activity for Frigg's sake! Frig the occult scene!
We do magick because we want to know what makes things tick; what "irrational" or "unscientific" forces are involved in the True Nature of Everyday Life. T.N.E.L. is not half as rational or scientific as the "real world" of the media magicians (who direct the hive consciousness of our "civilisation") would have us believe. (There is no Priestess image in the media's vocabulary, think about THAT!!)
Magick is an experimental process. Neglecting to investigate the Tradition (both its techniques AND its allegories) leads to dead letter procedures where techniques gain an almost symbolic value of their own, and become collectable while trendy values replace genuine occult principles. To reverse this trend we need to ask questions & look for answers. (Why do Magick? What is Magick? Where is it going? What are its fundamental bases? etc. etc. etc.)
Now, put simply, there is one reason why novices do what THEY do, & that is, presumably, to learn magick & become a magician. But why do magicians do magick? All the talk of spells to obtain results of the "wine, women and song" or "mink, money and men" variety is so much crap. Any half decent human being can get these things if they want them and learn a bit about the True Nature of Everyday Life in the process.

This image was also from 'Summer Magic', first printed in seven episodes in progs 571-577 of *2000 A.D.*, running April through June, 1988.

It read: "And when the master has added something of significance to the art, he can be content to take a back seat to nature..."

Real Magick in essence asks (and seeks answers to) the same questions as philosophy & science, basically "What is the true nature of the reality my senses and consciousness imperfectly reveal and can I do anything about it?" Note that as all experience is necessarily subjective the expression "objective results" is largely meaningless. Magick takes as its experimental fundamentals the only (transpersonal) constants in our experience: Physiological, Astronomical & Numerical "facts". Magick is at root identical to Tantra, it is a way of action rather than of faith. It assumes we CAN interact with the Universe actively, and sets out to do so. That's the definition, the rest is experiment. This is the Quest for the Holy Graal that leads to the Chapel of Abominations.
The great creative matrix of magick is language; Alphabet Soup is the Primordial Soup. Ideas in action are embodied in language. Language is an entity (akin to the old theory of Collective Consciousness or the Astral Light) in which Archetypal Ideas or Forces live & evolve. The root of magickal language lies deep in man's past; the process is not synthetic but organic. It is not we who give meaning to language but language which gives meaning and direction to our experience. The Runes of the Norsemen & the Goths and the Oghams of the Celt are the ancestors of our alphabet, rather than either Latin or Greek, and certainly not Hebrew. The runes were "obtained" or "inspired", not devised, any more than our letters & the structure of the alphabet are either "accidental" or "artificial".

Language expresses our attitudes, our orthodoxy & our inhibitions and reinforces or reduces them at will - whose will we leave for you to decide. Language not only expresses our experience, it defines & sets limits to what we can experience & how.
The most significant results possible in shaping our experience & attitudes could be readily obtained simply by placing a word in the language. John Dee put a word into our language which had not been there before, & FORMULATED a concept. The word is UNIT; before it existed we had the idea of a Unity, but this actually excluded the idea of units. A unit is not merely a part or division of a whole, it is an entity in its own right. The implication of THIS tetragram are truly huge.
Magicians like Burroughs & Gysin have sought to blow a hole in the consensus reality by producing new "linguistic structures" which express and access an EXPERIENCE of reality which science & philosophy only hypothesise about. Such a process is entirely in keeping with the role of the magician in all times.

"He's left his calling card...

"The Hierophant"

"There is a word to say about the Hierophantic Task. BEHOLD!"

We now sum up our conclusions on the question "Why do Magick?" before moving on. We have already broken down the various arguments into neat sterile definitions, i.e. Enlightenment/Knowledge versus Results/Power, and we have seen that with both these approaches, when the frigging about is over the big question "So what?" looms large. (Consequently we have offered a third alternative: Survival alias Cultural/Evolutionary Magick.) These two are by no means mutually exclusive, but let us further define our terms before moving on to "What is Magick anyway?"
People labour under the wierdest illusions, thinking meditation alone will make them calm, when the reverse is true; you must be calm in order to meditate. All that "stillness" and "radiant aura" stuff has more to do with the achievement of a reasonable state of physical health & ease of circumstances in order to get on with one's meditation in the first place. The meditation itself may well turn you into a howling animal as your "complexes" emerge in your peaceful laboratory! If you're not riddled with complexes then the awful realisation of what makes the world tick will certainly ruffle the composure of the naive idealist who began this meditation, and may even upset the psychotic cynic who completes it!
So much for Knowledge!
As for Power, the art of getting what you want; quite how this is intended to result from manipulating "subconscious forces", I'm at a loss to understand. Whilst the so-called "excitatory" & "inhibitory" gnoses may well put one in touch with one's subconscious, but is this likely to result in objective results, like money or women or destruction of enemies (for instance)? On the other hand such techniques may work some other way in which case the subconscious is nothing more than a handy little "spirit" or "talisman" disguised in 20th Century "Emperor's new clothes"; or even a complete red herring!

In any case the late, great William Sargant in his "Battle for the Mind" (essential reading folks) shows clearly that the active and passive modes are equally and inseparably involved in each single conversion/ecstatic/brainwashing experience, rather than forming distinct and separate disciplines.
It is obvious to me that real power is obtained simultaneously with

knowledge as we have defined it. The question is then not "Can you do magick?" so much as "Are you prepared to?" MAGICK WORKS, often despite the magician, frequently misinterpreted or ignored by him. There is NO POINT thinking "Is it going to work?" because SOMETHING is definitely going to happen, & the best you can hope to achieve in all honesty is to understand it when it does. Gain that understanding or clarity (the ability to ask the right question rather than score cheap debating points) & virtually Nothing is impossible. Knowledge and Power are synonymous; the only recourse is experiment, with one proviso, don't confuse the planes.

If you are using a particular system, understand it in its own terms, whether it's a philosophical model or a technique. You can, & should, experiment with a wide range of methods, symbols & approaches, from a variety of cultures and periods; but one at a time, avoid blurring, seek clarity & completeness although both are supremely elusive. You've got your whole life to mess it up, so why rush?

Here endeth the first lesson.

CHAPTER TWO: (IN WHICH MAGNUS REPEATS HIMSELF AND PLAGIARISES EVERYBODY.)

The Fire fell from Heaven,.....it passed through the Spheres of Power, Illusion & Change, across an abyss of thought & through the Spheres of Restriction, Expansion, Contraction, Harmony, Emotion, Intellect and Instinct, receiving packages of various different shapes, sizes and colours from the officials of these Spheres. All this before finally gaining a shape, as it floated, warm and serene, awaiting the moment of Truth. Then came a terrific struggle as the Waters were parted & the Fire came into the World, & SCREAMED.

What it was trying to say was "Oh no! Fooled again!"

I don't know what They promised you kid, but I guess by now you know that Here we count those Spheres & call them "planets", & the process you experienced is called "being born" which is part of what they call the "human reproductive system".

It's very mysterious territory alright, & you'll need a chariot to get around in - well, more like a sphere really, wheels within wheels. Build it out of numbers, star stuff and sex. Different parts of the wheels for different roads & routes. You want a fighting vehicle? Count Five, press the Red button & get dominant baby!

What magick offers a culture or civilisation is an Idea, a "myth" or "symbol" that explains "society" to itself. Religion has occasionally provided this Idea through the things it "borrowed" from Magick. To explain a culture to itself, in clear, coherent imagery, give it a reason for being, explain its phases and crises and its direction, devise rites of passage between infancy and adolescence, adolescence and adulthood, to reinterpret the archetypes for the age which man & women can understand & identify with, & in effect become. Without "that" civilisation doubts itself & declines in confusion & dismay; or vanishes in fire to make way for a bolder, more primal culture.

Magickal symbols, such as runes and sigils, are understood by the "right hemisphere of the brain" or the "noumenal consciousness"; whereas their "linear" equivalents, i.e. letters, are interpreted rationally by the "left hemisphere" or "reasoning mind". (Pardon the rattle of terminology.) It is well known that the ideographic scripts such as Futhark (runic) & Proto-Canaanite (Hebrew's pagan ancestor) were derived from "pre-literate" magickal symbols. It is also fairly obvious that the Latin characters (i.e. the English alphabet) closely resemble their Futhark equivalents. That the

> "Listen, I may be old-fashioned..."
>
> "Oh there's no 'may be' about it!"
>
> "But unless we act now, **billions of lives will be lost!**"

Book of the Law should refer to the "runes" as well as to the "order & value of the English Alphabet" is no accident.
"There is A WORD to say about the Hierophantic task: Behold."
The word of the Hierophantic task is "Behold". It is his task to "show the sacred things" (hierophanes) i.e.: to make use of symbols present in the experience of the initiates, and of the people.
Hence the importance of turning our letters into runes, so to speak. Indeed of turning the whole apparatus of the media, particularly the "Words of Power" & the symbols and archetypes of Hollywood and TV good to account. Mass media - a combination of Pluto and Neptune keywords - techniques make use of catchwords, symbols, music, slogans, stereotypes, fantasy imagery (erotic/ego rewarding), relentless repetition (mantra) & other such "occult" techniques.
An interesting booklet on this theme has recently been republished by TOPY / U.S. entitled TELEVISION MAGICK, I will refrain from quoting it here as the material is explored in some detail and my space is limited, so buy yer own!
We might add that the media magicians are not held back by ignorance of Hebrew or Freemasonic symbolism! either on their part or that of the people (I do not say of the initiates). Propaganda is in essence the major application of magick in ANY culture. In a crisis, such as faces governments and businesses every day, the "right word" or "gesture" so long as it is clearly heard or seen is generally more effective than any rational theory or enshrined tradition, or indeed any actual WORK.
In fact in most situations this is the case. It is well known that a uniformed parade & plenty of drum banging is a surer recruitment technique than grave rumblings about the worsening international situation & an open debate on the political future of the appropriate nation.
A politician's career can suffer worse from a photograph showing him locked out of his own home than years of bumbling ineptitude in office. Adverts attract more custom than high quality craftsmanship. Need I go on? I'm sure you can develop a thousand such examples & have more fun doing it. I shall not waste more space, or the students valuable time by adding diagrams of the brain or a glossary of right-on jargon or a list of persons plagiarised. The student is, after all, far too busy introducing insidious sigils, maddening mantras (jingles?) & self-fulfilling prophecies into the "consensus reality" - "bypassing the rational mind" like wolves in sheep's clothing. But remember the great word of power: T.R.I.V.I.A, which being interpreted means Totally Reliable Invasion Via Insidious Action, or Transcending Reason, Ideas Vault Into Actuality, & so on.

"Can't... get up... stairs..."

"You? How can YOU possibly solve a mystery which tantalises the mind of a master of khaos?"

"Gravity again! Slowing him down! Yeah, I think I've got the answer!"

YOU KNOW NOTHING!

One way to demonstrate the above fact is to develop three theses on one subject. All must a) be equally convincing, b) make use of, or at least make sense of the same data, c) be capable of implementation "experimentally", granted that someone possessed appropriate facilities. Let us give an example, choosing for this purpose an area of fundamental significance, we shall ask "what is the "original" significance of sexual symbolism &/or activity in magick?"

THESIS ONE. STUDENTS NAME: IULUS DE MONSALVAT.

The significance & purpose of sexual symbolism & activity in occultism is clearly a veiled reference to an occult selective breeding programme & the preservation of a sacred bloodline. The endless genealogies of the Bible, tracing the line of Adam through its various offshoots to Jesus Christ & the future President/Pope of Europe; the stories of sons of god consorting with the daughters of men; the divine right of kings, all lend weight to this interpretation.

The cult of the ancestor; the mother goddess; the Sangraal or Sang Real ie holy blood; the power of sites & symbols associated with our own cultural predecessors & the importance placed on "exploring the river of the soul, where and whence thou art come"; the initiatory question "From whence do you come?" all hint at the same primal mystery of our genetic (dare we say racial) heritage.

The tabus of earlier stages of our culture & the specific occasions on which they were periodically relaxed frequently make sense only in this light. The "orgies" of "primitive" religions were the means by which the divine bloodline was perpetuated. For instance the Vestal Virgins as well as "guarding the perpetual fire" had the additional role in ancient times of conducting such "orgies" with a select "college" of "sacred kings". Thus they perpetuated the divine bloodline of Rome, which later degenerated into Emperor worship. (The worship of a man is the worship of the Beast.)

> "I realised **mind scanners** checked that robots entering the tomb were there to **repair** the system, not **destroy** it..."

In modern times we have the debutante season & the pedigree guides to maintain similar tribal tabus. (Okay shut up you Trojan philistine. Ed.)

SECOND THESIS. STUDENTS NAME: SMALLUS PRINTUS.

The original and primal significance of sexual symbolism and activity in magick and religion arises due to its aptness as an allegory of the union of the worshipper with their god, or the knower uniting with the known in meditation.

There is a physiological & mental analogy between the ecstatic states attained through sex and those obtained in prayer, meditation & similar practices. As an extension of this idea we have the tantric or quasi-tantric approach where sexuality is directly employed as a means of worship &/or meditation.
This kind of technique is based on the unspoken assumption that these analogies are not merely accidental or irrational, but real. In the "Alchemical Marriage" of the Empress and the Hierophant, or mind with its thought, these dualities are abolished, and reality is perceived by a "new" being or in a "different" way (very poetic I don't think. Ed.) Variations on this theme range from the rather puerile: "Honest to god guvnor, it's not a dirty book it's the Song of Solomon, I only borrered it." "Wretched man 'tis an allegory of God's love for his church." to the sophisticated "human reproductive cycles & their phases are analogous to astrological cycles & their phases." ("Who said that then?" Ed. "What, do you mean who said it first?" "O never mind!" Ed.)

"That's why only you, Blackblood and Mek-Quake were attacked... I've suspected for some time that the only reason the three of you came this far was to make sure we **FAILED**..."

"The black hole destroyed earth... and your precious khaos triumphed..."

THESIS THREE. STUDENTS NAME: CARLOS COSTABRAVA.

The significance of sexual symbolism relates neither to "tribal" breeding rites & tabus nor to ecstatic states but to occult biochemistry. Like blood, the sexual secretions contain life force or life potential **which may be conditioned in various ways; chiefly yoga, astrological ritual and diet.** This potential is the basis of magickal power. Magickally charged sexual secretions may be utilised to empower spells, to consecrate talismans, or to act as alchemical agents charged with whatever force is **successfully** invoked in the **preparation** or distillation. (There is also the matter of ascertaining what properties are inherent, in the different secretions as separate and distinct substances, if any.
The fertility rites of ancient times sought to utilise these powers for various purposes. The fertility of the land, (& thus the preservation of the race) was chiefly, but not exclusively, the object of such rites.
Enter Magnus at stage right clutching a letter: "You three can go & talk among yourselves now." He puts down the letter, it's a T.
Now whether any such three theses be partially or wholly compatible is neither here nor there for the moment. The point is that a thesis is only a thesis, and any idea is capable of being distorted, exaggerated or downright wrong, not to mention obscure, forgotten, twisted, misquoted or taken out of context.

"Sorry Deadlock. Afraid the solution was just **TOO SIMPLE** for a master of khaos!

"Ciao!"

Fundamental Realities are capable of being misunderstood, but it is much more difficult to erase them altogether. You cannot abolish seventeen, nor forbid Jupiter to form a sextile aspect with Venus. All you can do is try and get people to call it something else, or distract people's attention from the real significance, or the very existence of such abominable things.

So remember, you know Nothing! Have no established mental criterion! Attempt to make sense of our misunderstood & ill-perceived reality without such superfluous mental luggage as opinions or theories bogging you down before you start, or indeed during the journey itself. What you need is signposts, like the ones our paleolithic ancestor used: PHYSIOLOGICAL, STELLAR & NUMERICAL constants are the only factors, aside from the qualities of matter, upon which any kind of empirical knowledge, or any transpersonal, "suprarational" standard of symbolism can be based.

SPECIAL SUPPLEMENT: UNCLE MAGNUS GOES PSYCHO-EXPERI-MENTAL.

In scientific experiments any preconceived ideas about the result nullify the validity of the experiment. For trainee magicians this is a recurring problem, they expect to be told in advance why and what will happen, well tough on them!

Experiment One. Obtain a new notebook and pen & write in the book your every desire, no matter how minor or how grandiose. This practice must be maintained daily for a whole fortnight. The completed catalogue of desires is to be treated as a talisman, according to the ingeniuum of the compiler.

Experiment Two. This requires two participants, one male, one female. Let them be seated comfortably, in asana or on cushions. Let them concentrate upon each other's eyes, not suppressing smiles or shudders but remaining in eye contact. Let this practice be continued for at least one hour, & repeated as often as possible, preferably daily, or if this is not practical twice weekly or some other regularised pattern. (Technique buffs might notice a superficial resemblance between this method & the "death posture" technique where the operator concentrates on their own eyes in a freestanding mirror. This technique we therefore name the Life Posture.)

Experiment Three. In this the magickal weapons are the Hand and Eye (I.O. in old letters). Let the magician hold their right hand before them, either in the sign of the fig or open, & vibrate silently or with their breath a Word of Power chosen from among these: "HAD", "ABRAHADABRA", "AOUIE" (Ah-Oh-Oo-Ee-Air); repeat the word as a mantra, slow and drawn out, concentrating on the hand until the vibration is felt in the hand rather than the throat or diaphragm. This practice should be performed twice daily, for at least one month. (Again, the resemblance between this technique & the Lucid Dreams technique where the magician concentrates on both hands before sleep, may be noted, and forgotten.)

In the latter two experiments a record should be kept of duration, results etc.

MAGNUS DICTUS.

Illustrations by Simon Bisley, Copyright (c) 1988, 2000 A.D.

MANTRAS AND SPELLS

The most simple & obvious way of using our alphabet/language ideographically, i.e. magickally rather than as a linear & psuedo-rational process, is in talismans & ritual magick. The sigils of Zos Kia Cultus are an obvious example. The runic alphabet, the direct ancestor of our English characters, is also ideal for this purpose. See the accompanying table of runic equivelents drawn from the many variants & allowing for such accidents of history as reversal, i.e. ↑ = ↓. Likewise the symbols of Trigrammaton may be used in talismanic & other "traditional" ways, either as they are or as the basis of linear figures, in much the same way as Francis Barrett & the Golden Dawn used the symbols of geomancy to obtain "characters of the planets" etc.

In the second number of the Equinox we described the process of "counting well" longhand, a process which can be performed more rapidly shorthand [value of word (a) x no. of letters in word (b) + value of word (b) x no. of letters in word (a).] A method of constructing Magick Squares & Rectangles having specific numerical values can readily be devised from the longhand technique. The idea being that the numerical value of such a square is appropriate to a particular operation & the "Practical Qaballist" will either discover the ones he needs or devise them, as & when that particular operation becomes "necessary".

Two examples are given: BLACK counted well with STONE = 600, 6 = LAW, multiplied by 100 suggests extending it into the Three Worlds (or digits), i.e. Establishing the Law of Thelema; the second example is HOLY counted well with GRAAL = 248 suggesting its use to materialise the serpent fire (24=T= ♌/▽).

85

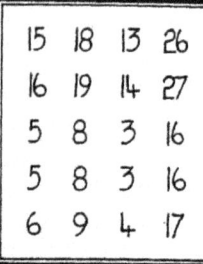

Also illustrated are two examples of Talismans as described above, one of Jupiter (values of 143), another of Sun-Jupiter (values of 179). An appropriate verbal spell for use with these squares and talismans could be devised as shown in "Mantras and Spells" (2), alternatively or additionally this spell devised by AOS could be used:

O mighty **Rehctaw!**
Thou who exists in all erogenousness,
We evoke Thee!

By the power of the meanings arising from these forms I make.
We evoke Thee!

By the Talismans that speak the secret leitmotif of desire,
We evoke Thee!

By the sacrifices, abstinences and transvaluations we make,
We evoke Thee!

By the sacred inbetweenness concepts
Give us the flesh!

By the quadriga sexualis
Give us unvarying desire!

By the conquest of fatigue
Give us eternal resurgence!

By the most sacred Word-graph of Heaven
We invoke Thee!

ANTON K. JETTSTRAKE

BLOOD & GUTS

It's become quite the thing among occult lounge lizards nowadays to proclaim in a languid drawl "traditional magic is dead" or similar pretentious nonsense. One is of course meant to assume that these self sacrificing souls spent years working out exactly what traditional magick was about and then doing it, only to be bitterly disappointed. But nothing could be further from the truth.

The only way these people ever obtained a reputation (among the weak minded) was by continually dismissing things without really trying them. As the weak minded are even less capable of getting to grips with, say, astrological timing, they're very relieved to be assured by these self proclaimed experts that they needn't bother. The upshot of it is that scarcely anyone has a clue what traditional magic is, the so-called traditionalists included. One hundred years after the Golden Dawn and there has still not been a single book on astrological factors in ritual, and the so called synthesis of the Western Tradition has not grown by so much as a page. Nevertheless, the idea that traditional magick is dead is a complete misnomer; which tradition? The Indo-European shamanic tradition perhaps? Are modern magicians really incapable of being imaginative with traditional magickal ideas, of applying them in a new cultural era? The essential principles of magick haven't changed, despite the protests of modern 'wizards' who can't or won't apply those principles in the modern world. Word Games! Tradition isn't a right-on word, unless it's someone else's tradition, "Ooh isn't it just ethnic, Milo?" Virtually all modern magickal ideas have precise analogues in traditional magick, frequently concealed behind the "Emperor's new clothes" by those too arrogant or too stupid to recognise the work of their predecessors, ancient and modern.

A modernist, then, is someone who having recognised his ignorance, elevates it to a virtue. It's just as easy to conceal ignorance behind modern jargon as behind medieval gibberish. The modernists decry the complexity of occult symbols (offended, we are assured, by those who hide behind this complexity), but then they inform us that to understand why THEY are right we must understand Quantum physics and biochemistry. They say "use the modern technology", well thanks very much, we do, for Qaballa and Astrology.

The rational technocratic wizards (i.e. college kids) have painted themselves into a corner with this codswallop. 100 years of occult revival and scarcely one of them can read an ephemeris or erect a horary chart, they think gematria is some kind of cerebral emetic, and wouldn't know a Qaballa if it jumped up and bit them in the face. So they are reduced to pompous non sequiturs. The fact is that nearly every accusation they fling at their opponents (bless 'em) is truer of themselves. They see Qaballa & Astrology as dogmatic because THEY are dogmatic, they see gematria as a word game because they are into word games, and they see traditional magick as dead.......

Whereas we once saw chaos magick as young and alive because we were young and alive. Now we know things for what they are; now it's time the real candidates for initiation, the true investigators, the imaginative loners got into traditional magick, because ALMOST no-one else has ever done any.

JAKE STRATTON-KENT.

EVERY WOMAN IS A STAR

The question of sexual politics in magick is reachining mammoth proportions of late, so much so that the politics have obscured the magickal principles involved. In a recent article in Nuit-Isis no. 6 an excellent summation of the situation was given by Sister Shantidevinath 93:

"....the idea that somehow women have, by virtue of having a womb, some remarkable form of power which men do not naturally possess. Although this might seem an attractive idea, particularly in contrast to the shame that women frequently feel regarding their bodies, and their menstrual cycle in particular, I think it is in fact in the long term an oppressive one. For one thing, both Ann Campbell and Kenneth Grant agree that there is some power in Women that CAN ONLY BE TAPPED IN PARTNERSHIP WITH A MAN." (Emphasis in the original, and rightly so.)

Now I don't happen to think that the view of the Female sexuality possessing magical power is necessarily oppressive, but then I do most definately dispute the idea that this power must be used in concert with a man.

This point has been hinted at as a most sacred arcanum in this magazine and its predecessor time and time again. Within the lodges of the A.'.A.'. that arcanum has been put into practice effectively for the last 15 years to my certain knowledge and possibly long before. I quote from number four of this journal:

"In sexual contexts, the word is not spoken in the great rites. What is the difference between worship and the communication of a word? A word could not be spoken using - - (woman to woman) as IT WOULD MANIFEST A POWER OF BALANCED FORCE (emphasis added) also during a + - (man to woman) ritual where NOT one seed is given."......."The ritual of 107 is the worship of the Virgin Goddess DIRECTLY by woman (emphasis added)......the ritual is the worship of woman and Goddess by man.....Man worships the union of woman with the Goddess because this is the ultimate truth".

It is this directness that lifts her to "pinnacles of power", for whereas in rites where many worshippers of either sex worship the enthroned priestess under the stars as it were, the power is largely mystical in nature and union is concealed; in the rites where priestesses alone worship the enthroned priestess the power is directly magickal and union is also direct. In my own experience the priests, even the chief invokant, must leave the Temple and allow the priestesses to continue the rite before the Goddess power can truly manifest itself in the priestess. They may enter again later and resume the ritual, but what happens between their departure and return are the mysteries of Isis, of which I am not permitted to speak further, and without which there is no true magick.

<u>LIBER AL</u> II.22. I am the Snake that giveth Knowledge & Delight and bright glory, and stir the hearts of men with drunkenness. To worship me take wine and **strange drugs** whereof I will tell my prophet, and be drunk thereof!

<u>LIBER VII</u> VII.1. By the burning of **the incense** was the Word revealed and by the **distant drug**.

<u>LIBER VII</u> VII.2. O meal and honey and oil! O beautiful flag of the moon, that she hangs out in the centre of bliss.

There have been many interpretations over the years of the references to drugs in the Holy Books of Thelema. The idea is that they represent 'secretions', particularly those of the Priestess in "tantric" rites, wherein the analogy between stellar cycles and the female reproductive cycle becomes 'vivid' and actual. The incense referred to is the "cakes of light" of AL III. vs 23/25.

Qaballistically, "STRANGE DRUGS" and "DISTANT DRUG" are identical, for both have the value 143 by English Qaballa. This number is also the total of all the **numbers** in the two lines of the Cipher of AL.II.76.

$$\left. \begin{array}{l} 4\ 6\ 3\ 8\ \text{ABK}\ 2\ 4\ \text{ALGMOR}\ 3\ Y = 30. \\ + \\ X\ 24\ 89\ \text{RPSTOVAL} = 113. \end{array} \right\} = 143.$$

143 is the value of the **words**: JUPITER. COMPLETE. PERFECT. MIGHTIER. TERRIBLE. WORSHIPPER. DELIGHTING. and of the **phrases:** MANTRAS + SPELLS. ARDOURS OF HADIT. SACRAMENT + GRAAL. O WINGED SNAKE. SNAKE

OF LIGHT. THE BLUE & GOLD. KING OF CUPS.

The idea of a drug, secretion or incense of the nature of Jupiter, which is perfect and complete in itself, being "distilled" by a distinct alchemical - which is to say "tantric" - process, is implicit in "The Paris Working", where Crowley and Neuburg concentrated specifically on the "benefic planets" (omitting Venus, due, it seems, to the absence of a Priestess) and particularly JUPITER in a series of sexual invokations. It is my contention that Crowley was unaware of the esoteric aspects of astrology - indeed during one of these operations Mercury gave him the sound advice "make a particularly careful study of the stars" - and his experiments consequently were rather crude in many ways.

The Typhonian OTO on the other hand has emphasised the "science of the kalas" or "vaginal essences" and frequently connected them with stellar or astrological symbols. This is in fact the basis of the "physiological gnosis". In practical terms, however, symbols themselves are useless. Magickal power is obtained from techniques and "physical" realities. Experimentally, ANY planetary power may be invoked into an enthroned Priestess, although Jupiter, Venus, Moon and Sun are distinctly to be preferred to Pluto, Neptune and Uranus, and considerable experience is required before aspects like Sun-Mars can be successfully worked; whilst the Restriction of Saturn is best left uninvoked and unpersonified by the group and its individual members, at least as a general rule. Mercury is a fairly neutral planet astrologically; quite why Crowley considered him a benefic planet is beyond me, unless it be on a crude Venus = Girl, Mercury = Boy hypothesis.

The essentials of such a ritual are:

The "preliminary invokation" or Bornless Rite performed by the Temple Master.

The dedication by the Priestess of Her Body to the Goddess (the Opening of the Vault of the Adepts).

The Adorations of the enthroned Priestess: 1. The chapters of Treasure House of Images appropriate to the signs occupied by the planets invoked; 2. The 169 Cries of Adoration. In the former case, the word God is replaced by Goddess throughout, in the latter the worshippers should participate in the responses "I adore Thee Evoê, I adore Thee IAO".

Each of these stages of the Ritual may be developed separately as things in themselves. At this stage the Temple Master commences to "Invoke...with a pure heart & the serpent flame therein" using no script but as it were improvising, identifying each part of the Priestess & each reaction of the Priestess with the Goddess. He shall also channel the Kundalini through his chakras, thus by "sympathetic magic" encouraging that of the Priestess (experience in the Middle Pillar exercise or Bornless Rite will be very useful to him). She, for Her part, should RESIST the power of the Goddess until she can no more.

This invokatory power is very subtle, and few in the West possess it consciously. The poet who knows that the function of poetry is to INVOKE HER, the shaman/showman, & insignificant little guys like Hitler and Napoleon possess it in abundance, but few know how to use it. Few indeed possess "a pure heart" or "the serpent flame"; those who possess both are rarer still.

Let us sum up this rather fragmented article by insisting that:

a) An Oral Tradition, or living magickal current, can only grow where such "worship of Nu" is regularly attempted. The attitude of reverence for woman, for sexuality physical and metaphysical and for our own ideals - which is implicit in Tantra in the East and in the Graal in the West - must be carefully nurtured and cultivated. "To worship me", ME = 46 = WOMAN.

b) Aligning such "feasts" with astrological configurations "regenerates the Earth" and gives continuity to the groups celebrating them. Each time such a ritual is repeated, it will be with increased experience and renewed power. Astrologically Timed Ritual is, by its very nature, worship of the Star Goddess, and of WOMAN by extension.

c) The Book of the Law and its Qaballa are the ideal basis for such "experiments", distinctly to be preferred to any technical theses or "comparative" and "eclectic" methodology.

d) The existence of a Sisterhood is synonymous with magick as a living & continuous process (an Oral Tradition). The emergence of such sisterhoods simultaneously with the discovery and development of a native QABALLA (=46=ONE) is no coincidence. Both are equally essential to any true occultural renaissance - BOTH HAVE OCCURRED.

SOPHIE ZUMM

JOTTINGS

Recently one of our Adepts was studying Frederick Carter's "Dragon of Revelation", wherein the author construes the Book of Revelation as an astronomical ritual. Central to his thesis are the Zodiacal Signs: Gemini, Sagittarius, Libra and Pisces. Immediately our honoured brother totted up their combined values by English Qaballa, and lo! he obtained 418. Intrigued we set our computer to discover how many groups of four signs have the total 418. As well as our consecutive group Libra, Scorpio, Sagittarius, and Capricorn and that detailed above we found Gemini, Leo, Sagittarius and Capricorn. Inspired I took the seven signs from these three groups Gemini, Leo, Libra, Scorpio, Sagittarius, Capricorn and Pisces and added them together, and LO! I obtained 666. Furthermore these seven signs represent the seven planets of traditional astrology: Mercury, Sun, Venus, Mars, Jupiter, Saturn and the Moon (if we take the tarot trump representing Pisces rather than its conventional ruler, Jupiter).

Nor was this all, we set the computer searching for ANY combination of signs totalling 718, and it found only two such groups, each of seven signs, and of these two only one was consecutive, viz: Sagittarius, Capricorn, Aquarius, Pisces, Aries, Taurus and Gemini. The non-consecutive group consists of Aries, Sagittarius, Cancer, Scorpio, Pisces, Capricorn and Gemini. The total of the nine signs comprising these two groups is 889, which, if we subtract 718 gives 171.

Readers of our first issue (which is now extremely rare) will have seen the two twenty-six pointed stars which turn the ABC into the ALW order and vice versa; recent geometrical research reveals five such stars; another pair which produces the AJS order from the ABC and vice versa, and a fifth which produces the AFK order clock wise and returns it to ABC anticlockwise. These alternative orders do not produce any particularly intriguing results as gematrias, but it is intriguing to note that virtually every way of producing the ALW order will produce the AJS order, ie the grid of sheet sixteen and the tables of John Dee which will contain all continuous Julian Cyphers within the English Alphabet (12 x 13 = 156) etc. Blah blah blah.

In our second number we spoke of the SUN VENUS (= 107) and how the cycle of their conjunctions produce a pentagram. The cycle of SUN MERCURY (151) conjunctions produce a Hexagram, as we may have noted elsewhere, Astro-Qaballists will note that 107 x 5 + 151 x 6 = 1441, which divided by 11 (points of the combined stars) gives 131 = UNIVERSE.

ALTHOTASH

A WORD TO SAY
SUNDRY OCCULT ITEMS VAGUELY CLASSIFIABLE AS PSYCHO-LINGUISTIC

There is a recurring idea that the name AIWAZ is that of some obscure Sumerian deity; I have seen no evidence to support this supposition, which is no reason to dismiss it out of hand although my research into the Sumerian Tradition† has not been exactly superficial.

The astounding fact is that it is far easier to find the origins of AIWAZ/AIWASS in a good ENGLISH dictionary than in a work on Mesopotamian archaeology! I am not aware that this information has been remarked on in any Thelemic literature, and given the nature of our preoccupation with the English language it is fitting that it should first appear in this Journal. I quote the Oxford English Dictionary: "**Ay, aye**...[Middle English ai, ei - Old Norse. ei, ey = Old English a. Old Saxon eo, Old High German eo, io. Gothic **aiws** age, eternity :- Germanic * **aiwaz**, related to Latin ævum age, eternity, Greek aei, aeon ÆON.] 1. a. Ever, continually; b. on all occasions. (Now only in Scottish and northern dialect.).

It is significant that the word "Yes" does not occur in any Class A work, and that the word Ay and/or Aye occurs frequently, possibly with the meaning given here. The reason that YES does not occur in the speech of the deity is identical to the reason why Do what thou wilt SHALL BE the whole of the Law, rather than IS. Such an affirmation on the part of the deity would affirm the perfection - and deny the purpose of - existence.

(The asterisk preceding **AIWAZ** in the O.E.D. signifies that this root is inferred rather than found, which is to say that such a word or root had to exist in order for other words to be derived from it!) We heartily recommend that all persons involved in the exploration of AL and its Qaballa direct their attention more towards the O.E.D. and Skeats etymological dictionary, and less towards Hebrew Sepher Sephiroth and such like works of comparative religion. The reader will have more fun, and to more purpose, delving into the nature of the English words language than exploring such cultural cul de sacs.

A further note regarding the numerical qaballa, the last words in the Book of the Law, in which words it is declared "Written and Concealed", are "AUM. HA." - those readers familiar with the 'counting well' formula of value of first word times number of letters in second word and vice versa will discover this phrase to have the value of 93. The nature of the Double Current in one phase is to write and to conceal simultaneously. On this basis alone many present day occult authors must be accorded more respect than they at present receive.

SMALLUS PRINTUS

† According to Crowley "our work is historically authentic, the rediscovery of the Sumerian Tradition" that worthy gentleman Kenneth Grant has been credited with this achievement, but on studying his Typhonian Trilogy we discover that the only reference to Sumeria is to claim that the Bornless Rite is of Sumerian origin, when it is quite clearly of Graeco- Egyptian in origin and contains no God Names related to any Mesopotamian civilisation. It is to be hoped that at some time in the future my projected work on the Sumerian Tradition will be published and make clear the true historical significance of Sumerian culture in the development of Astrological Magick.

Zos Kia Cultus and the English Qaballa

The following account of the Death Posture of the sorceries of Zos is important enough on its own account - however the possible connection between the "visualisation" involved and the nature of the letter X described in previous Equinoxes will we hope justify its quotation in full in these pages.

"Lying on your back lazily, the body expressing the emotion of yawning, suspiring while conceiving by smiling, that is the idea of the posture. Forgetting time with those things which are essential reflecting their meaninglessness, the moment is beyond time and its virtue has happened.

Standing on tip-toe, with the arms rigid, bound behind by the hands, clasped and straining the utmost, the neck stretched - breathing deeply and spasmodically, till giddy and sensation comes in gusts, gives exhaustion and capacity for the former.

Gazing at your reflection till it is blurred and you know the gazer, close your eyes (this usually happens involuntarily) and visualise. The light **(always an X in curious evolutions)** that is seen should be held on to, never letting go, till the effort is forgotten, this gives a feeling of immensity (which sees a small form ⊘), whose limit you cannot reach. This should be practiced before experiencing the foregoing. The emotion that is felt is the knowledge which tells you why."

From 'The Book of Pleasure' Ch. The Ritual and Doctrine, by Austin Osman Spare. 1913.

MANTRAS AND SPELLS

The Book of the Law, as has been remarked by various authorities, is a Tantra or Grimoire of inestimable power. What is not generally understood is that by definition this implies that timing factors, as well as ritual instructions and so on will be found in the text. An indication of the extent to which AL is an astrological grimoire is found in the references to colours in the text. Precisely seven colours are referred to in Liber AL:

BLACK.	- AL CH.1. vs. 60. CH.2. vs. 52.
BLUE.	- AL CH.1. vs. 60. CH.2. vs. 50.
RED.	- AL.CH.2. vs. 50.
GOLD.	- AL.CH.1. vss. 51 & 60. CH.2. vs. 50.
GREEN.	- AL.CH.2. vs. 50.
PURPLE.	- AL.CH.2. vss. 50/51.
SILVER.	- AL.CH.1. vss. 51 & 60.

These colours tally exactly with the traditional planetary correpondences found in the grimoires, though obviously differing from G.'.D.'. and other Qabalistic schemes. In the table below we list the probable correspondences to the Gods mentioned in the adorations found on the Stele of Revealing, and to a proposed Temple layout based on the Solar Stations of Liber Resh, with other considerations derived from Liber Pyramidos et al.

NO.	LET.	PLANET.	COLOUR.	POSITION IN CIRCLE.	GOD-FORM
3.	W.	SATURN	BLACK.	NORTH.	KHEPHRA.
4.	H.	JUPITER	AZURE/BLUE.	CENTRAL POINT.	MENTU.
5.	S.	MARS	RED.	APPROACH TO CENTRE.	RA HOOR.
6.	D.	SUN	GOLD.	EAST.	RA.
7.	O.	VENUS	GREEN.	SOUTH.	AHATHOOR.
8.	Z.	MERCURY	PURPLE.	CIRCUMFERENCE.	TAHUTI.
9.	K.	MOON	SILVER.	WEST.	TUM.

For practical purposes Mars may be considered as guarding the approach to the Centre from the EAST, and Mercury as standing beyond the Altar in the WEST. The Magician, identified with Ankh-af-na-Khonsu, the Prophet of Mentu, stands centrally, in the position of his God.

The essential prerequisite in astrological magick is that the structure of the ritual be analogous to the aspects being celebrated. There are certain obvious points involved here. For instance, if the Moon be translating light between two or more planets involved in the ritual, then Sister Moon (one of the Priestesses) can take the talismanic basis of the ritual around the circle, presenting it in turn to the officers of the Temple representing those planets, and this should preferably coincide with the actual times involved. These kinds of considerations are essential. Likewise the nature of the aspect should be considered, whether the Moon be Void of Course, for instance in which case a form of words such as these, extracted from "The Supreme Ritual", may be used:

O. "What is the hour?"
I. "When time hath no power."
O. "What is the place?"
I. "At the limits of space."
O. "What God do we wake?"
I. "The Lord of the Snake!"
O. "With what do we serve?"
I. "Bone, Marrow, and Nerve!"
O. "The shrine in the gloom?"

[O. gives sign Puella as Babe of the Abyss, I. "destroys" this with Sign Puer, answering:]

I. "Is the Mouth of the Womb."
O. "And the Priest in the Shrine?"
I. "Is this Madness of Mine!"

[I. repeats sign Puer (Mentu) and O. gives sign Mulier (Isis or Baphomet).]

Thelemic ritual and the Holy Books contain much material of enormous value in Astrological Magick. We may instance Liber Israfel as being of value in Invokations of Sun conjunct Mercury, likewise the Opening of the Pyramid from Liber Pyramidos. The appropriate planetary verses of Liber Ararita are useful when Fortuna conjuncts the planet in question, or when Luna conjuncts them.

This last is particularly useful when Fortuna or Luna transit a tight planetary grouping such as a multiple conjunction, itself conjuncting each in rapid succession; the officers of those planets may then assume the Godform and pronounce the appropriate verse of Ararita. On a broader note, when a particular planet is being invoked the appropriate planetary chapter of Liber Lapis Lazuli may be read aloud (with vigour!) by the chief celebrant. (The chapters are attributed in the order Mars, Saturn, Jupiter, Sun, Mercury, Moon, Venus.)

So far we have been considering what for want of a better word we call "Formal Rituals" due to their structured form, which is finalised in advance. Informal rituals, which may or may not be Opened and Closed by some formal rite such as the Pentagram, are generally only linked to stellar events by the time of their performance. That is to say, if for instance a chant such as the UN mantra is to be used, it may commence and/or climax at some appropriate astrological moment. Likewise the sacrament and spontaneous Toasts may take place at some specific time, but these phases of the ritual are looser than their formal counterparts and are not necessarily analogous to celestial events, although useful and appropriate in the celebration of those events.

Rituals may be entirely formal, entirely informal or a combination of the two. Bear in mind that these titles are not indicative of rigidity and laxness. Informal rites are frequently of a "higher" nature than the formal, which are generally speaking very joyous affairs. Structure does not exclude spontaneity or the unexpected, any more than the apparently loose form of the informal rites does.

We have spoken of Planetary officers in the Temple, and now we wish to speak of the Zodiacal signs and how they are best worked. It is obvious that the planets and luminaries occupy the signs, and that at the time of a ritual those signs are going to be significant in regard to the anticipated or actual result. The way in which the signs themselves influence the structure of the ritual itself seems to be twofold in operation. Firstly, if the aspect celebrated be a conjunction, which are generally the most powerful rites, then the planets will usually, again obviously enough, be in the same sign. In this case it is fitting to decorate the temple accordingly, and to consider the nature of the planets involved and their connection with the sign. If for instance the ritual involves Jupiter and Venus in Pisces (OH IF!!!) we may wish to recall Venus as born from the sea, or Jupiter as brother of Neptune in mythology. As Ruling and Exalted planets respectively in relation to Pisces, the ritual is likely to produce spectacularly benefic results.

The Temple in any case will whenever possible be decorated according to the nature of the Sign involved, although one's right ingenium is called for in this, even more so if more than one sign is involved. The nature of the invokations is particularly relevant to the signs, as the nature of invokations involves receptivity to the higher, then the sign as the 'present address' of the planet is the best current model of receiving the powers of that planet. The chants from the Treasure House of Images are related to the Zodiacal Signs, and have a rhythmic quality which is appropriate to a seated chant, with the participants facing the Priestess. Here we have less problem with planets involved in the rite occupying two or more signs, since we can always use more than one chant, allotting them as appropriate to the ritualists taking part.

Among the other Thelemic rituals which are appropriate in Astrological Magick, we must take account of the Rites of Eleusis, each of which is attributed to one of the seven planets of antiquity. These are ripe for plunder, in whole or in part, for the celebration of Astrological Feasts.

FEAST AND REJOICE

Which brings me to another principal part of the modus operandi. Feasting, not only inculcated in the Book of the Law, but in such places as the Arabic Astrological grimoire known as the Picatrix, is the most vital and most underrated element of astrological magick. The Foods must obviously be considered for aptness, as Peaches for Venus, Curry for Mars etc., etc., but the point in the ritual at which the feast is consumed must also be carefully considered, and not merely to avoid indigestion either - Thelemic magicians need to be made of sterner stuff than that!! If the Feast is consumed before the ritual, exceeding by delicacy, then one is ingesting the nature of the god or goddess invoked. This will sustain you for the rite and enable you to enter more fully and joyously into the nature of the occasion. If the Feast is consumed during the ritual at an appropriate point then it MAY coincide with a specific sacrament as well. If this is the case similar considerations to those outlined will be involved, but ritual discipline must be more strictly maintained, which is facilitated by reading from the Holy Books or continuing with some appropriate invokation or music. Latterly there are occasions when the feast ends the ritual. Here the energy is as it were earthed, and the ritual is its own result. This must be carefully considered and understood. Although psychologically a feast before is a lead in and preparation from which one will continue and build, while a feast at the end is a wind down, which may degenerate if care is not taken into a mere binge and loss of power, on the magickal plane other rules apply with equal force. A feast at the end is a climax in the sense of a peak or orgasm; there will be, in all likelihood, no other result from the ritual - all the energy is absorbed and digested with the food. This is empirically observed data, not a gourmet guide; distinguish carefully.

93 PERIODS

93 = TIME, also THAT HOUR, indicating that there is a specific point at which the 93 Current can be invoked. There are many suggestive clues as to the NATURE (=93) of this TIME (=93) in AL vel Legis itself, with its frequent references to Stars and Stellar rituals. Most suggestive of all is the reference to the "Five Pointed Star with a circle in the middle and the circle is red" which symbol suggests a connection between the stars and female periodicity. The Sun Venus conjunctions form a pentagram (see Equinox VII. No. 2 and elsewhere) and the nature of the Rite is such that the female cycle is linked with the astrological cycle, with the result that an **ALCHEMICAL** cycle of Initiation (through the signs and months) is triggered in the celebrants. So the elixir is formed whilst the Sun and Venus are conjoined.

On the other hand 93 = SCORPIO (N.B. on the Tree of Life the Path from Venus to Sol is attributed to Scorpio), suggesting that the "Enemy Naming Ceremony" should ideally be performed during the Moon's transit through Via Combusta (the dreaded Moon in Scorpio of modern folklore), using the Blood of the Moon or Red Elixir as its Prima Materia. V.C. is 15 degrees Libra to 15 degrees Scorpio during the Moon's monthly circuit (most potent of all when Sun is also in Scorpio), at which time the Horned Goddess menstruates. The process sublimates while She is in Sagittarius, and when She enters Capricorn the result appears (Capricorn = Rex Mundi).

In Horary astrology V.C. indicates a time at which NOTHING can be predicted; this is equivalent to the "recent" idea of CHAOS setting limits to predictability in "Scientific forecasting" - as in Crowley's lifetime the major breakthroughs in mathematics and physics paralleled the Book of the Law's cryptic utterances, so is it now - only now we are armed with the Qaballistic key to this ultimate grimoire. The implications of 93 Periods go beyond astrological forecasting; NO method of divination can be successfully employed at these times, either when the Moon is in "the Burning Way" or when these same degrees are ascending.

The term "Via Combusta" suggests the existence of other such 93 Periods than those of the Lunar cycle, for "Combust" has the additional meaning in astrology of "Under the rays of the Sun", which is to say that when either Conjunct the Sun or within a 17 degree orb of that body, the affairs "ruled by" the planet involved are to say the least unpredictable.

The connection between Via Combusta (15' Libra to 15' Scorpio) and these other 93 Periods is implicit in the Qaballa of AL: LIBRA + SCORPIO = 151 = SUN + MERCURY, which is to say Sun conjunct Mercury, or Mercury Combust. This suggests a formula, associated with the so-called formula of ALIM (see Magick in Theory and Practice), and is perhaps the only rite where male/male polarity is appropriate. The Sun and Mercury are conjunct approximately six times a year, and form a complete cycle in that time - tracing the points of a Hexagram, as the Sun Venus cycle forms a Pentagram. Given the numerical connection between this Sun Mercury cycle and the Libra-Scorpio phase of 418, astrological rituals performed when Sun-Mercury conjunctions occur in Libra Scorpio are almost certainly implied. It is regretted that so far the A.'.A.'. has not explored this particular avenue in great depth. However, judging from other experiments with Mercury it seems wise to advise caution; when Mercury is retrograde not all the facts involved are known - and when he is conjunct the Sun serious mental confusion can result. However even when retrograde he may be invoked, but be prepared for panic as the unknown factors emerge between the ritual and the result. If a good aspect, say Mercury-Jupiter, is worked with Mercury retrograde, as has been done, the eventual resolution is very satisfactory, but all hell can break loose between rite and result if your nerves are not made of steel.

This brings me to a final and most important point, although unfortunately also a most incredibly subtle and evasive one. Real objective results with some planetary alignments in particular require great vigilance. Opportunity must be recognised and seized as it arises; the precise nature of the aspect being worked, if understood correctly, will enable you to identify the general area in which results will manifest, but you must be prepared to "strike while the iron is hot" as it were, or a potentially great result may evaporate before you move. This seems to be particularly the case with Mercury aspects, as one might expect. It must also be said that some opportunities disguise themselves as problems, particularly to the novice, and again courage and nerve are vital, lest the "gold turns to dead leaves" as in the old tales.

ANTON K JETTSTRAKE

RETURN OF BLOOD AND GUTS

That distinguished old duffer G.K. Chesterton once remarked that Christianity had not been "tried and found wanting but found difficult and left untried", whereas good ol' Prof. A.J. Ayer [every time you write about these characters they die! Ed.] called it "intellectually contemptible and morally outrageous". Now with Thelema the situation is necessarily different. Thelemites cannot allow Thelema to be a borderline religion.

Thelema is entirely intellectually coherent and internally consistent. This is no excuse to abandon sheer hard work. The tenets of Thelema require that the work continue, that Magickal and Mystical methodology be put on a scientific footing of continual reassessment and experiment. That test driven methods be put before the public in journals such as the Equinox, and that Thelema itself should be the guiding force in the development of civilisation into the future.

At the present time we cannot help but be aware that Christian Fundamentalism and Freemasonic conspiracies run riot in the political and cultural life of the Western World, whilst Islamic fundamentalism makes a mockery of the tolerance, learning and culture of medieval Arabia. Despite the evident fact that these power groupings are magically, mystically, intellectually and in all other ways utterly contemptible, they possess sufficient wealth and influence to make the parochial little circles of occultism pale into utter insignificance.

Why? You may well ask! While Bankers swing from Bridges, while ancient Aristocratic cliques in France and Germany prepare to elect a God-king over a united Europe, perpetuating the worst kind of theocratic dogmatism; while Mad Mullahs threaten the innocent and the talented, and Popes ordain that the Third World abandons contraceptives despite massive levels of starvation and infant mortality through want and disease; while these and worse offences against LIFE are perpetrated, we see self proclaimed experts on occultism arguing over points of little real significance instead of providing direction to the young aspirants whose vigour and energy is so urgently required to reverse these sickening trends. We see impotent "magicians" who find their own circumstances beyond their control yet find ways to gather circles of admirers. Good grief! There is a real world out here, beyond your garrets and basements and ivory towers! The existing curriculum of the A.'.A.'. does contain sufficient store of magickal training to produce a new aristocracy of real magicians, and if teachers cannot be found then persistent individual work will more than compensate for the deficiency. Any person who has seriously considered the bare facts of magickal work will be aware that correctly applied it produces fearless and self reliant individuals; yoga training and concentration will provide means to act under terrific stress, and inure them to all but the most lethal forms of hardship. These kind of people are dangerous, and can be produced by any intelligence agency or religious cult worth its salt, yet where do we find them among occultists today?

Certainly not among the psuedo sophisticates of the occult scene - so called occultists who "aren't into astrology man" and don't acknowledge the importance of alchemy and the "traditional" procedures of ritual magick, who prate of "subjectivity", "paradigms" and "solepsism" as if they were new words of power - there is nothing subjective about belladonna except one's body weight to height ratio, nor are the aspects of the planets dependent on the "belief structure" of the magician - intellectual fashion does not dictate the rules of the game in the real world. MAGICK WORKS period. The posturing of the chaos magicians‡ and green fairies would be laughable, were it not for the lamentable state of Thelema itself. We cannot afford to laugh at these second rate mock-ultists while Thelema is in such sordid disarray.

The various OTO bodies have proved slow to adapt to the Twentieth century, and though this is perhaps not the place to examine the track records of any of them we may at least complain that the Eighties have been dominated by the same old charter and copyright bullshit. Whatever happened to "Refuse none"?

Despite Magnus' attempts to promote some kind of Thelemic Glasnost [his wot! Ed.] a distinct Cold War permafrost holds the movement in its icy grip. It is strange, but sadly true, that the most radical occult thinker in three centuries has spawned a cult following that is rigidly conservative, in every meaning of the word.

Talking of words, let us observe how the world has changed in the last two or three years by examining its vocabulary. Political words were always pretty meaningless - but in the last couple of years there have been some startling new developments in the political language. We hear of "Conservatives" among the Communist leadership, we hear of "moderate" guerrillas among the mujahedin who are none the less ferocious for all the moderacy of their political allegiances. We even hear of "Moderate Islamic Fundamentalists", supporters of the Saudi variant.

What has this to do with Thelema? Plenty! This stretching of the available vocabulary to breaking point has come about through the impact of magickal forces on the mundane world. As Jimmi Rocket correctly

‡ Not to diminish the value of Chaos Magick as a counter-blast to dead letter traditionalism.

avers in his ONE HORIZON article (see issue 4) the changes in the world in the last decade, and particularly, in my view, in the last two years, are entirely due to the existence of several thousand magicians. Most particularly perhaps to a mere handful of them, but the consensus reality of those who continued the work of the pioneers has had an earthing effect, bringing mighty ideas to fruition.

Narrowness of vision in this crucial period is the rigor mortis of a movement that will not move with the times. The token followers who stand in for the electorate in my analogy between politics and magick cannot forever dictate the policy of the leaders, whether those leaders be grandiosely titled or simply the pushiest or most capable of their peers. We need leaders of the calibre of a Gorbachev or a Walesa, people who can change what could not be changed.

We need to escape from the treadmill of tradition, the anguish of authenticity. We need less arguments about who is more Thelemic than whom, who owns the copyright to what, who knew Crowley and who didn't. These arguments are sterile and counter productive. What is needed, above all, is recognition and tolerance. Recognition of the ability and work of others, whether individuals or groups - oh bugger it let's give some examples! Grant, with his excellent work on the kalas and the double Tree of Life; the Caliphate with its protracted and extensive researches into Enochian magick; and US with our state of the art Astrological Magick and the English Qaballa. These are great achievements, and though the novelty of mutual back slapping might soon fade the divisions in the Thelemic movement would be over, THELEMA would become STRONGER!!! As a representative of the least well established of the three parties mentioned it is all very well if I stand up and say "Well done, you are every bit as Thelemic as me" to the others, and their like. I have done similar things before, and been labelled "ecumenical" for my pains. But while the various Thelemic groups continue their bickering over points of very little interest, or even of any particular occult significance, they are simultaneously disillusioning the cream of generation after generation of young and intelligent persons whose attention is needed for the future of magick, and by extension, of this planet.

The way out? Glasnost! Break some established patterns, make the enemy and the heretic of yesterday the ally and co worker of tomorrow. Shout from the rooftops that you can see value in the work of so called rivals - the result will not be to decrease your power and influence, on the contrary, it will extend it. A man who claims much for himself but whose weaknesses remain obvious to discerning people has only sycophants for followers, whereas a man who does what he does best and encourages and admires those who do likewise finds fierce allies and firm friends.

Reluctance to take the kind of risks in occult politics that Gorbachev has in foreign and domestic affairs is understandable. It is not laudable, it is not really even practical, but it is understandable. But it is idle to stand in the shadow of "the Master" four decades after his death, as if only Crowley could settle these problems. It is too late, HE IS DEAD. He hasn't had a bright idea in forty-three years! Complacent inertia is not the way of the Tao; there is a world of difference between Doing by Not-doing and simply doing nothing. It is time that Thelemic groups, indeed Thelemites individually, realised we do live in an exciting and fast changing world, that it is of our making, that we can make of it what we will, and do so together. And do it now.

Movements fail when they fail to respond to changing situations, or respond in an inept fashion. The occult revival is a movement standing in imminent danger of failing in this manner.

The world is changing. Exponents of the "science and art of causing change to occur in conformity with the will" are an inconsequential factor in the dramas unfolding in the world today. What we might call the ideology of occultism is under serious attack, and has failed to catch the attention either of the educated classes or the young blood which it needs to survive as a significant world view or experimental process.

The features of occultism which the average person is likely to contact are a) small, secretive societies with obscure or suspicious motives; b) descriptions or parodies from non-occult or unsymathetic sources; c) occult propaganda, largely aimed at the converted, and frequently attacking equally obscure rival occultists. This last reveals a lot about the parochial and internecine nature of occultism. Occultists have a tendency to be obscure and inhibited. They are interested in bizarre things, they are occasionally lucid, when not bombed out of their minds, and they do little to reassure people about their reputation for being evil, child-murdering perverts.

All heretical or alien beliefs have at some time been accused of being E.C.M.P.'s. The Jews throughout history have been accused of it, the Gypsies have been accused of it. A friend of mine recently observed that anti-occult evangelists don't dwell on theological matters which alienate or bore their listeners, they come straight out and exploit people's fears of occultism. It's never "theology objects or begs to differ on this or that" always "occultism threatens so and so, don't we care about so and so?"

Occultism has tried to influence politics, as when such groups as Pagans against Nukes organised large scale anti nuclear rituals. While rituals may not be an appropriate way of dealing with the problem, they form a group identity and offer possibilities of forming a collective movement which is better magic than isolated insecurity. The calls to occult unity we hear derided so often are actually a sensible response at gut level to the forces of change and the understanding of the urge to act. Who are we? What do we stand for? And how much will we stand for before we get organised?

Occultists are not a uniform cult; there are many methods of working or worshipping. Unfortunately this has led to division and internecine conflicts, when our principles should lead us to protect the right to be different in the face of mounting adversity.

The derision or indifference which are meted out to the average occult activist by their fellow occultists is symptomatic of the waning vitality of what is becoming a cultural anachronism. Of course occultists want to spend time being themselves and pursuing their destiny individually, of course research or group activities demand time and effort - but there are means and means.

Collective rituals to avert catastrophe - it's rather cute and naive, but it's idealistic, and it brings people together. That is a start down the path to becoming a force in the world. There are also the myriad benefits that come from keeping up with the work and methods of your peers. It is well worth maintaining links with various organisations, magazines and information networks. A cellular structure, propoganda outlets, cooperation over campaigns. Today the soapbox, tomorrow the world!

JAKE STRATTON-KENT

LIBER ACHAD

There is one true Order of initiates, the which encompasses all enlightened persons. The A.'.A.'. is one name for this Order; and the "A.'.A.'." developed by Aleister Crowley WAS a formalised cell of this eternal congregation of the Saints. Although it is correct to refer to the eternal Order as the A.'.A.'. it must not be supposed that this limits the activities of this Order to the pursuit of Crowleyan magick, which - whatever its virtues - is restricted by adherence to antique forms, and by the limitations of knowledge at the time of its formalisation.

It has been supposed that Crowley's Order functioned through a continuous chain of grades. Some have argued that once this chain was broken the Order ceased to exist. This is palpably ridiculous. Firstly, Crowley himself took the Oath of Probationer <u>after</u> he "founded" the Order in 1907, but backdated the Oath to 1904 (see introduction to the Law is for All). Secondly, neither he nor Karl Germer, Madame Blavatsky or Oscar Eckenstein, all of whom, Crowley maintained, held the highest grades in the A.'.A.'., ever worked the curriculum Crowley himself advocated in the manner and sequence he delineated. For evidence of this compare Crowley's records, both before and after 1907, with the curriculum he set. Of the other known members of the A.'.A.'., such as Leah Hirsig (8=3), J.F.C. Fuller (1=10), Charles Stansfield Jones (8=3) or Marta Kuntzel (8=3) etc., there is again no evidence that they worked the curriculum in the strict fashion laid down. Nor is there any evidence that they maintained the chain of grades by ensuring that each grade had at least one incumbent member. The A.'.A.'. cannot be said to depend for its existence on this - in many ways admirable - curriculum nor on the hierarchical structure that is part and parcel of it.

The Order publishing this "Liber" maintain that they are also a "formalised cell of the eternal Order". This is not through its members' work with the curriculum, for many do not undertake it, nor are they required to do so. Although a minority of members do work the curriculum and have to an extent revived the chain of grades, this is not the basis of their claim to represent, however transiently, the eternal Order.

Crowley's authority to work in the name of the A.'.A.'. was obtained when he became the scribe of Aiwass - the true author of Liber AL vel Legis (and - perhaps - the other Class A texts also). Crowley's right was absolutely legitimate, for Aiwass, through him, had provided the West with a Holy Book superseding those of the Old Aeon; he had no need to claim authority from older organisations, for their shrines were desolate, whereas his was radiant with the LVX. Crowley's curriculum and his neo-Golden Dawn approach to the formalisation of the A.'.A.'. have no authority in AL, and little enough in the Class A as a whole. AL speaks of 3 Grades, "the Hermit, the Lover and the man of Earth". Although other Class A texts speak of the grade structure of the A.'.A.'./G.'.D.'. (Liber Tau does so in parentheses, which may not be part of the text) some of these at least are of lesser authority, and to an extent are the creation of Aleister Crowley, which AL is not. The works of Crowley the occult scholar deal with what he knew, guessed at or wished for. They cannot be relied upon to speak for Aiwass and the work He intends for the race. Nor does this contradict the Class A Comment on AL itself, "all questions of the Law are to be decided only by appeal to my writings" for this Comment is that of the scribe Ankh-af-na-Khonsu, and refers not to Crowley's works, but to the Book of the Law only. Solve the riddle by the riddle, not by academic research: "the study of this Book is forbidden".

The A.'.A.'. is, the A.'.A.'. was and the A.'.A.'. will be. Those shallow fellows who suppose the eternal assembly of the Saints to have been "Crowley's cronies in the twenties", to have ceased to be when he thought the OTO was more like the way to get on, are unworthy to be associated with it. The A.'.A.'. is the Sanctuary Crowley sought before he found the Golden Dawn, it is the Sanctuary from which the Golden Dawn, the OTO and the Rosicrucians of yore emerged into the world, from which Crowley's A.'.A.'. itself emerged. If proof of membership were required, which would be absurd, then no document signed by Crowley or his successors or imitators would be valid. Those who sense, believe or know this to be true may be members of this august body already. There are many more ways to enter it than to write care of the editors, although that is one.

Let us speak plainly: there may be Orders in the world who vampirise the energy contained in Thelemic legend, pseudo A.'.A.'.'s or fake OTO's, or perhaps these groupings serve a purpose. But the real A.'.A.'., in Thelemic terms, is greater now than ever it was in Crowley's day. The real A.'.A.'., in a sense, was recreated when Regardie put the Oaths and Tasks of the Grades in the back of "Gems from the Equinox". Those who took those Oaths and performed those Tasks are as genuine or more so than any charter holding claimant. Our fear of falling into the clutches of false messiahs or phoney Great Wild Beasts is a lesser thing than the danger of overlooking the existence of the Eternal Order.

THE THREE GRADES.

The Three Grades mentioned in the Book of the Law are the only real Grades of the A.'.A.'., as opposed to the largely synthetic grades 0=0 to 10=1, which are merely a convention. AL says: "there are three ordeals in one, and it may be given in three ways". What this means in practice is that the first initiation that the candidate receives involves all three levels, so that they may function on whatsoever level their own capacity requires or facilitates; this negates the difficulties of the other scheme, where contradictions arise very easily. For instance, there is no difficulty with a capable occultist functioning in a grade higher than that which he/she nominally held in the Tree of Life scheme, which in the old way of things he/she is barred from holding by reason, say, of lacking the required ability in Asana. One might nominally be a Zelator, yet function quite happily as Adept or even Magister Templi. Our primary initiation involves a period of seclusion for the Hermit, a formal rite resembling the G.'.D.'. Neophyte ritual for the man of Earth (the G.'.D.'. rite describes the Candidate as a "Child of Earth"), and a rite of tantric worship such as the Sun-Venus for the Lover. As Liber Tau makes clear, the Three Orders of the Tree of Life grades, the so called "G.'.D.'., R.'.C.'. and A.'.A.'.", are all resumed under the headings of "the Hermit, the Lover and the man of Earth". There have been attempts to interpret the grade structure of the OTO in terms of the Three Grades, breaking down the grades 0 through XI into groups under the headings man of Earth, Lover and Hermit, though since the OTO also disclaims any equivalence between OTO grades and the A.'.A.'. grades this hypothesis must be considered suspect, despite some obvious symbolic connections between, say, the Rosicrucian content of 5=6 A.'.A.'. and fifth degree OTO. That there are further mysteries involved in this triad of grades is obvious enough, but this should suffice as clarification of the method of initiation in the A.'.A.'.. INITIATION IS NEVER WHAT YOU EXPECT.

A word on the glamour inherent in hierarchical grade structures: a distinguished scholar, Gerald Suster, has remarked that his mentor, the late Doctor Regardie, was fond of saying "we are all students". The grade structure begins with the non-grade of student, and although Dr. Regardie was also given to signing G.'.D.'. documents "A.M.A.G. 5=6" and making no bones about who "A.M.A.G." was, we are bound to say that the whole question of grades is riddled with opportunities for egoism and accusations of the same. Indeed, it might even be worth claiming a suitably ostentatious grade publicly in order to make a study of the "less egoistic than thou" responses. The necessity of courage in undertaking the task of a grade in earnest might be better understood after thus exposing yourself to such ridicule. The only purpose to such designations as 5=6 on esoteric documents is to indicate the level upon which the author is writing. Most other uses are simply advertising. Nevertheless, the ritual of Opening by Watchtower requires the magician to perform the Grade-Signs and vibrate the Pass-Words of the Elemental Grades 1=10 to 4=7, and to affirm to some degree either the intention to undertake the work of 5=6 or their having done so. In essence most acts of magick operate in the realm of the four elements and spirit; the grades relate to these more in a departmental fashion than a hierarchical system. There is little point enquiring which of the elements is first in priority, since the objective is to balance them, not to emphasise one at the expense of the others. So for the grades, the skills of each of the Elemental Grades are essential to any particular magickal operation; one must have harmonised these abilities and techniques into a whole. Whoever says they are Lord of the Forces of some particular grade shows merely that they have failed in the overall aim of these related tasks.

THE EQUINOX PROGRAMME

The purpose of the Equinox publishing programme and its attendant work is threefold, and is aimed at three types of individual.

AGENDA:

1. To provide a coherent and operable scheme of magical technology without resort to comparative religion, a priori notions or indeed any material outside the Class A books, which have sole authority. This scheme is the real core of our work, involving the Qaballa of AL and the Initiation cycle of Sun-Venus (Rose-Croix). The purpose of Initiation is to produce Adepts, or attainment to the Lover Grade. Initiation is by Ordeal - the Grade of Adept is not conferred but implied by success in this Ordeal, actual Knowledge and Conversation of the Holy Guardian Angel, which truly conferrs this Grade, is not an automatic function of the Ordeal X.

2. To provide a means by which persons working the traditional A.'.A.'. syllabus could be aided and supported by competent persons; and thus to some extent to reconstruct the chain of grades, though without placing any special emphasis on hierachical structure or other side issues. For reasons which will be apparent to those familiar with the syllabus, and for other, strictly practical purposes, this "over-seeing" must be restricted to the elemental grades, up to and including Dominus Liminis. Any advancement beyond these grades is either of an interior nature - i.e. the operator's own work with the Holy Guardian Angel, while technically constituting him or her an Adeptus Minor, will not result in any certification - or of an honorary nature, i.e. when an individual's function in the Order necessitates their being given some formal title. In the latter case this will be administered through the Gnostic Alchemical Church of Typhon-Christ, and implies no strict familiarity with the A.'.A.'. syllabus beyond Dominus Liminis.

3. To provide an avenue through which real occult work, chiefly astrological, alchemical and qaballistic work, could be encouraged and facilitated in a modern context - whilst simultaneously attacking

and discouraging the placebos with which the present generation of young aspirants are distracted and then disillusioned by cynical or misguided self-styled teachers and leaders. These last of course will find it in their best interests to misrepresent our intentions, motives and methods; since this will only affect those too idle or too gullible to investigate matters for themselves, we consider their efforts to be in our own best interests!

THE INTENDED AUDIENCE:

1. Those persons working in isolation or in assemblies separate from the so-called occult scene. In this regard we have been successful beyond our initial projections.

2. Those persons working with the A.'.A.'. syllabus, particularly those under Oath to perform the Tasks of the Grades.

3. Those persons with little or no knowledge of occult methods - with a healthy distrust of the various high-profile groups or methods - who are responsive to an integrated "unified field" theory and practice which maintains the methods and ideals of the tradition without seeking to revive its outmoded forms.

These aims and persons are not so clearly distinct in practice; for instance, an individual in category 1 may have qualities classed under 2 or 3, but this outline is intended to inform, not to promote a rigid structure. Still less is it intended to imply any kind of hierarchy, either implicit or explicit.

To this end we produce our Journal along lines which are "formally" recognisable to "Traditional" Thelemites, though recognisable as a departure; and we claim no links with established groupings, even where such links may exist. Similarly we published the Oath of Probationer in order that the Magical Link with the Order could be established by aspirants to the Order. To this end also we avoid all discussion of bygone methods, save where it may assist comprehension, and keep historical and structural details to a minimum.

Our actions and motives have been misinterpreted by various parties, with, we suspect, either malice or ignorance as their excuse. To a degree, we accept responsibility for their errors, or for the plausibility of their distortions. We have endeavoured to mislead those who see the cover and not the content. We have deliberately facilitated the misrepresentation of our purpose in order to save ourselves, and our true fellow aspirants, the indignity of associating with fools or time-wasters. We make no apology for these diversions, since anyone who investigates the material we present will be aware of the truth, and those who do not do no real harm through their uninformed calumnies.

In order to place the whole matter more clearly in perspective, it is necessary to define the Equinox programme further with a brief manifesto:

1. The Equinox and its attendant bodies exist primarily to make known the English Qaballa and the Astrological Magick it describes.

2. The Equinox programme provides <u>additionally</u> the facilities for work with the traditional A.'.A.'. syllabus and curriculum so far as it is possible. This work is pursued only by those particular participants in our work who desire to work the tasks of the grades 0 = 0 to 5 = 6. This is not demanded of any participants and confers no status as such on those who pursue it.

3. Participants are involved in Astrologically Timed Ritual and Tantric Worship in English. The modus operandi and other considerations are derived wholly from AL and the Qaballa of AL. However, members need not be either astrologers or qaballists.

4. As a Qaballistic Order, our work is based on the Book of the Law and the other Class A books.

5. Progress is by Ordeal, not attainment in the A.'.A.'. syllabus or by technical knowledge of any kind.

6. The heart of the work is the Knowledge and Conversation of the Holy Guardian Angel. Here the A.'.A.'. syllabus and the principal work of the Equinox programme coincide. This being so there is identity of EQUINOX with A.'.A.'..

7. The principle feature of the work is the ritual of Sun conjunct Venus. Also the conjunction of Sun and Mars, and the movements of planets and luminaries through the four signs Libra - Scorpio - Sagittarius - Capricorn.

8. The Class A, particularly AL, the E.'.Q.'. and the rituals should be known to all, but let each embellish their work as they will, be they herbalist, ritualist, healer or what not.

9. Our standard of truth is Physiological, Astrological and Numerical (P.A.N.), not vague vision or sectarian doctrine; nothing is dependent on personalities or lineage.

10. We consider further elaboration redundant, and criticism unsupportable, no matter by whom.

Finally, in sincerity and reverence, I have only one more speech to make. It has been said that if God did not exist, then it would be necessary to invent him; but since God is dead, and the A.'.A.'. serves a more useful purpose, I say this; if the A.'.A.'. ceased to exist with Aleister Crowley, or if its historical descendants have withdrawn from the world, as numerous supposed authorities maintain - then it is IMPERATIVE that it Manifest again. For this reason, and with assistance beyond any person's abilities to provide, it has been created anew. The existence of the A.'.A.'. is simply a function of the Universe as is apparent to any who have aspired towards it.

JAKE STRATTON-KENT

D.I.Y. THELEMIC FUNDAMENTALISM

000. Buy ye olde copy of "Ye Gemmes from ye Equinox" and read instructions for Probationer Grade in the back. Sign the Oath in presence of whatever divine being takes your fancy and do the work for a year.

00. Do the other degrees work too, and the work associated with each path and sephirah in logical sequence. Read "Magick" several times. Get really familiar with all the stuff on the reading list, all the rituals, all the Holy Books. Drive yourself nuts reading The Vision and the Voice and sussing out which bits are Class A and which bits are Class B, and which parts are Crowley's subconscious getting rank or malicious.

0. Take the Oath of Dominis Liminis and keep your eyes and ears wide open for signs. Throw your lot in with the most conspicuous bunch of Thelemic loonies around and do exactly what thou wilt until you feel like you're ready for "ye bigge one".

1. Tell them all that you and your Holy Guardian Angel are off to take on the Universe. A good parting line is "I'm going to be mad for six months, so goodbye everyone."

2. Go mad.

3. See God and all his angels and devils.

4. Conquer hell.

5. Obtain magick powers.

6. Master your new knowledge.

7. Start new (and/or return to old) Thelemic group and watch out for fanatics like yourself.

ULRICH VON HUTTEN

THE HEADLESS ONE.

"O Holy Exalted One, O Self beyond self, O Self-Luminous Image of the Unimaginable Naught, O my darling, my beautiful, come Thou forth and follow me." LXV. 5 42.

This essay is an analysis of the ritual known variously as The Preliminary Invokation of the Goetia, The Bornless Rite and Liber Samekh, although as we shall see these are by no means the only names by which this ritual is known. In the course of this survey we shall consider these several points following:

(1) The Origins, Language and Antecedents of the Ritual.
(2) The History of the Ritual in Modern Times.
(3) The use of the ritual by Crowley and others.
(4) Its relation to the system of Abramelin & to the instruction of the VIIIth Æthyr.
(5) The Qaballistic scheme via Crowley's reconstruction.
(6) Its relation to Kundalini Yoga and sexual magick.
(7) The work of the present writer and his conclusions.

I shall discuss all these points under separate headings, although naturally there will be some unavoidable overlapping. First I append the text of the Ritual in the version described in Liber Samekh, each section of which bears a letter which I hope will aid in the comprehension of this somewhat tortuous essay.

a)
Thee I invoke, the Bornless One.
Thee, that didst create the Earth and the Heavens.
Thee, that didst create thee Night and the Day.
Thee, that didst create the darkness and the Light.
Thou art Ra Hoor Khuit: Whom no man hath seen at any time.
Thou art Ia-Besz.
Thou art Ia-Apophrasz.
Thou hast distinguished between the Just and the Unjust.
Thou didst make the Female and the Male.
Thou didst produce the Seeds and the Fruit.
Thou didst form Men to love one another and to hate one another.

b)
I am N******** thy Prophet, unto Whom Thou didst commit Thy Mysteries, the Ceremonies of ALBION.
Thou didst produce the moist and the dry, and that which nourisheth all created Life.
Hear Thou Me, for I am the Angel of AIWASS: this is Thy True Name, handed down to the Prophets of ALBION.

c)
Hear Me:- AR THIAO RHEIBET A-THELE-BER-SET A BELATHA ABEU EBEU PHI-THETA-SOE IB THIAO.
Hear Me, and make all Spirits subject unto Me; so that every Spirit of the Firmament and of the Ether: upon the Earth and under the Earth, on dry Land and in the Water; of Whirling Air, and of rushing Fire, and every Spell and Scourge of God may be obedient unto Me.

d)
I invoke Thee, the Terrible and Invisible God: Who dwellest in the Void Place of the Spirit:-AR-O-GO-GO-RU-ABRAO SOTOU MUDORIO PHALARTHAO OOO AEPE The Bornless One.
Hear Me, and make all Spirits subject unto Me: so that every Spirit of the Firmament and of the Ether: upon the Earth and under the Earth, on dry Land and in the Water: of Whirling Air, and of rushing Fire, and every Spell and Scourge of God may be obedient unto Me.

e)
Hear Me:-RU-ABRA-IAO MRIODOM BABALON-BAL-BIN-ABAOT ASAL-ON-AI APHEN-IAO I THOTETH ABRASAX AEOOU ISCHURE Mighty and Bornless One!
Hear Me: and make all Spirits subject unto Me, so that every Spirit of the Firmament and of the Ether: upon the Earth and under the Earth: on dry Land and in the Water: of Whirling Air and of rushing Fire: and every Spell and Scourge of God may be obedient unto Me.

f)
I invoke Thee:-MA BARRAIO IOEL KOTHA ATHOR-E-BALO ABRAOT

Hear Me: and make all Spirits subject unto Me: so that every Spirit of the firmament and of the Ether: upon the Earth and under the Earth: on dry Land and in the Water: of Whirling Air and of rushing Fire: and every Spell and Scourge of God may be obedient unto Me.

g)
Hear Me:
AOT ABAOT BAS-AUMGN ISAK SA-BA-OT IAO
This is the Lord of the Gods:
This is the Lord of the Universe:
This is He whom the Winds fear.
This is He, Who having made Voice by His commandment is Lord of all Things; King, Ruler and Helper. Hear Me, and make all Spirits subject unto Me: so that every Spirit of the Firmament and of the Ether: upon the Earth and under the Earth: on dry Land and in the Water: of Whirling Air and of rushing Fire: and every Spell and Scourge of God may be obedient unto Me.

h)
Hear Me:
IEOU PUR IOU PUR IAOTH IAEO IOOU ABRASAX SABRIAM OO UU AD-ON-A-I EDE EDU ANGELOS-TON-THEON ANLALA LAI GAIA AEPE DIATHARNA-THORON
I am He! the Bornless Spirit! having sight in the feet: Strong and the Immortal Fire!
I am He! the Truth!
I am He! Who hate that evil should be wrought in the World!
I am He, that lighteneth and thundereth!
I am He, from whom is the Shower of the Life of Earth!
I am He, whose mouth ever flameth!
I am He, the Begetter and Manifester unto the Light!
I am He, the Grace of the Worlds!
'The Heart Girt with a Serpent' is my name!
Come thou forth and follow me: and make all Spirits subject unto Me so that every Spirit of the Firmament and of the Ether, upon the Earth and under the Earth: on dry Land, or in the Water: of Whirling Air or of rushing Fire, and every Spell and Scourge of God, may be obedient unto Me!

IAO SABAO

Such are the Words!

(1) The Origins, Language and Antecedents of the Ritual.

"I am the heart, and Thou the serpent. Wind Thy coils closer about me, so that no light nor bliss may penetrate." LXV. Ch. II. vs. 53.

The original ritual was written in Greek, and is typical of the Graeco-Egyptian papyri exemplified by the Leyden Papyrus. Although Grant ascribes Sumerian origin to it there are no Sumerian god-names in the ritual. There are related forms of the ritual where there are. Its original structure is quite different from the form it has in most modern versions, as may be found in the translation below. (- The original Greek may be found in Regardie's "Ceremonial Magic").

A)"I call thee, the headless (1) one, that didst create earth and heaven, that didst create night and day, thee the creator of light and darkness. Thou art Osoronophris (2), whom no man hath seen at any time:
Thou art Iabas (3), thou art Iapos (4), thou hast distinguished the just and the unjust, thou didst make men to love one another and to hate one another. I am Moses thy prophet, to whom thou didst commit thy mysteries, the ceremonies of Israel (5); thou didst produce the moist and the dry and all manner of food.
Listen to me: I am an angel of Phaphro Osonnophris (6); this is thy true name handed down to the prophets of Israel. Listen to me..(Names of power omitted)..hear me & drive away this spirit.
I call thee the terrible and invisible god residing in the empty wind (7), (names omitted) thou headless one, deliver such an one (8) from the spirit that possesses him. ..(Names)..strong one, headless one, deliver such an one from the spirit that possesses him. ..(Names)..deliver such an one. ..(Names)..This is the lord of the gods, this is the lord of the world (9), this is he whom the winds fear, this he who made voice by his commandment, lord of all things, king, ruler, helper, save this soul. ..(Names)..I am the headless spirit, having sight in my feet (10), strong, the immortal fire; I am the truth (11); I am he that hateth that ill deeds should be done in the world; I am he that lighteneth and thundereth; I am he whose sweat is the shower that falleth upon earth that it may teem; I am he whose mouth ever burneth; I am the begetter and the bringer forth; I am the Grace of the World; my name is the heart girt with a serpent (12); come forth and follow".

8) **The celebration of the preceding ceremony.**- Write the names upon a piece of new paper, and having extended it over your forehead from one temple to another address yourself turning towards the north (13) to the six names (14), saying: "Make all the spirits subject to me, so that every spirit of heaven and of the air, upon the earth or under the earth, on dry land and in the water, and every spell and scourge of God, may be obedient to me". And all the spirits shall be obedient to you.

1. The Greek word used here is Akephelos, literally "headless".

2. Asar un Nefer, i.e. Osiris; a curious detail if it identifies Osiris with his arch enemy, but in a gnostico-magical text its unorthodoxy in terms of conventional Egyptian religion is unremarkable.

3. Ia-Bes in Samekh, the god Bes.

4. Ia-Apophrasz in Samekh, the god Apep.

5. Replaced with Ankh af na Khonsu for Moses and Khem for Israel in Samekh.

6. Ptah-Ra-Osiris?

7. Alternatively translated "the void air". Crowley reads air as spirit in line with certain conventions, appropriate in Greek and Hebrew, but possibly inappropriate to the Sethians.

8. The ritual was designed to exorcise spirits from possessed persons: "such an one" would be replaced by the name of the victim - in Western books the symbol "N" for "Name of client" is common.

9. Possibly cognate with the Western term "Lord of this World", appropriate to an invokation of Set.

10. A reference to a form of priestly foot-wear bearing an Anubis head on the upper part of the foot, see illustration, also found in other rituals as "wearing a nose at his feet", see Leyden Papyrus, Col. IV, line 8 and notes. It apparently represents wariness and swiftness, although the Ankh sandal strap is considerably more elegant!

11. Compare with the famous cry of Mansur-al-Hallaj (III' OTO and Holy Books of the Yezidi).

12. This phrase, enshrined in the title of one of the Thelemic Class A books, very likely refers to Osiris the heart of the deceased, and Apep or Set the serpent. See note 2.

13. Holy place of the Yezidi and orientation of many Thelemic rituals, as well as the witch cult &c.

14. Probably this means the six series of names in the text.

The famous "Come thou forth..." refrain which recurs throughout later versions of the ritual is here found only in the rubric, in shorter form that that generally found. We also note that the bulk of the ritual is to be written as a kind of talisman or phylactery, rather than for recitation.

The Leyden Papyrus, which has so much in common with this ritual, dates from the 3rd Century AD and was found in the tomb of a Theban magician. Thebes, it will be remembered, was the cult centre of Amon-Ra, of whom Ankh-af-na-Khonsu was priest. A close relative of the "Headless" ritual can be found in this papyrus; it is an invokation of Typhon-Set and its purpose is to inflict catalepsy and death upon the magician's enemies.

Leyden Papyrus. Col. 23. A spell to inflict catalepsy.

A) **Formula.** Take an asses head * and place it between your feet opposite the sun in the morning when it is about to rise, opposite it again in the evening when it goes to the setting. Anoint your right foot with set-stone of Syria and your left foot with clay, the soles (?) of your foot also, and place your right foot in front and your left foot behind, the head (of the ass) between them +. Anoint your hand, of your two hands (palms?), with asses blood, and the two corners of your mouth, and utter these charms towards the sun in the morning and evening of 4 days, then he sleeps. If you wish to make him die you do it for 7 days, you do its magic, you bind a thread of palm fibre to your hand, a (rolled?) mat (?) of wild palm fibre to your phallus and your head; very excellent.

B) **Incantation.** "I invoke thee who art in the void air, terrible, invisible ╪, almighty god of gods, dealing destruction and making desolate, O thou that hatest a household well established ¶. When thou wert cast out of Egypt and out of the country thou wast entitled, "He that destroyeth all and is unconquered."
I invoke thee, Typhon-Set, I perform thy ceremonies of divination, for I invoke thee by thy powerful name in words which thou canst not refuse to hear: IO-ERBETH, IOPAKERBETH, IOBOLKHOSETH, IOPATATHNOX, IOSORO, IONEBOUTOSOUALETH, AKTIOPHI, ERESHKIGAL#, NEBOPOSOALETH ƒ, ABERAMENTHOOU ¤, LERTHEXANAX, ETHRELUOTH, NEMAREBA, AEMINA, entirely come to me and approach and strike (so and so) with frost and fire: he has wronged me and has poured out the blood of Typhon beside him; therefore I do these things."
Common form. (ie conventional Greek).

* The wild ass, particularly if red in colour, was associated with Set.

+ May describe Sign of Set Fighting, see illustration; note variation from G.'.D.'. form.

╪ In the empty wind, translated by Crowley in romantic vein as "the void place of the spirit". Compare also "the terrible and invisible god"; these are conventional forms in the rituals involving Set, particularly Set Akephalon, vide infra.

¶ May connect with "the ill-ordered house in the victorious city" where A.C. found the Stele.

Queen of the Sumerian Underworld.

ƒ Nebo or Nabu is the Sumerian Mercury or Thoth, a magician god with underworld roles.

¤ ABRA-MENTU. As well as its connections with Thelemic magick this name is also associated with Gnostic ideas and with Set Akephalon, see below.

"In the magic of the later period [i.e. the Graeco-Egyptian period under consideration. Author's note.] Seth (the Biblical patriarch) is identified with the monstrous Greek genie Typhon, son of Tartarus, who has a serpent's body. He is supposed to have an ass's head, a feature which recalls the elongated snout and long ears of some African animal, with which Seth (Set) is sometimes identified in Pharoanic iconography. More often he seems to be identified with **a sort of headless demon** whose eyes are placed in his shoulders, **the Akephalos**". (Quoted in S.B.E.G. from K. Preisendanz, AKEPHALOS, DER KOPFLOSEGOTT. Leipzig 1926.)

"In the Gnostic mythos - which transforms the God of Genesis into an evil god, and similarly turns the various other values of Biblical doctrine upside down, this Seth - the enemy of the chief Egyptian gods...acquires a definite position....(see the) Egyptian figurines of the God Seth, cast in bronze which are perfectly appropriate to it. The most significant represent the god walking with the hieratic gait (see Invokation of Typhon-Set above), his body girt with a loin cloth...the asses head...There is no doubt about the identification of the god worshipped in this guise, as one of the great figures of Gnosticism: the pedestal is engraved with the name **ABERAMENTHÔ** which denotes Jesus."

Elsewhere in this valuable book we find reference to the Bornless Rite itself, under its original name, the name which we find, in Greek, at the head of the papyrus from which it was first translated - "(in) an incantation entitled "The Stele of Jeou the Painter" the text of which is preserved in a Greek papyrus...the "headless" god is..referred to as "creator of earth and heaven". We have now placed the ritual in context: it is very late Egyptian, it is an invokation of Set seen through Gnostic eyes, and is closely related to a whole family of Graeco-Egyptian magical papyri, of which the Leyden Papyrus is simply the best known.

THE GOD SÎT, FIGHTING.

(2) The History of the Ritual in Modern Times.

"With courage conquering fear shall ye approach me: ye shall lay down your heads upon mine altar, expecting the sweep of the sword." Liber XC. vs. 16.

The ritual commonly known as "The Preliminary Invokation" or "Bornless Rite" was originally published as a "Fragment of a Graeco-Egyptian work upon magic, from a papyrus in the British Museum, edited for Cambridge Antiquarian Society, with a translation by Charles Wycliffe Goodwin" in 1852. Crowley took the phrase "headless one" - which recurs throughout the original - as meaning "without beginning" and accordingly altered the phrasing to "Bornless One". At one time I was quite content with this adjustment, but having worked with this ritual for many years I am no longer so sure.

Since Goodwin presented this ritual to the English speaking world in 1852, it has become part and parcel of the "Western Tradition" represented by 19th Century revivals such as the Golden Dawn, who incorporated it into their modus operandi. Indeed it may have been Mathers rather than Crowley who amended it into something like the form in which we find it in the "Goetia", and in Leah Hirsig's Diary, with "Moses" and "Israel" etc. as in the original, but having the "Come thou forth" refrain attached to each separate string of barbarous names. The Goetia edited by Crowley bears the date 1904, and we know that he was familiar with it at least two years preceding this date from entries in his diary and references in Equinox of the Gods. Sometime between these two dates, some person or persons unknown adapted the ritual and altered the name "headless" to "bornless", on the assumption that since "Resh"in Hebrew means head or beginning then the term "Headless" might be read as "Thou who art without beginning - unborn and undying". This does not stand up in the light of current Egyptian studies. Nevertheless the phrase itself is significant. The Golden Dawn used part or all of this ritual at various times, and in all likelihood Crowley's use of it derives from his period of apprenticeship to Alan Bennett, since virtual quotations from the ritual occur in Liber Israfel, originally composed by Bennett, but amended by Crowley at some later date. We shall examine more closely its use by Crowley and his associates in our next section, but in the meantime it is enough to say that the "Come Thou forth" refrain seems to have been adopted quite widely in invocations, and the ritual as a whole has been adapted primarily for invocation rather than exorcism.

(3) The use of the ritual by Crowley and others.

"Therefore I say unto thee: Come Thou forth and dwell in me; so that every my Spirit, whether of the Firmament, or of the Ether, of the Earth or under the Earth; on dry land or in the Water, or Whirling Air or of rushing fire; and every spell and scourge of God the Vast One may be THOU. Abrahadabra!" (The Invocation of Horus.)

Of the many occasions when Crowley used this ritual two of the most significant for our purposes were performed in Egypt, in 1903 and 1904. The first Crowley describes as "an exhibition game of magick in the King's Chamber of the Great Pyramid in November, 1903, when by his invocations he filled that chamber with a brightness as of full moonlight. (This was no subjective illusion. The light was sufficient for him to read the ritual by.)"

The next occasion in 1904 is of profound significance for Thelemites. When Crowley described "The events leading up to the Writing of the Book", (i.e. the Book of the Law) this was his first entry:

"MARCH 16. Tried to show the Sylphs to Rose† . She was in a dazed state, stupid, possibly drunk; possibly hysterical from pregnancy. She could see nothing, but could hear. She was fiercely excited at the messages, and passionately insistent that I should take them seriously. I was annoyed at her irrelevance, and her infliction of nonsense upon me. She had never been in any state resembling this, though I had made the same invocation (in full) in the King's chamber of the Great Pyramid during the night which we spent there in the previous autumn.

† I invoked them by the Air section of Liber Samekh, and the appropriate God-names, Pentagrams, &c."

The rest, as they say, is history, but it is worth noting as we consider this momentous event that Crowley's adaptation of the ritual to invoke the Air spirits resulted - not in the appearance of "the sylphs" à la "Compte de Gabalis" - but in the remarkable series of events that within days was to produce the announcement of a New Era for Mankind through the reception of a cryptic book which encodes the formulae of the Aeon of Horus: Liber AL vel Legis. This is perhaps an indicator of the limitations of the will of the magician, who, producing a ritual for a specific purpose, on synthetic lines, overlooks the possibility that what he is adapting has a life of its own. This ritual certainly produced a significant result, but not the result intended. This is a point I wish the reader to bear carefully in mind in later discussions of the rite.

Crowley's diaries, works and the Class A books themselves all stand testament to the importance of this ritual in his magical work. There are references to it in "John St. John" and "Rex de Arte Regia" where he describes a ritual involving a) Liber Israfel, b) the Enochian Calls appropriate to the Elemental Watchtowers and c) The Bornless Rite. The ritual also played a prominent part in Crowley's invocations of the "Secret Chiefs" Abuldiz and Amalantrah. His first contacts with Ab-ul-diz were rather unsatisfactory, but Crowley was told both when next to invoke, and with what ritual. Accordingly, on November 28th 1911 at 10.38pm he opened the Temple and at 10.45pm he invoked Ab-ul-diz by the Bornless Ritual - and at exactly eleven o'clock the Spirit appeared. The circumstances are somewhat similar to the Cairo working of 1904, with Mary d'Este Sturges playing the part of Rose Kelly, having confused visions which lead to an invocation, and to a Book, for the writing of "Magick in Theory and Practice" was on the instructions of the intelligence contacted in this operation.

In August 1920 he records yet another similar event. This time the seeress is Leah Hirsig, Crowley performs the Bornless Rite, and the visions become a series of conversations - this time with Aiwass, although Crowley at first suspected that either Amalantrah or Abuldiz were involved. Indeed there is hardly an important event in Crowley's magical career where the Bornless Rite was not involved. His walk across China involved performing it several times daily. The ritual played a significant part in the John St. John retirement, appropriately enough since this operation was a "retreat and communion with the Holy Guardian Angel, whose Knowledge and Conversation I have willed, and in greater or less measure enjoyed, since Ten Years." It is Liber Pyramidos that he uses for the attainment of this new stage in his relations with his Angel but the Bornless Rite is involved at every turn:

"The Second Day...12.20. In Hanged Man posture, meditating and willing the Presence of Adonai by the Ritual "Thee I invoke, the Bornless One" and mental formulae...[These are either the Shin of Shin operation, see notes at end of this section, or the corresponding part of HHH, probably the former. Author.]

10.50pm. Have done "Bornless One" in Asana. Good; yet I am filled with utter despair at the hopelessness of the Task. Especially do I get the Buddhist feeling, not only that Asana is intensely painful, but that all conceivable positions of the body are so.

The Fifth Day...8.45 I have dressed and from 8.35-8.45 performed the Ritual of the Bornless One. Though I performed it none to well (failing, e.g., to make use of the Geometric Progression of the Mahalingam formula in the Ieou section, and not troubling even to formulate carefully the Elemental Hosts, or to marshal them about the circle) I yet, by the favour of IAO, obtained a really good effect, losing all sense of personality and being exalted in the Pillar. Peace and ecstasy enfolded me. It is well.

The Sixth Day...12.35...I am so sleepy that I cannot concentrate at all. (I was trying the "Bornless One".) The magic goes well; good images and powerful, but I slack right off into sleep...12.45. Have risen, washed, performed the ritual "Thee I invoke, the Bornless One" physically.

The result fair. One gets better magical sight and feeling when one is performing a ritual in one's Astral Body, so called. For one is on the same plane as the things one's dealing with.

If, however, serious work is wanted, one must be all there. To get "materialised" "spirits" - pardon the absurd language! - one should (nay, must!) work inside one's body. So, too, I think, for the highest spiritual work; for that Work extends from Malkuth to Kether."

The Seventh Day...9.30..."that Dweller-of-the-Threshold-thought...comes again and again urging me to quit the Path...At least, though, I am thrown into the active again; I shall rise and chant the Enochian Calls and invoke the Bornless One...Not a bad idea to ask Thoth to send me Tapthartharath with a little information as to the route...This shall be my ritual.

1. Banishing Pentagram Ritual.
2. Invoking ditto.
3. "The Bornless One."
4. The Calls I - VI with the Rituals of the Five Grades.
5. Invocation of Thoth. [Liber Israfel presumably. Author.]
6. No: I will **not** use the New Ritual, nor will I discuss the matter.) An impromptu invocation of Adonai.
7. Closing formulae.
To work then!"

This last section seems to be the same ritual as that mentioned under 1925 in Rex de Arte Regia, see above. The Calls and Grade rituals may be found in Gems from the Equinox; as opening rituals of the grades they here represent an ascent through the Sephiroth in order to invoke Tiphereth.

Of course, the ritual also played a part in the work of the Thelemites of the time. The Liber Samekh version of the ritual was devised at Cefalu for the use of Frank Bennett - Frater Progradior. The Goetia version of it is written at the back of Leah Hirsig's diary, and was used by her to commence new periods, and as a preparation for visions, including the following series where she apparently forsaw the Intercontinental Ballistic Missile.

"January 17th [L Ed.] 9 P.M. After Amoun Invocation I asked for Light (IEHI AUR).
Thin stalked leaves with heavy birds on them as in a previous vision.
I said "I understand" and had a feeling of something definitely accomplished.
Later - Preliminary Invocation.
Started vision but couldn't hold it. A lion turned into a beetle which was really a sun
(Sign of) 7 = 4
Asked for someone of higher grade
(Sign of) 8 = 3 X I. (symbol) - a dog.
And no more!

Jan. 18th 9 P.M. Ra Hoor Khuit invocation.
Asked for light
"Stir not" (heard)
Elixir (seen)

Jan. 19th. 5.30. P.M.
Preliminary Invocation (33 L)
War Engine
Met a dragon - who looked mild after 93
Flashes of (symbol) etc.
A man - his name - AUM - 84
Showed me that War Engine was of metal (very fine) and to be hurled. Not electricity.
Danger of being seen hurling?
No.

Jan. 20th. 7.30 - 8.30
A period of silence in which I invoke Neptune to look after OPV + Mss.
An anchor and a white bird flying over it.

Later - Pre. Inv.
Concentration. - W.E. [War Engine]

(I forget much of what I saw.) A man in a simple dark robe carrying a red heart appeared eventually & showed me a room where a man, a woman, and a child were eating in a very poor room. I got the impression that the W.E. energy would be got for us by such a person - 93 changed the room and it was illuminated by an 11 pointed star.

I was shown a rocky country - perhaps Russia - presumably the place where the energy would be found or created.

More - but nothing definite."

Notes on the G.'.D.'. 0=0 ritual.

The Golden Dawn 0=0 rite: "...the Candidate repeats the Obligation after the Hierophant...As the Candidate affirmeth his own penalty should he prove a traitor to the Order, the evil triad riseth up in menace, and the avenger of the Gods, Horus, layeth the blade of his sword on the point of the Da'ath junction [i.e., of the brain with the spine] thus affirming the power of Life and Death over the natural body...the Form of the Higher Self advanceth and layeth its hand on the Candidate's head for the first time, at the words: "So help me the Lord of the Universe and my own Higher Soul". And this is the first assertion of the connecting link between them."

The Shin of Shin Operation: Shin of Shin is a part of a document analysing the 0=0 in terms of various Magical Operations. The Shin of Shin involves "Spiritual Development", i.e. invoking the HGA.

"On the 16th April he [Crowley] journeyed to Amecameca, from which place he visited Soror F, by projection, and thence up Popocatapetl, encamped on whose slopes he resolved the Shin of Shin into seven Mental Operations:

1. Ray of Divine White Brilliance, descending upon the Akasic Egg set between the two pillars.
2. Aspire by the Serpent, and concentrate on Flashing Sword. Imagine the stroke of the Sword upon the Da'ath junction (nape of neck).
3. Make the egg grow gray, by a threefold spiral of light.
4. Make the Egg grow nearly white. (Repeat spiral formula.)
5. Repeat 2. Above head. Triangle of Fire (red).
6. Invoke Light. Withdraw. See Golden Dawn Symbol.
7. Let all things vanish in the Illimitable Light."

Liber HHH: the first section of HHH, as is well known, is itself an analysis of the 0=0, and is clearly based on the above sevenfold process. The second section may well correspond to the unpublished paper, Liber Cadaveris. The final section is SSS, dealing with Kundalini, which I shall examine in the sixth section of this paper.

These excerpts show the extraordinary versatility of the ritual, although in at least one instance, in Cairo 1904, the preconceived purpose of the ritual was not even related to the (admittedly extraordinarily important) results achieved. It should be borne most carefully in mind, however, that although the ritual seems admirably suited to precede visionary experiments, to commence invocations of Spirits and to invoke the Holy Guardian Angel, it undoubtedly had an original purpose, and was devised in its original form along lines which assuredly made more sense to the composer of the ritual than to Goodwin (the translator) or Crowley (the adapter). I now proceed to the core of the matter, so far as Liber Samekh is concerned, if not the other forms of the ritual.

(4) Its relation to the system of Abramelin & to the instruction of the VIIIth Æthyr.

"I am like a black eunuch; and Thou art the scimitar. I smite off the head of the light one, the breaker of bread and salt." Liber VII. Ch. III. vs. 34.

This ritual stands at the centre of Thelemic magick, as the ritual par excellence of achieving Knowledge and Conversation of the Holy Guardian Angel. Its central importance is to be understood in terms of Crowley's mission to bring all men to this sacrament (" I am indeed sent to do something. For whom? For the Universe?...What shall I teach men? And like lightning from heaven fell upon me these words: 'The Knowledge and Conversation of the Holy Guardian Angel.'") which is essentially identical with the discovery of the True Will. The precursors of this method are to be found in "The Sacred Magic of Abramelin the Mage."

The Abramelin Retirement is a major magical operation in which the phrase "Knowledge and Conversation" first occurs in extant occult literature - it is to be found in a MS purporting to date from 1485, translated by the able hand of Macgregor Mathers. The entire scheme of the work is outside the scope of a resumé such as this. Briefly, however, the operation extends over six months, during the first two months of which the operator rises at dawn and invokes his Angel with prayer, and makes the study of the Holy Books of his religion his principle pastime. For the second two months, he increases the intensity of his devotions, making his invocation at dawn and sunset. During the third two month period he makes the invocation at dawn, noon and sunset.

The instruction in the Eighth Æthyr of the Enochian system detailed in "The Vision and the Voice" is aimed at the same attainment. Essentially the details of the preparation of the place and the operator are not too dissimilar from the Abramelin scheme, but the time scale differs in that it extends over 91 days or eleven weeks. The prayer cycle is more intense than Abramelin, partially perhaps due to the shorter time span: "he shall pray thrice daily, about sunset, and at midnight, and at sunrise. And if he be able, he shall pray also four times between sunrise and sunset......and in any case he shall pray seven times daily during the last week of the eleven weeks."

The rubric of Liber Samekh ends with these words, which we may compare with the above: "Let the Adept perform this ritual aright, perfect in every part thereof, once daily for one moon, then twice, at dawn and dusk, for two moons, next, thrice, noon added, for three moons, afterwards, midnight making his course, for four moons four times every day. Then let the Eleventh Moon be consecrated wholly to this Work; let him be instant in continual ardour, dismissing all but his sheer needs to eat and sleep. For know that the true Formula whose virtue sufficed the Beast in this attainment, was thus:

INVOKE OFTEN.

So may all men come at last to the Knowledge and Conversation of the Holy Guardian Angel: thus sayeth the Beast, and prayeth His own Angel that this book be as a burning Lamp, and as a living Spring, for Light and Life to them that read therein."

Crowley's use of the Bornless Rite for this purpose, as set forth in Liber Samekh, was performed over a four month period, "invoking often" during a journey on horseback in China in 1906, two years after the reception of the Book of the Law. This was not the only such retirement he undertook; his relations with his Holy Guardian Angel involved numerous such retirements. The magical strain produced by such efforts cannot be perfectly described. It involves distortions or interruptions of normal consciousness, in which time and the apparent laws of our day-to-day existence are meaningless and frequently suspended. The diaries of these retirements themselves can give only an imperfect sketch of these phenomenon, by which resistance to the consummation of this communion is broken down to the point at which the Angel can overcome our defences and finally render us passive and receptive to His force. The only analogy to this that is remotely suitable is the relation between the Spheres on the Tree of Life, each of which is active in relation to that below it and passive in relation to that above. This passivity is incredibly difficult for the magician to achieve in their relation with their Angel, and the strains of the operation, against which he or she ACTIVELY struggles day by day eventually produce a state of, if not collapse, at least resignation. In this surrender, achieved by such pains and trials, the Knowledge and Conversation is finally granted.

(5) The Qaballistic scheme via Crowley's reconstruction.

"Fear not at all; fear neither men nor Fates, nor gods, nor anything. Money fear not, nor laughter of the folk folly, nor any other power in heaven or upon the earth or under the earth..." AL.III. vs.17.

The attributions of the elements to the quarters in Samekh does not follow the scheme used in the other Thelemic rites, such as "The Star Ruby" or the "Star Sapphire" or even the Gnostic Mass, but retains the well known East = Air, North = Earth, rather than the more usual Thelemic attribution of Earth to East and Air to North. &c. This may be because the ritual predated Crowley's adoption of these attributions, or it may be quite simply, as Crowley himself remarked from time to time, that this operation differs in many respects from every other, and, indeed, reverses the usual methods. Judging from my own experience with the rite, and from various considerations arising from this work and from the orientation in the original Graeco-Egyptian ritual, I consider it to be desirable, once one acquires perfect comprehension and competence with the rite, to switch the attributions as outlined in the final sections of this paper.

There is no necessary connection between the ideas involved in the Barbarous Names of the Ritual and the Elements to which Crowley has ascribed them in the structure of this rite. To take an example, KOTHA meaning "The Hollow One" is as appropriate to Air as to Earth. Crowley and/or Mathers deleted at least some names and altered others: i.e. PHOTETH for the original THOTETH - the interested student should see the Greek in Regardie's Ceremonial Magic. This being the case, there remains the likelihood that the six "Names" or sections spoken of in the original - and the six corresponding sections in Crowley's recension - relate to SOMETHING, which Crowley interpreted as the Four Elements and Spirit Active and Passive, but which could equally well be the Six Spatial Directions: Up, Down, East, South, West and North, or some similar pattern in common currency among Graeco-Egyptian sorcerers!

Analysis of the Elemental Sections.

Below may be found the various visualisations, gestures and sigils associated with the ritual. Accompanying them are the outlines of two schemes of elemental attributions. These attributions relate both to the four quarters and to the chakras, and are derived from Samekh and my own work with the ritual since 1981.

(For references c) to h) see text of ritual at beginning of this article.)

c)
Air.
Enochian Sigil: Air.
Gesture: Grade sign of 2=9 (Moon) or alternatively Puella.
Visualisation: a golden bird or angel.
Colour of phallic wand and auric egg: yellow.
Chakra: Groin. (Attributed to either Air or Earth, see Solve/Coagula table.)

d)
Fire.
Enochian Sigil: Fire.
Gesture: Grade sign of 4=7 (Venus) or alternatively Puer.
Visualisation: a red lion.
Colour of phallic wand and auric egg: red.
Chakra: Stomach.

e)
Water.
Enochian Sigil: Water.
Gesture: Grade sign of 3=8 (Mercury) or alternatively Mulier.
Visualisation: a blue dragon or eagle.
Colour of phallic wand and auric egg: blue.
Chakra: Heart.

f)
Earth.
Enochian Sigil: Earth.
Gesture: Grade sign of 1=10 (Elements) or alternatively Vir.
Visualisation: a green hippopotamus or bull.
Colour of phallic wand and auric egg: green.
Chakra: Throat. (See notes on Air section.)

g)
Spirit Active.
Sigil of NOX.
Gesture: Grade signs of LVX, or alternatively Rending of the Veil.
Colour of phallic wand and auric egg: white.
Chakra: Forehead.

h)
Spirit Passive.
Sigil of NOX.
Gesture: Grade signs of LVX, or alternatively Closing of the Veil.
Colour of phallic wand and auric egg: white.
Chakra: Above Head.

(6) Its relation to Kundalini Yoga and sexual magick.

"But to love me is better than all things: if under the night-stars in the desert thou presently burnest mine incense before me, invoking me with a pure heart, and the Serpent flame therein, thou shalt come a little to lie in my bosom." AL. I. vs. 61.

Liber Samekh commences with the significant instruction to perform the ritual armed with the Wand and Cup. This is an obvious reference to tantric elements in the ritual, which we may compare with the ritual called the Star Sapphire, allegedly the cause of the OTO accusing A.C. of revealing their sex-magical secrets. A method of arousing the Fire Snake with this ritual was described in The New Equinox Volume 6 number 1, and by Francis King in his excellent work "Tantra for Westerners". King also "feminises" the God invoked, on the basis that Kundalini is personified as a Scarlet Goddess in tantric sources. In many respects this book is among the best extant for applying Tantra in a Thelemic context. That neither of us were "exceeding our brief" is obvious from the reference to the magical weapons mentioned above, standard allegorical terms for the Lingam and Yoni in modern occultism.

I would strenuously advise anyone undertaking an Abramelin style retirement with this ritual to take very seriously the injunctions Crowley makes in the text. Prepare yourself by reading LXV, which we can and should expand to include the Holy Books of Thelema in general, and AL in particular.

You will benefit from experience in the expansion of the Body of Light along the lines of Liber 536, BATRAXOPHRENOBOOCOSMOMACHIA:

The Expansion of Consciousness.

"Seated in the open air, let him endeavour to form a complete mental picture of himself and his immediate surroundings. It is important that he should be in the centre of such picture, and able to look freely in all directions...Let him gradually add to this picture by including objects more and more distant....let the Practicus form a mental picture of the Earth, in particular striving to realise the size of the earth in comparison with himself...Let him add the Moon, keeping well in mind the relative sizes of, and the distance between, the Earth and its satellite........add in turn Venus, Mars, Mercury and the Sun.....the Asteroids, Jupiter, Saturn, Uranus and Neptune [Pluto was not discovered at the time of writing. Ed.] The utmost attention to detail is now necessary, as the picture is highly complex, apart from the difficulty of appreciating relative size and distance..........let his contemplation become vast as the heaven, in space and time ever aspiring to the perception of the Body of Nuit." Liber BATRAXOPHRENOBOOCOSMOMACHIA.

An alternative to this method is to use the wide focus view method found in Liber Null (Pete Carroll), coupled with an appreciation of the Sun and Moon's positions in the Ecliptic, studying daily the astrological picture of the heavens and striving on one's walks to locate where each part, whether visible or not, is located in relation to oneself. If the ritual can be performed outside in the country (albeit internally or without full ceremonial) at some stage in the walk after expanding the consciousness by such means, all the better.

Some measure of success in the practices in Liber Nu, where the first of the three Results is "Expansion of consciousness to that of the Infinite" would serve the same general purpose.

The analogy between these exercises and certain tantric meditations, where the operator visualises such vast pictures of the Universe in conjunction with the Compassion meditation (Peace to all beings), will be noticed. This practice of expansion relates to various aspects of the rite, in particular:

The Assumption of God Forms.

"In these invocations he should expand his girth and stature to the utmost (having experience of success in the practices of Liber 536), assuming the form and the consciousness of the Elemental God of the quarter."

The Extension of the Will Symbol.

The Will in this ritual is formulated visually as a phallus; "Let then the Adept extend his Will beyond the Circle in this imagined Shape and let it radiate with the Light proper to the Element invoked."

The Geometric Progression of Divine Names.

This Will symbol is the channel for the divine names. "Let each Word issue along the Shaft with passionate impulse...Let also each Word accumulate authority, so that the Head of the Shaft may plunge twice as far for the Second Word as for the First, and Four Times for the Third as for the second, and thus to the end...". This practice may be compared with the Kundalini exercise in Liber HHH. If the operator works the rite in the chakras rather than the quarters, the close identity of the practices, and the reason for the emphasis on HHH throughout the Elemental Grades, will be clear to him.

The Arousal of the Fire-Snake.

"In this practice the cavity of the brain is the Yoni; the spinal cord is the Lingam...concentrate thy thought of adoration in the brain...begin to awake the spine...concentrate thy thought of thyself in the base of the spine, and move it gradually up a little at a time...adore the brain...figure to thyself its content as infinite. Deem it to be the womb of Isis, or the Body of Nuit...identify thyself with the base of the spine..figure to thyself its energy as infinite. Deem it to be the phallus of Osiris, or the being of Hadit...imagine the hunger of the one for the other; the emptiness of the brain, the ache of the spine...if thou hast experience of the Eucharist in both kinds, it shall aid thine imagination herein [i.e., in the case of the male having experienced penetrating and being penetrated. Author.]...let a current of light, deep azure flecked with scarlet, pass up and down the spine, striking as it were upon thyself that art coiled at the base as a serpent...Then at last being well-fitted in body and mind, fixed in peace, beneath a favourable heaven of stars, at night in calm and warm weather, mayst thou quicken the movement of the light until it be taken up by the brain and the spine, independently of thy will." Liber HHH. Cap. SSS.

(7) The work of the present writer and his conclusions.

"He shall await the sword of the Beloved, and bare his throat for the stroke." Liber VII, ch. 5. vs. 47.

My own work with this ritual has extended over ten years, and I thus consider myself qualified to not only write this article regarding what it is and might be, but also to conclude with my own interpretation of how it is best performed. We should remember that the original use of the rite involved states of possession, which we might consider in terms of willed states of possession rather than unfortunate obsessive conditions. In such cults as Voodoo, as ably described by Maya Deren, the state of possession commences with a force ascending through the body, analogous if not identical with the Kundalini serpent.

In the course of the ritual's performance, the operator "assumes" beast forms & "vibrates" the Names along a phallic shaft of will, "Unto the ends of the Universe", i.e. up the spine to the brain, the body "visualised" as immense in size; each series of words relates, in ascending order, to the "chakras", viz: Air=Groin, Fire=Solar Plexus, Water=Heart, Earth=Throat, Spirit Active=Pineal Gland, Spirit Passive=Above Head. Why are the elements in this order? Surely it would make more sense to have Genitals as Earth & Throat as Air? Yes, it would; indeed the elemental attributions to the quarters in, say, the Star Ruby are arranged exactly like that. But! As Crowley emphasised, the Holy Guardian Angel ritual is different from and even the reverse of usual procedures. The "Bornless Rite" was originally the "Headless Rite", and magicians who use the Rite, and analogous yogic and tantric processes, find the Da'ath Chakra or larynx is or feels "blocked". Qaballistically this is the Abyss. Remember all the sword and neck symbolism?

Throat=Pentacle (or Platter), Genitals=Dagger (or Sword). Solve et Coagula, or "fixing the volatile & making volatile that which is fixed", is, so to speak, turning Air into Earth and vice versa. Thus the ascending Kundalini passes the Da'ath centre when the "Flaming Sword" cuts off the head. Unfortunately for the Golden Dawn methodology, the "divine white brilliance" only descends when it's good and ready; it is the "ascending mode" which is important initially, not only throughout yogic tradition but in other living traditions such as Voodoo.

Here follow some extracts from my own Magical Records.

Retirement 1980/81.

In 1980 I undertook the Magickal Retirement described in Samekh, involving an eleven month period (actually somewhat longer as I worked with the ritual for several months prior to the Retirement itself), as outlined above. From the beginning I observed Dawn, Noon, Sunset and Midnight & performed the Solar Adorations from Liber Resh. At the appropriate stages of the retirement I performed the Bornless Rite once, twice, three times and finally four times a day, reading the Class A, particularly AL, and interpreted those parts of it that gained relevance through various states and intuitions with the aid of the Holy Qaballa, in this case the E.'.Q.'..

March 1 '81...Less and less of my thoughts concern anything but Adonai and magick, each day is directed towards Him and the attaining of His Knowledge and Conversation.

Bornless Rite, a great thrill of exaltation at achievement of the "Star Spate" "psychic orgasm". I think the achievement...is partly due to practice of assuming phallic god form earlier today, a course certainly to be emphasised...it goes well with Ptah posture.

March 3 '81...Complete disassociation of self from actions and perceptions...on leaving Temple I found myself automatically back into mantra, as often happens but not on exiting temple when usually it is the Bornless Rite re-echoing fragmentarily....another memory of results occurs to me, during the Hexagram ritual there was a great profusion of arrowheads of brilliant silver light in the North, and while performing mantra yoga coming home tonight I broke spontaneously into the adoration that is equivalent to this mantra (Unity uttermost showed) and saw the Stele and the Godforms of the Thelemic cosmogony in brilliant light.

June 21st. 8.40 to 9.25. Japa (mantra) till sunset. Bornless Rite, fearful, noises as of animals or creeping persons all around, saw a lion while facing North, beside me, its head to South, quite a jolt at this. XXV-water and fire - Bornless Rite difficult among the trees, but earnest. All Four Demons (the beast forms) piling in at end with Pillar of Light/White Phallus reaching sky (but not hell) between their enormous forms.

July 22nd. I'm not sure what's going on! I went in at 4.45 I think and did alternate mantra - Pentagram - Fire - Water - till Dawn Adoration at 5.10. Then I started pranayama and lost 15 minutes, one minute it was 5.13, the next the clock said - or appeared to say 5.30, I carried on until what looked like 5.45 then did the Bornless Rite (which should take at minimum ten minutes) until what looked like 5.50 ish and went to phone the speaking clock, which said 5.42, I looked at the clock and it was back at 5.42. What the hell happened? I can read a clock at point blank range! Also the pranayama FELT like 30 minutes in asana, and the candles LOOKED like they'd burnt away. In fact I didn't lose any time at all, the clock just appeared to gain while in the Temple, and then come back to "normal" on phoning the time, if anything I gained time that didn't exist, but it's damned curious and I'm a bit freaked out by it all!

August 2nd. 11.35 (?) till 12.45. Clock seemed to retrogress but is correct on leaving temple!

August 9th. 8.30 to 9.35. Adored Sun, Bornless Rite, prayers from Treasure House, Sagittarius, Unity, 169 Cries...I note an irritating but possibly suggestive tendency to forget results till later on, so I can't be sure always which time they occurred, e.g. at Midday performance of 169 I had a tinkling of bells interiorly; e.g. at several unspecified performances I've been the god looking at me, not me looking at the god in the quarters, especially West, this since taking up use of appropriate pentagrams and Grade Signs etc.

<u>Retirement 1988</u>

6th April. Sun at Noon. Sun at Sunset and Bornless Rite, visualisation good, otherwise not brilliant. Sun at Midnight and Bornless Rite. Better, saw a red pyramid inverted fall down shaft into heart, red ruby light to it. Serpent arose facing opposite direction to my physical sight, (towards me but inside me) to heart centre.

8th. Sunset adorations and Bornless Rite + mantra and "entered in" finale from Phoenix. Some swift and nasty headaches recently, physical or psychic?

19th May. Sunset. Resh and Bornless in "astral body" as Middle Pillar Exercise, vibrating names up the lengthening spine. Oh for BATRAXOPHRENOBOOCOSMOMACHIA!

22nd May. Bornless Rite last night v. good indeed, no writing materials available, in car to Bristol.

Spirit Passive=Above Head.
Spirit-Passive=Pineal.
Earth Section=Throat=Head on Platter.
Water Section=Solar Plexus=Grail.
Fire Section=Stomach=the boiler room!
Air Section=Groin=The "Beast in the East" see Star Ruby.

Realised feasibility of disincarnation. Contact HGA to save you from your own folly! Nearly "holied out", strongest since March events. You really are living on borrowed time once the contract is fulfilled.

June 1st. Midnight, mantra etc. began rite with:

"Now I begin to pray: Thou Child,
Holy Thy name and undefiled!"

Bornless Rite etc. as above. Goodish; breakdown of ideas: Pentagram in chakras rather than quarters Air, Fire, Water, Earth as in Bornless. Final Qaballistic Cross as Spirit Active and Passive from above head to brow.

Purifications, in spine, Graal above Head, the "water" Triangle or "blessings" descend.

Consecrations, Fire ascending from base of spine to heart, the Fire triangle meets the influence from above, thus forming Hexagram. Invocations follow.

Bornless Rite in chakras, "head on a plate" strong in QBL + and Bornless at Earth section. At the end spontaneously moved into NOX signs as yogic dance thus fixing the volatile Earth Fire Water Air and making volatile that which was fixed.

[Table showing relation between two schemes of Elemental Attributions]

SOLVE					COAGULA
LAMP	- SPIRIT PASSIVE	- CROWN	- SPIRIT PASSIVE	-	LAMP
	SPIRIT ACTIVE	- HEAD	- SPIRIT ACTIVE		
DAGGER -	AIR	- THROAT	- EARTH	-	DISK
CUP -	WATER	- HEART	- WATER	-	GRAIL (emotions)
WAND -	FIRE	- BELLY	- FIRE	-	LANCE (appetites)
DISK	EARTH	- GENITALS	- AIR	-	DAGGER

Visualising the animal god forms, the fire phallus, pentagrams, hexagrams and wheels and vibrating Names, extending the pillar into infinity, with assistance of A.'. because I never learned to do these things like they're happening now, it's subtler but stronger and more exacting than the ('81 Retirement codename).

Oct. 5th.

ASTROLOGY tells you WHO you are,
QABALLA tells you WHERE you are going,
ALCHEMY tells you HOW to get there.

Alchemy involves "Time Jumps" speeding up the evolutionary process. The process takes place in time, say Aries to Pisces but time is "condensed" (?), past and future are transmuted in the present. Oh blah blah, what do I know?

Oct. 6th. The Great Winds may be connected with the recent Sun trine Jupiter ritual, and there's another in January. Went out in it about 9.30, mantra and Bornless Rite, or the headless Rite as I'm now beginning to understand it. "I cut off the head of the light one, the breaker of bread and salt" = Jesus, Tiphereth, or rather John. See Blue Notebook for Headless One.

Oct. 7th. 8.45pm. Bornless Rite in krystal. Altar. [No longer understand this. Author.]
The West. Da'ath centre expecting the sword.

Midnight 25th. Notes on Resh adorations: There are definite distinguishable differences between standing in Apophis and Typhon posture facing different directions at different times. Might be light and shadow, might be blood or brain, might be gravity or all these, but making samahdi on self-sun at these times is qualitively different.

Midnight Nov. 9th. Adored Khephra. Saw "aura colours" when arms went into Apophis and Typhon - produced "wings" mainly of red and brilliance. This occurred quite frequently during the Bornless Rite period earlier this year, but I don't think I recorded it.

The realisation of the nature of these processes and their connection with the Headless motif of the Rite was a long time coming, through the feelings and experiences attending my performance of this rite and the various parts of the curriculum connected with it - influenced no doubt by my close relationship with the Class A and the various ritual and meditative processes surrounding them. I hope this relationship has been made a little clearer by this article. All I would like to add to the above is my earnest wish that the student makes use of the ritual, in conjunction with the Abramelin retirement in some form, with a close and reverential attitude to the Holy Books of Thelema as their guide through the maze of initiation.

So mote it be, Amen.

JAKE STRATTON-KENT

Works cited:

Pete Carroll.	Liber Null.
Aleister Crowley.	Liber Samekh.
	The Goetia of Solomon the King.
	Magical Record of the Beast 666.
	The Law is for All.
	The Equinox of the Gods.
	John St. John.
	Complete Astrological Writings.
	Liber HHH.
Maya Deren.	Divine Horsemen/Voodoo Gods.
Jean Doresse.	The Secret Books of the Egyptian Gnostics.
J.F.C. Fuller.	The Temple of Solomon the King.
Kenneth Grant.	The Typhonian Trilogy.
F.Griffith & H.Thomson.	The Leyden Papyrus.
Leah Hirsig.	Magical Record of the Scarlet Woman.
Isya Joseph.	Devil Worship; The Sacred Books and Traditions of the Yezidis.
Jake Stratton-Kent.	The Ordeal X. (TNE/BJM Vol.6.No.1.)
	Magical Diaries.
Francis King.	Secret Rituals of the OTO.
	Tantra for Westerners.
Israel Regardie.	Ceremonial Magic.
	The Golden Dawn.

MAGNUS RIDES ROUGHSHOD (or MORE MAYHEM WITH MAGNUS)

In the Book of Long Words - & elsewhere in my works - it is asserted that empiricism is the great magickal virtue. By empiricism, of course we mean an eagerness to experiment & learn by experience. Ideally the magician should commence his career with no other yardstick. There are many reasons why this is desirable, as will become clear, but let's lay down a few anti-rules.

TAKE NOTHING FOR GRANTED.

Do not assume any explanation or theory regarding magickal phenomena is a hard fact rather than a convenient idea, or worse, a deception. Further than this, do not assume your results or lack of them are caused by any straightforward means. Yet more vital, do not assume that you have noted all results or attendant effects; there will always be lots going on you haven't noticed, YET!

TAKE EVERYTHING FOR GRANTED.

When working with a particular system be wholehearted about it; as whatever you believe is untrue on some plane or another there is all the more reason to use the complete thing-in-itself; it takes a whole aspirin to cure a headache, the individual ingredients achieve nothing by themselves. Keep a really thorough record - there are lots of good reasons for this: i) patterns may emerge over a period of time; ii) the intellectual process of recording workings helps the "banishing" or "coming down" process; iii) it might be useful to others, like us for instance!

Be eclectic. Try everything; every culture & time period has left writings, rituals, ideas & tools, be as wide as possible in your use of existing materials. About the best place to start is with our old friend the grimoire. Any grimoire will do, although perhaps the best of all for our purposes is "The Secret Grimoire of Turiel", due to its coherence & schematic completeness. The first thing one notices with almost every grimoire is that its operations are astrologically timed & departmentalised. Every operation is under some planetary heading & the position of the Sun &/or Moon at very least must be considered in each operation. Correspondences are invariably astrologically classified too, & Qabalah plays at best a secondary role.

This is important, since astrological magic has a superbly empirical basis. Astrological observations have attended magic since the paleolithic era - if any magical results are provably repeatable then those under astrological aspects are among the most eligible for research. Biological causes, such as drugs, the sexual cycle, "excitory" & "inhibitory" exercises are fairly constant & repeatable, likewise astrology. These two areas are of most direct use for building up useable data by the empirical method. I've said all this before, but as no-one else is saying it I'm entitled to repeat myself.

So, assuming that we have found a suitable grimoire & learnt how to set up an astrological chart - not to mention how to read an ephemeris - we should be able to conduct a series of experiments, working through each class of operation systematically. There are those who say magic should never be performed out of curiosity - fine - don't call it curiosity, call it scientific research! Keep an open mind, perform the rituals thoroughly, be prepared to improvise when necessary & DO NOT PANIC! Sure, some operations are dangerous & you may go mad, but if & when you recover you will be better informed than most so-called occultists who try & dissuade you! You will find a wide range of techniques in the course of your research: dancing, chanting, sensory stimuli, gestures & so forth. Work with them & understand them. If you want to do anything, do it magickally - I really can't emphasise this enough, so I will just say it again, if you want to do anything do it magickally!!! You want to know how so-and-so is and how it is with them? Well, DON'T ASK THEM! That's the normal thing to do & it doesn't work! Use the Tarot, then they don't even have to be there! You want to invoke Mars & Venus? DON'T look for a free weekend, look for a conjunction of Mars & Venus! You want a loan from the bank, arrange an appointment for Jupiter conjunct Fortuna. Magick works, & in the real world, not the laboratory where conditions are artificial, but in the streets & fields, where Nature rules supreme. Use magick, not half baked humanitarian or sociological hogwash. Magick works! Do people vote for the politician with the best policies or the one with the best image? Answer, they say one thing but they do the other. "Vote for Maggie, she's tough & sexy! who cares about policies?" Who cares about politics? It's entertainment people want, & behind the stereotype lurks the Archetype, the magickal symbol. Of course, symbols aren't potent in their own right, TECHNIQUE AND REAL SOLID FORCES are potent, but just the same, techniques involving recognisable archetypes don't seem to have let the media down so far, do they?

You want to fly through the air? Wipe out enemies at a distance? Collect legions of bunny girls? Get yourself a batch of gold talismans & an IMAGE! If you can just get enough gold talismans you can achieve EVERY purpose known to magick! How do you get the talismans? Why, MAGICK of course, after all, statistics prove that most people who REALLY work for a living are either too poor or too busy to have any fun. The Protestant work ethic is dead; Magick is easy, nothing is impossible. Sure, most would-be magicians need the esoteric enema of the Ordeal X before they know what magick is....so what's the problem, fear of failure? Do it! & to hell with the consequences! The only guide you need is your Holy Guardian Angel, the only tools you need are yourself, the Book of the Law & MAGICK! Welcome to the Invisible College.

EVERYTHING IS TRUE - NOTHING IS PERMITTED.

The limitation of empiricism: I only eat what I've eaten before. So you starve to death. Solution, suspension of disbelief. Scepticism is positive, cynicism negative.

The best empirical magician of the last generation thought he could disprove Qaballa by enumerating a Volkswagen manual; unfortunately he forsook empiricism & neglected to study even an enumerated magickal manual, let alone the VW manual.

Had he done so, he might have noticed that the VW manual & the Holy Book had unusual letter frequencies when compared to ordinary literary use of language - S more frequent than E, for starters. The mistake this magician - for such we must call him - made was not merely forgetting to do his homework FOR OR AGAINST but in planning to use statistics rather than MAGICK. In other words, he wore the "blinkers of because". Notwithstanding the fact that Gauguelin's statistical surveys of astrology converted him from the anti to the pro camp, statistics are NOT astrological - nor by extension magickal.

English - the language of the Angles or Angels - in the Class A's is the Serpent Tongue, the Angelic Language. What does that imply? That we're not harmless eccentrics, but dangerous right wing mystics? (Right Wing = belief in the power of Archetypes.) The Queen's English what's more, American is Ben Franklin's. Trust the Hellfire Club to mess things up, "my color is black to the blind"?? At least they got the Pyramid right. The Invisible College is the Fourgated Palace, the Chapel Perilous.

In magick, the ability to learn fast must be matched by the ability to unlearn carefully. We usually acquire much superfluous knowledge & obsolete technical data in the course of - hopefully - uncovering some fundamental principles which lie beneath the debris of dead ages & archaic civilisations. Once these principles are firmly grasped, we must either abandon the dead letter or be buried with it.

Such principles are not hard to find - once you've seen the fnords - but in the meantime the glamour of the astral conspires against you; with decayed religions, unreadable tablets of clay & stone, unpronounceable names of gods long dead, mythical kings & iguanas, not to mention all the lights & colours. I'm not saying these things aren't fun - they make great videos & role-playing games - but they don't help you cause change to occur in conformity with will - they make sure it all remains the same. So UNLEARN CAREFULLY & examine what you REALLY KNOW & can use, & what is just tinsel on the Xmas Tree.

On the other hand, we should not overlook the possible benefits of some of our mistakes, or seemingly trivial discoveries. For instance, you may discover that a particular herb, far from producing an enhanced understanding of life - or even a delusion of such an understanding - actually emptied the contents of your stomach; this might teach you caution & may even provide a fast working emergency cure for more digestible poisons! You will have found a way to influence the environment: "Hey, great! I can make people puke!" And with such a weapon, it may be that after many diverse doses & purges you will find the "enlightenment" herb & exclaim "Hey, great! I've found a way of lobotomising revolutionaries!"

I've said it before & I'll say it again:

HAVE NO ESTABLISHED MENTAL CRITERION.

The most enlightened views can be distorted into bigotry or pathetic excuses. The most irrational ideas can be useful. I.e. "There is no God" frees us from superstition & from obligations to outmoded institutions like the Church. On the other hand, a god can be a "psycho-experimental construct" of great value in practical occultism. It is somewhat depressing to observe that many modern magicians feel able to personify their complexes, limitations & what not as demons & banish them, but incapable of personifying their ideals, motives & such like as gods & worshipping them. It is the quality of devotion which renders magick an organic & continuous process, rather than a mechanistic & sterile technique. This devotion is traditionally attributed to the Sephirah Netzach or Venus, & the work of this grade precedes the "Knowledge & Conversation of the Holy Guardian Angel" - it is the last, & most critical, step in completing the work of the "elemental grades" in which "the Temple is builded that the God may indwell it".

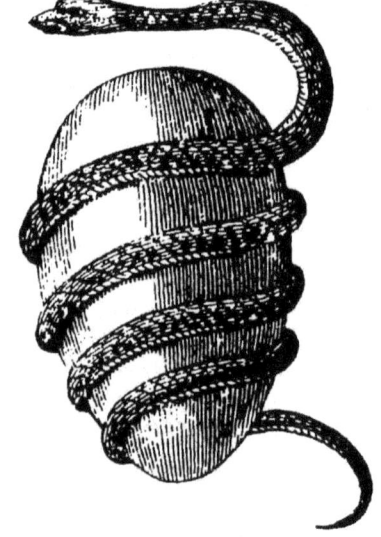

This devotional attitude may be cultivated through the painstaking procedures of ceremonial magick, in which everything is prepared in the most perfect possible fashion. Such simple actions as preparing the lustral water or adoring the Sun in the four stages of his 24 hour cycle develop an attitude of reverence, if to nothing other than the work itself. This is the real dynamo of initiation. It is this attitude of reverence which distinguishes the live snake from the dead snake. If this attitude of reverence is absent then sexual magick is impossible. The real identity of ritual magick & tantra is in DEVOTION rather than any similarity of procedure. None of the dull intellectual evasions of supposed modernists or any other species of mental chicanery are worth a damn if this quality is absent. SO THERE! I, MAGNUS, HAVE SPOKEN!!!

The etymology of "God" is in the Indo-European root GHU - "to worship". The etymology of "Worship" is in the Anglo-Saxon "Weordscipe" - "to honour" as in "Worth" or "Worthiness".

Have no established mental criterion; "believe twelve impossible things before breakfast". Opinions are vile, ideas are at best useful. Hitler appealed to the emotions & consciously avoided stimulating the minds of his audience; had he propounded an intellectual system, however appealing, the mind, once awakened, would inevitably diversify. An intelligent person who begs to differ - however loyal - is more truly dangerous than a traitor who thinks much as you do. [Hang on a minute, what are you driving at Magnus? Ed.] All ideas are false, yet freedom lies in variety without attachment, rather than in mental oblivion.

It might be objected - by really incredibly lazy & boring cretins - that Qaballa & Astrology are incompatible with such freedom of thought. This is not so in PRACTICAL terms, for both are empirical, that is to say, experimental. On the contrary, the value of both schemes is their non-dependence on intellectual premises, unlike various theories of mind (& its relation to the world) which are based on synthetic models & present a fixed practical technique. The nature of symbolic schemes in general is to supply a model by which we can interpret our experiences & direct them. It should be noted that whilst many schemes - including scientific & psychological theories of universe & mind - are based on abstract hypotheses, astrology is based on physical, external & impartial principles. While these principles may be "only symbolic" they are not prone to the vagaries of intellectuals who - presented with the same psyche - argue with Freud that it is expressing suppressed infantile sexuality, with Adler that it is expressing the Will to Power, or with Jung that it doesn't know its arse from its anima. As for verification, whilst we admit - within certain limits - that one interprets reality in terms of one's own predilictions, what is better to base these predilictions on? Eternal laws of physiology, astronomy & number, or pseudo-rationalistic drivel which only panders to the whims of fashion-conscious intellectuals? Empirical results can be obtained, interpreted & repeated with principles as fundamental as those afore-mentioned, & are thus to be preferred to any intellectual conceit or airy fairy nonsense.

People keep coming up to me in the street & saying: "Surely astrological magick is rather old hat, don't you think any symbol system will work if you put enough energy into it?" What they mean, of course, is that they don't want to have to put in as much energy as astrological magick demands. It may or may not be true that any symbolic system will work, although if it is true, there is still the question of quality to consider - i.e. how flexible & useful are the factors involved in the schema? On the other hand, if we assume that any scheme will work, WHY NOT ASTROLOGY?! It is at least pretty coherent, there is no shortage of material to work with, & it is independent of any cultural bias. There are no short cuts in magick except those that lead back to square one.

Astrology is based on an EXTERIOR order which is MOBILE rather than static, & independent of any intellectual fashion. Qaballa similarly is based on number & permits of transformation & inter-relation; the value of such fundamental yardsticks as opposed to any secondary hypothesis is in the constancy of their natures; the value in practical terms is in their infinite elasticity.

Many so called "intuitive" types, when confronted with tables & diagrams, experience a kind of mental block & assume astrology is "too technical", conveniently forgetting that the shamans & druidesses whom they romantically idealise had a first hand knowledge of the stars & calculated extremely precisely without being any the less "intuitive". Similarly, it is often said that Qabalah does not appeal to women, & has been called "male chauvinist"; the same tendency can be discerned at work here - the so called "intuitive" is simply an inverted intellectual snob who insults the ancient shamans & modern women by unconsciously implying they were/are too stupid to handle these equations. The truth of the matter is that these persons, rather than shamans or women, are too lazy &/or too stupid to cope with the fundamental bases of magick, but have found a handy & fashionable catch-phrase to conceal this uncomfortable fact.

Too many modern "occultists" are victims of this "intuitive" malaise, & as many are guilty of misrepresenting qabalah & astrology as immutable dogmas. Few groups or individuals operate experimentally, either with traditional materials or with new ones! Consequently, they are prone to insidious dogmatism, since without experiment there can be no flexibility, & the rallying cry of revolution becomes simply another dogma of intellectual dictatorship. There are dangers involved with such experiments, but the alternative is the loss of genuine "occult" knowledge; i.e. it will remain "occult", which is to say "hidden" from occultists as from all others. One should take nothing for granted, not even the most seemingly sensible notions. On the other hand, a knowledge of symbolism might prepare one for some dangers, by perhaps indicating the type of problems or manner of resolution. Example: wealth attracting rituals involving Scorpio may have the effect of gaining inheritances (VIIIth House/Scorpio "rules" legacies) & this may cause distress. The lesson is clear; abandoning the study of occult symbolism is fine as a tactic, but as a general strategy it is a dead loss. [Neglecting the why, what & when for the how? Ed!] It seems a logical assumption to me that a period of hard work with the known techniques should lead to an enhanced understanding of the allegories of traditional occultism - including under this heading tantric & alchemical

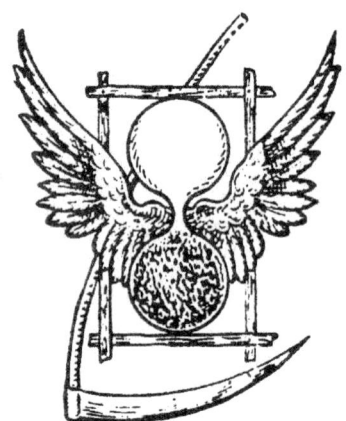

symbolism as well as qabalah & astrology. It has become fashionable until quite recently for "magicians" to talk of "abandoning" traditional magick; how does one abandon what one never possessed?

Of course, I realise that when the Sophisticated but Insecure Western Occultist understands me he will accuse me of plagiarism, & when he doesn't he will accuse me of obscurantism, but this is simply symptomatic of his insecurity. Well, so much for sophisticated occultists; I shall continue to aim at the naive & idealistic ones - after all, there are fewer of them, they could constitute an elite with just enough pressure of the right kind! So the sophisticates had better frig off, go on, clear off; I'm going to whisper dark secrets to the elite of tomorrow, & I don't want any know-alls eaves-dropping.

OK, oh naive ones, harken to the secret which has already been revealed, but was not grasped by the sophisticated. Empiricism is frigged, it's a dead end, it's hopeless! If the only yardstick you have is your own experience, you will actually understand nothing, at least nothing new or important. Oh, sure, empiricism implies the willingness to experiment & learn from experience, but all too often the empirical man is the man with the blinkers - "I never eat anything I haven't eaten before" - the guy will starve to death! Numerous examples may be found in the Chaos Magick camp. They PROPOSE experiment rather than dogma, they PROPOSE freedom of belief, but their every action reveals a stick-in-the-mud who won't examine what lies outside their own preconceived notions. These are the blinkered Colonel Blimps of our times; who having ignored every sign of life in our movement for years go on to pronounce us dead. They add insult to injury by expecting us to justify our continued existence in "their" terms - which are in any case watered down & vulgarised imitations of our own.

MAGICK IS NOT SAFE. Magick, by which I mean Initiation, is not comfortable, or convenient. It is not possible to be moderate in magick, it is not safe, & dilution & compromise are false friends; magick does not operate by laws of mediocrity or half-heartedness. Those who say that they are not involved in magick for initiation but for results are phonies or lunatics. You do not & cannot know what awaits you before you start, & often for long after. It is not possible to preserve a persona with the same opinions or characteristics throughout one's career as a magician.

MAGICK IS ALL THE TIME. All operations of magick work, & indeed are more reliable than any rational process when it comes to dealing in practical terms with problems philosophers only discuss & scientists omit from their lab reports. The main such problem is people, i.e. yourself, & other people. These problems are with us always, which is one reason amongst many why magick is all the time. As magickal operations all work, so long as you know which you need in any given situation there should be no problems - the problem is knowing. The largest difficulty in any operation is knowing what action, if any, would be appropriate. In such cases astrology should prove more reliable than any other form of divination. This is why astrology is so little understood, most forms of divination are the prerogative of either a philosophical or religious caste. Astrology is the principal exception, being outside of caste, on the plane of macrocosmic & magical forces.

EVERYTHING IS TRUE - NOTHING IS PERMITTED.

MAGICK IS NOT SAFE. The Dark Night of the Soul, or Ordeal of Initiation, is not a bowl of cherries. Magick is an extremely delicate & dangerous process. Initiation does not start nice & get nicer, turning you by degrees - no masonic pun intended - into a Walt Disney Boddhisattva; it may be attractive & fun at first, but "progress" is painful. There are a thousand ways to avoid the issue, & most "commercial" cults avoid it very neatly: one whiff of an unstable "punter" & it's expulsion time - after all, madmen & flagellants aren't good for business. Unfortunately, some of us are such thick skinned weirdos - with nasty squares & oppositions in our charts - that the least contact with real magickal forces is likely to induce major personality disorders. If we survive these & win through, the result is an initiate possessing genuinely useful knowledge, & with it generally a certain "power", the power to assist candidates to deal with the archetypal powers we call "spirits" or "gods" in works of evocation & invocation. If we don't, then the result is either madness or "avoiding the issue".

SUBJECTIVITY SUCKS!

Well, I'm not going to avoid the issue; as a wise madman recently wrote to me: "I didn't like the old Truth is relative syndrome...[i.e. in The Book of Long Words] Truth is constant; it's just that some people make mistakes at times. I mean, ascertaining the Truth might be difficult under some situations, as in aural time lapse, but if you know about the Doppler effect...you can rectify the situation." (Quoted from private correspondence with Jimmi Rocket.)

OK, so now we are working with the premise that there IS an ULTIMATE TRUTH, sod relativity & subjectivity, they are a meaningless cop out!

EVERYTHING IS TRUE - NOTHING IS PERMITTED.

Magicians, divided into their various camps, are notoriously intolerant of points of view other than their own. The so called freedom of belief which Spare & Crowley so ardently cultivated & advocated seems to be almost entirely absent from contemporary occult circles. We hear a lot about the supposed healthiness of discussion, we hear experts demanding respect for their opinions, & offering to "respect" yours by agreeing to disagree. When a man offers to respect my opinion I don't know whether to blush or to hit him! What the hell are we doing with such surplus baggage? Opinions are for people who need blinkers. Opinions are one sided, reality is not.

Think about this for a moment: we have heard the famous saying "When two wise persons meet, they laugh", well, when two occultists meet, they invariably argue! Now, I can accept this situation; if we are all such power-hungry bastards that we actually have nothing in common, let's just concentrate on our individual efforts at world domination! Lets just go our separate ways & try & accumulate as much personal power as we possibly can, & screw the other guy! That would be honest, if somewhat puerile. If on the other hand we see magick not merely as a results technique or spiritual path exclusively but as the vehicle of cultural forces, then we have not only a possibility but a downright necessity of working together.

Magick, it may surprise you to learn, works Magically. Occult groups do not develop due to recruitment drives or discussion groups, but through alignment with the current. Occultists do not develop through collecting a new technique a week or a new mythology or system, but through understanding things magickally & dealing with them magickally.

These criticisms are not new, or startlingly original, except in so far as they apply right across the board, rather than to some group or individual I'm pissed off with at the moment. Goddammit, they apply to me as well. Oh well, this will never do, insulting the readership isn't a good idea. Let's change the subject, a little.

Occultism is in crisis. We have seen the deaths of many leaders of the movement in recent years: Israel Regardie, Grady McMurtry, Rheinhold Ebertin & Alex Sanders to name but a few. The question arises, does there exist today a magickal movement with an evident dispensation? The fragmented "occult scene" is on the run - internal division, reluctance or plain inability to recognise the work of others, defensive reactions to imagined persecutions, personality differences & sheer lack of imagination hound it to its grave. Well, rot in hell occultism! Who needs to hide anything anyway? The Occult is dead (Dictionary: occult = hidden, i.e. hidden knowledge). There are no secrets any more, except what we hide from ourselves & others. The Great Arcana have all been revealed (well, nearly all), & an occultist is someone who tries to conceal them again, or conceal their own ignorance. A despicable character. So forget occultism & all the other faddy euphemisms like Shah-manism & other bloody charades. Let's do magick & leave posing to the media & its celluloid heroes.

To continue then; there is no clear picture of ritual magick in any published work. The grimoires are little more than shorthand notes for particular phases & purposes during a rite; they do not describe the rite itself.

The lengthy preparations that these books describe & recommend are in fact NOT avoidable. The threshold of convenience, when perseverance must surmount the obstacles of doubt, of boredom, of flippancy & the defensive machinery of sophistication which protects Westerners from the reality they inhabit - this Ring-Pass-Not - must be crossed, must be passed, not ignored. It is the apparent simplicity of these procedures, rather than the unfamiliar words & concepts, which really deter the uptight dilettantes.

Magick made easy is either a placebo or not really easy at all. Say I tell some fellow "Oh, magick, that's simple, go & stare into a woman's eyes for three hours, & breathe gently & completely." Ten minutes later, the guy "can't do it", he's found a problem, & doesn't appreciate me not appreciating his problem. It was no easier in the old days, believe me; the process has never been "convenient".

To sum up I shall move into the mysterious realm of Voodoo, or as we prefer to call it:

THE OBEAH AND THE WANGA.

Obeah is a technical term within the Voodoo tradition; it points directly to the essential core of this magickal religion, which is divine possession, possession by a "loa" or god. It is important to note that the English word "enthusiasm" comes from the Greek term "inspiration or possession by a god". It is not very fashionable to be enthusiastic or religious about anything nowadays; the sophisticated but apathetic citizens of our sceptred isle only feel comfortable about enthusiasm when the god is Mammon; greed is acceptable in our "rationalistic" age.

Crowley's slim volume "Energised Enthusiasm" is about the clearest account of what a ritual IS rather than "what words to say over what when". The fact is, the Western Tradition is nearly dead because atheism & devotion don't coexist very well. The Ring-Pass-Not of western magicians is Devotion. Ritual magick is incredibly painstaking, not to make it difficult, but to get through the barriers of thick skinned people who are in too much of a damned hurry.

Try approaching your whole life as a ritual, it is anyway, so make it a good one. Perform some small action with devotion (& regularity) at specific times of day. I.e. wash your face, hands, feet, armpits, anus & groin; put on a light & open robe, & raising your arms in a large V, slightly tipping the head back, cry aloud in praise to the Sun - preferably at dawn, noon, sunset & midnight, or alternatively on rising & retiring. This has very deep connotations of a very subtle nature, but the mainspring is developing an attitude of devotion, to the process at least if not to the deity. This state may take a long time to acquire, or even to recognise, but in magickal terms it is worth a million times more than any extreme alterations in consciousness.

WE take the word Inspiration in the same sense as Robert Graves, taking it to refer to the prophetic frenzy. This process is described in AL: "The inspiration is sweeter than death, more rapid & laughterful than a caress of hell's own worm."

In qaballistic terms INSPIRATION = 172 = THE SILVER STAR. UNIMAGINABLE. THE PROMISE. GLORY OF THE STARS. THE HOLY OF HOLIES. THE SPLENDOURS & also THE EMPRESS - the Goddess Venus (or Pisces, combining Jupiter with Venus) "who seeketh seventy to her four", SEVENTY + FOUR =172 = THUS IS IT KNOWN:

A	L	W	H	S	D	O	Z	K	V	G	R	C
1	2	3	4	5	6	7	8	9	10	11	12	13

N	Y	J	U	F	Q	B	M	X	I	T	E	P
14	15	16	17	18	19	20	21	22	23	24	25	26

EVERYTHING IS TRUE - NOTHING IS PERMITTED.

Let us end by revisiting the idea of stretching the imaginative muscles. The above dictum, which I earnestly adjure you to consider in all its implications, is one hell of a start in that direction. Think of it this way for a moment: if everything is either true or as close to the facts as you are going to get - the Kennedy assassination theories, U.F.O's, the secret chiefs etc. - if whatever you believe has an odds on chance of being related to the truth, the awful & tiresomely complex pattern of reality, beyond the scope of newspapers and computers, let alone the paltry human mind to encompass - then isn't it about time we all got off our asses & stretched those muscles of the mind every day! Never mind the Jane Fonda workout, how about the Albert Einstein keep fit class! How about the artistic, scientific & philosophical muscles that have been put out to grass in a field of couch potatoes! Why are they in a couch potato field? Because Nothing is Permitted, that's why!

We live in a world that is chock-a-block with all kinds of information: ideas, religions, crackpot theories, news broadcasts, telethons, & the propaganda machines of umpteen competing factions. There are also all kinds of controls: disinformation, censorship, intelligence agencies, counter intelligence agencies, conspiracies both real & imagined & convergent arcs of the two, so that the only possible recourse is to believe what is useful & disbelieve what is not. This is not the same as believing what you like & disregarding what you dislike, since what you dislike is as liable to be useful as what you don't. Mental flexibility is all very well, but it must be real. Simple scepticism is not enough. Scepticism is the first virtue on the occult path (Virtue of Malkuth), but the next is Acceptance! (Virtue of the 32nd Path.)

So let's re-cap a bit on this point, as it is a major one. I'll indulge in a bit of technical jargon, so at least you have an even chance of understanding, not only what I am saying, but why & on what level. I have mentioned the question of virtues on the Tree of Life, so this sudden departure from the world of "Hard Facts" is connected with my intention that you should not remain poor putrid probationers, or even noxious neophytes, forever. I am trying to kick you up the Middle Pillar towards Yesod by telling you to put away your sceptical machine & get out the mental elasticity generator. That way you may become a zoomorphic Zelator, & eventually - so 'elp us - an addle pated Adept or miserable Magus. Whatever cock & bull story I am working round to, you want to be ready to take it on board, since even if it is not the absolute truth, it is a truth of sorts. It is true on its own plane, if not on others.

So the shock I have been working round to is simple enough. The world on T.V. & in the newspapers, the world described in class & the world your parents talked about is baloney! The real world is run by magicians, & the magicians are run by the secret chiefs. This is so secret even most of the participants seem to be largely unaware of it. Manipulation is everywhere: the language has been manipulated, political movements have been manipulated, consciousness & world events, all kinds of events, from birth to individual experience & to the greatest scientific & artistic creations & movements, have been carefully orchestrated by a power which we may as well call divine. Divine is a big enough word to cope with the job, & cannot be any more misleading than any of my inspired guesses, or sound more implausible than the truth anticipated by those few really perceptive souls whose vaguest inkling is scrupulously concealed lest they be obliterated. Not only do massive forces shape our world & our interpretation of it, but those forces do not act in concert. There is WAR IN HEAVEN. Earth & your soul is the battleground.

MAGNUS DICTUS

SETHIAN INVOCATION FOR VISION OR KNOWLEDGE.

The following Ritual was compiled from several variant texts and related materials from the Leyden Papyrus with additions where appropriate. It forms a postscript to the Sethian materials in "The Headless One" in the previous issue and to "Sothis" in this one:

Let the operator prepare an altar of "sweet wood" such as cedar, rosewood or pine, supported upon talismans in the manner of Dr.Dee's experiments. Let it be covered from top to bottom in fine cloth, and place it in the central part of the chamber of practice - which shall be pure and undisturbed. Before the altar, raised up upon a pedestal or further talisman, place an incense burner and charcoal. The incense should consist of either some Holy Incense such as Abramelin or Kyphi, or alternatively an intoxicating mixture as used by the Elus Cohens and elsewhere in the history of magick. In this latter case the operator should have a large cloth which will cover their head and hang down over the censer. [The Leyden Papyrus replaces the wax talismans of Dee's altar with "new bricks, which have not been turned", so that the upper part, on which the legs rest, has never touched the ground, & the lower part has never seen the Sun. The "secluded spot" is described as a dark sunless recess or windowless room.]

Facing East at Sunrise let the operator who would undertake the ritual of the Holy Magick perform thus:

First adore the Sun as Ra, as laid down in Liber Resh; then this adoration following.

"O Great God SABAO I invoke Thee in the Names BASOUKHAM. AMO. AHK-AKH-ARKHAN. BO-UN-ZANO-UN-II. EDIKOMPHTHO. KETHOU. BAS. ATHOORI. THELEMA. AL. O. That which I undertake cometh to pass!

IO. SABAO. SOKHOM-MOA. OKH-OKH-KHAN-BOUZANAU. ANIESI. EKOMPHTHO. KETHO. SET-HOORI. THELEMA. AL. OUA. PHO. KHRI. The words of my lips become flesh!

IO. SABAO. SOKH. AUMGN. O. A. OKH-AR-KHAN. BOUZANAU. ANIESI. EKOMPHTHO. KETHO. SET-HOORI. THMAI-LA-AL-OUA. HOOR-RA. That to which I apply my hand cometh to pass!"

By the use of this ritual the Egyptians prepared themselves for divinatory invocations with a boy taking the part of medium as in Abramelin and in the rituals of Cagliostro. It would therefore be appropriate prior to divination by Lamp, Crystal or direct Vision. Such "Egyptian" techniques as the inducing of vision by staring at an ink-pool in the central square of the "Square of Saturn" written on the palm of the medium's hand, or, more elaborately, replacing the ink-pool with a crystal (preferably dark) or mirror, retaining the Square for its Sethian connotations.

Let the operator prepare themself from Sunrise until Noon by abstinence from all but the lightest food. Wine may be consumed, but in moderation - all human society should be shunned, save the company of the medium if one is employed - and that only to instruct and prepare, or to pray together. The reading of the Holy Books and the preparation of the place and of the ritualist(s) may take place from Sunrise until Noon.

At Noon make the second adoration from Liber Resh and such other rituals and adorations as seem appropriate to the intention of the Ritual - particularly the Ritual of the Headless One. After this the retirement should become more complete. It may be well to stay in the prepared chamber so far as one may, certainly one should remain clean and unhindered by earthly concerns. One may continue reading the Holy Books aloud, and meditation or mantra-yoga may be employed to still the mind and ready oneself for the ritual and its resultant communion with the Genius or God.

At Sunset make the adorations from Liber Resh in their turn, as also further rituals of Sunset such as the Mass of the Phoenix, although the last section thereof should be omitted or adapted, for the operator will not go forth at this time, but continue with the seclusion and the ritual, making the following invocation, which may be preceded by Liber Israfel.

"I invoke thee who art seated in the invisible darkness.
Who art in the midst of the great gods receiving the sun's rays in his setting.
Who sends forth the luminous goddess NEBOUTOSOULETH.
The great God BARZAN. BOUBARZAN. NARZAZOUZAN. BARZABOUZATH the Sun!"

"Send up to me this night thine archangel ZEBOURTHAUNEN to answer with truth, certainly, without lie concerning this matter, for I conjure thee by Him who is seated in the flaming vesture upon the resplendent head of ABRASAX - the almighty four-faced daemon, the highest, the darkling guide of souls TAHUTI".

"Do not disregard me, but send up speedily in this night an injunction of the God. For I am the worshipper of the same, your god, the true worshipper of the Highest!"

Let the operator rest from this point, laid down before the altar, their head covered, and remain thus until midnight, when they shall rise and adore the Sun at Midnight according to the ritual of Liber Resh, then, still facing North, the direction of Ursa Major, make this further invocation.

"Ho! I am MURAI, MURIBI, BABALON, BAL-BIN-ABAOT. BA-MUI. ABRASAX. MURATHO. I am the God that ruleth in this hour, whose soul resteth upon the height of heaven. I am TAHUTI. BOUEL. MAU. TAHUTI. LA-II. BAL-BOEL. I-AA-TAT. BOUEL. VOHEL.

The minister of the great god.
He who giveth light exceedingly.
The companion of the Flame.
He in whose mouth is the flame that is never quenched.
The great God who is seated in the fire.
He who is in the midst of the fire which is in the lake of heaven.
In whose hand is the greatness and the power of god,
Reveal thyself unto me as thou didst to thy prophet before whom thou thyself didst create darkness and light.
Reveal thyself and give true answer, in truth, without lie.
Thou glory of Abydos!
Who exceedeth Ra and Khonsu for glory!
Thou minister of him who abideth upon the throne of the Aeons.
Thou great in glory PETERI. IO-PATER. ENPHE.

O god who art above the heavens.
Who bearest the double wand of light and life.
Who created deity, deity not having created him!
Thee, thee I invoke, that thou comest down into me,
Into this flame [lamp, crystal or what-not] that is here before thee,
Thou of Boel - and let be seen and heard that which I desire and ask of thee. Let it be seen - let it be heard. SISIHOOUT. ARMIOOUTH.
Come in before me and give me answer to that which I seek after.
O great god that is on the mountain of ATUKI, of GABAON.

IAO SABAO - such are the words!

Then you lay down without speaking or otherwise commence the vision.
(The Egyptians proceeded in the following manner. "Then he speaks with you "mouth to mouth" in truth concerning everything that you wish. When he has departed set out a tablet of reading the hours [corresponding to the Chaldean horoscope form used in geomancy] upon the altar. Write upon a piece of virgin paper the purpose of your ritual and place it upon the tablet. Then he maketh the stars to appear which are favourable to your purpose.")
The conclusion of this rite will be at Dawn, when the operator(s) will once more adore the Sun and depart from the Temple.

Jake Stratton-Kent

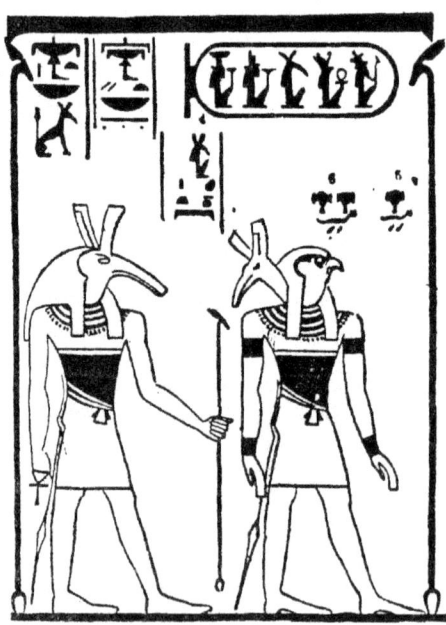

NUBTI SET, SON OF NUT.

HIGHER THAN EYESIGHT.

The Minutum Mundum in the Aeon of Horus.

The clearest possible distinction between so called low magic and High Magick is that High Magick derives its power from the highest plane - the interface between "Kether" and the Limitless Light - introducing new energy into the universe, thus depleting nothing but rather adding to that which already exists. (Sorcery on the other hand merely rearranges existing conditions - hence the origins of the confusion between magick and mere sleight of hand.) In this Seventh number of our Volume we accomplish this feat. Our predecessors "received" the English Qaballa from what can only be called higher sources - introducing something entirely new into the world. It is our honour and privilege to accomplish an extension of this system - not merely delineating their work, as we have done to a large extent in previous issues - but extending it. An entirely new area, absent from the brief of our predecessors, has opened up since our achieving independence from our parent order. It should be said however that the seeds of this new material were sewn at the earliest stage of our contact with them - but laid underground until the present time. The knowledge gained from them was based on pure Number; the material which we lay before you now is based upon another order of archetypal truth - that of Colour.

Those who understand the nature of Aeonic transition will know that the key task of the hierophant in such a period is the definition of the archetypes in the new order of things - accordingly for example as constellations move with the precession of the equinoxes, overlapping the borders of the so called "Signs", the symbols of the age are adapted to the new conditions - as once the symbol of the Virgin came to include a lion's tail in her hand reflecting the movement of Virgo into the "Sign" of Leo. Those who have tried to accomplish this in our time by adopting older forms of astrology such as the sidereal zodiac have misunderstood this task. They have tried to merely adapt rather than renew the symbols for our time.

The very nature of a true Qaballa arising "at the turn" of the Aeon is such that it will inevitably accomplish what these "sorcerers" have failed to do - bringing through the new archetypes - presenting a new and more perfectly evolved system of magick. The second phase of this task has begun, as will appear in these pages following.

PUBLICATION OF THE GNOSTIC ALCHEMICAL CHURCH IN THE GRADE OF NEOPHYTE.

"My colour is black to the blind but the blue and gold are seen of the seeing."

"The rituals of the old time are black."

"There is a veil: that veil is black."

"Now let there be a veiling of this shrine: now let the light devour men and eat them up with blindness."

The following text is constructed on extremely formal lines to prevent confusion of planes, and to deal with as much information as possible in a short space. It is therefore rather heavy going as detail is piled upon detail; our hope is that the true seeker after knowledge will read carefully, and that the fool will either pass on or have pause to wonder.

The colour references in AL and the Class A as a whole are a subtle route into the language and mysteries of AL and the English Qaballa. The references frequently appear in groups, and two such groupings are of particular interest.

AL. I. 60. The Five Pointed Star with the circle in the middle and the circle is **RED**, My colour is **BLACK** to the blind but the **BLUE** and **GOLD** are seen of the seeing. Also I have a secret glory for them that love me.

AL. II. 50/51. **BLUE** am I and **GOLD** in the light of my bride, but the **RED** gleam is in my eyes, and my spangles are **PURPLE** and **GREEN**. **PURPLE** beyond **PURPLE**: it is the light higher than eyesight.

Here we have two sets of elemental attributions of the colours: firstly Black for Earth, Red for Fire, Blue for Water and Gold for Air, a straightforward and traditional scheme if we read Yellow for Gold, though it should be kept in mind that Gold is the word found most appropriate by the "author" of the book, Aiwass. The second grouping gives another fairly recognisable schema, but it is apparent from the sense and tone of these verses that some deeper significance lies hidden. This scheme is Blue for Water, Gold for Air and Red for Fire as before, but now we find Purple and Green have replaced Black. Green is recognisable as Earth, the Earth of Thelema; Crowley speaks of this in The Book of Thoth in discussing the Universe Trump of the Tarot, attributed to Saturn and Earth and associated with the colour Black: "But the New Aeon has brought fullness of Light; in the Minutum Mundum [The Golden Dawn term for the Tree of Life coloured according to various esoteric principles. Ed.], Earth is no longer black, or of mixed colours, but is pure bright green. Similarly the indigo of Saturn is derived from the blue velvet of the midnight sky, and the maiden of the dance represents the issue from this, yet through this to the Eternal. This card is to-day as bright and glowing as any in the Pack." The reasons for this change may be intuited in consideration of the words "I fly and I alight as an hawk: of mother-of-emerald are my mighty-sweeping wings, I swoop down upon the black earth; and it gladdens into green at my coming." So reads Liber Tzaddi, echoing yet subtly transforming and transcending a similar passage found in chapter 77 of the Egyptian Book of the Dead. But this change is more subtle than a more optimistic attitude towards material creation. Why should AL give the old scheme as well as the new? Who are these "blind"? Could they be the "fools" of whom AL speaks elsewhere, as of candidates for initiation who will come through various ordeals and have their perceptions altered in consequence. In the "man of Earth" grade initiation, as seen in various forms, including the G.'.D.'. 0 = 0 ritual, North (frequently attributed to Earth in such rites as the Pentagram et al) is the "Place of Greatest Darkness", and is rightly black. But if this Black transforms through initiation into Green then many things become clear, for Green is also associated with Venus, the core of the cult, at least in the "worship of Nu" where astrological magic and the higher witchcraft are worked (ie magick as a cult of the Goddess). The secret glory may well be this Purple, which sounds rather like ultra violet or something of that sort, perhaps also associated with the Indigo of the Akashic Egg in the Tattvic colour attributions. (In Crowley's 777 he attributes ultra violet to the Tarot Card "The Moon" attributed to Pisces; the Golden Dawn attribution is given as Crimson, Ultra Violet is Crowley's amendment, given in brackets.) The phrase SECRET GLORY has the value 151, which in astrological terms is SUN + MERCURY and LIBRA + SCORPIO.

So far we have considered these attributions from a point of view both scholarly and comparative. We have not gone on to dissect, to analyse, applying Qaballistic principles, taking all the colour references in AL (and the Class A as a whole) and looking for patterns in isolation from their original context. AL speaks in all of seven colours, some of which are given synonyms, wherein lie deeps of all manner of obscurity. We shall attempt to bring these points out into the open in as clear and as concise a manner as we may, starting with a list of the seven and their synonyms.

1. BLACK
2. BLUE (also given as AZURE in similar contexts.)
3. RED (SCARLET is not entirely synonymous, Scarlet is ALWAYS connected with the Scarlet Woman, Red is not.)
4. GOLD
5. GREEN
6. PURPLE
7. SILVER (in the non textual "marginalia" found in the MS we find "Write this in whiter words", and WHITE may accordingly be taken as a synonym of Silver. Yellow, the natural synonym of Gold, is not mentioned in AL.)

There are good traditional sources attributing these to the planets of the Chaldean Scheme Saturn through to Luna.

We come now to the question of gematria, and the tying of traditional associations with the colours holds surprisingly well, with one or two surprises which it is important to remember in the study of this material in its entirety. The basis of the numerical attribution is to take the last number of the colour's value, for instance YELLOW = 54, 4 is the last number and thus Yellow in some sense might be connected with the ideas attributed to Jupiter. Yellow however does not appear in AL, and will be dealt with separately; its connection with Jupiter (4) and SET (equals 54) are not appropriate to the grade in which this paper is written.

CHALDEAN ORDER ATTRIBUTIONS OF COLOURS MENTIONED IN AL.

3. RED = 43, 3 = SATURN/43 = NOX, GOAT.
4. BLUE = 64, 4 = JUPITER/64 = LIGHT.
5. BLACK = 45, 5 = MARS/45 = HORUS.
6. GOLD = 26, 6 = SUN/26 = GOLD.
7. GREEN = 87, 7 = VENUS/87 = BURNT (FIRE = 78, VENUS = 71, NUIT = 78).
8. PURPLE = 108, 8 = MERCURY/108 = SPELLING.
9. WHITE = 79, 9 = MOON/79 = ABRAHADABRA, HEAVEN, HIGHER.

FURTHER ATTRIBUTIONS OF AN ESOTERIC NATURE.

SILVER = 77, 7 = VENUS/77 = DOUBLE, NOUGHT, KHUIT, VENOM.
AZURE = 63, 3 = SATURN/63 = MAUT, BURN, ABOVE.
SCARLET = 82 = CHOKMAH, higher conception of Luna, see notes on Feminine Wisdom in Equinox Three.

The last three associations have particular reference to the "Enemy Naming Ceremony" and other tantric practices, as may be seen by making a thorough perusal of their gematrias at length. Of the former seven many things are noteworthy, particularly the obvious reversal of red and black compared to their usual associations. On this point it is worth considering the connection of both these planets with Capricorn, ruled by Saturn, and in which Mars is exalted. The conception of the Moon as white glosses the idea that white and silver are equivalant as Gold and yellow are in traditional rituals. We must look further however, for 82 and 79 obviously represent different conceptions of the same thing, one places her in Chokmah the other in Yesod, so that these associations must refer to something quite specific, we are not talking in general terms. The ideas of Fire or Moon or any other symbol in AL might not mean what we usually take them to mean, or may reflect our "traditional" ideas while employing them in an unusual and enlightening way. AL does after all state quite clearly that the symbols to which the EQ will refer will not be altogether familiar - there would be little purpose in Aiwass producing a duplicate of an already known system.

ELEMENTAL ATTRIBUTION OF THE COLOURS IN CH. I. VS. 60.

"My number is 11, as all their numbers who are of us. The Five Pointed Star with a Circle in the Middle, & the circle is **RED**. My colour is **BLACK** to the blind but the **BLUE & GOLD** are seen of the seeing. Also I have a secret glory for them that love me."

Fire. RED = 43 = NOX, GOAT, &c. Planetary association Mars, exalted in Capricorn.

Earth. BLACK = 45 = BE, END, NOT, SLAIN, I AM, HORUS &c. Planetary association Saturn, exalted in Libra.

Water. BLUE = 64 = AMMON, LIGHT, DRINK, FRESH, LANGOUR, REASON, ROBE, WHEELS, PAIN, SEEK, STIR, WEAVE &c. Planetary association Jupiter, exalted in Cancer.

Air. GOLD = 26 = CAR, SAYS, SON, WHOSO &c. Planetary association Sun, exalted in Aries.

A more esoteric rendering of these symbols is found through gematria, via the method shown above wherein the last digit of each number determines its planetary rulership. Thus Red = 43, 3 = Saturn, Black = 45, 5 = Mars, Blue = 64, 4 = Jupiter, Gold = 26, 6 = Sun. This may be researched by the individual student.

ELEMENTAL ATTRIBUTION OF THE COLOURS IN CH. II. VS. 50.

AL. II. 50/51. **BLUE** am I and **GOLD** in the light of my bride, but the **RED** gleam is in my eyes, and my spangles are **PURPLE** and **GREEN**. **PURPLE** beyond **PURPLE**: it is the light higher than eyesight.

Water. Jupiter &c. as before.

Air. Sun &c. as before.

Fire. Mars &c. as before.

Spirit makes its appearance subsequent to the initiation of the "man of Earth" when the "blindness" of normal consciousness has given way to the higher consciousness. PURPLE = 108, which by the gematria rule described above gives its nature as Mercurial. The exaltation of Mercury is in Virgo, the only case in which the exaltation is also one of the rulerships. The esoteric meaning of Virgo may be divined through access to the Mysteries of the Sangraal.

Earth is renewed as shown above, "the little world my sister, my heart & my tongue, unto whom I send this kiss" (Kiss = X/22 , KISS = 42 = CROSS &c.). The planetary association is Venus, exalted in Pisces, see Trigrammaton commentary in Equinox VII No. 1. She is the Empress, who seeks "Seventy to her Four" - Seventy = Ayin in old letters, attributed to "The Devil", whereas Four is Daleth, attributed to the Empress. In EQ EMPRESS = 119 = SEVENTY + FOUR and THE DEVIL. All this is relevant to a higher grade than Neophyte, but careful study of these symbols and their relation to the Tree of Life will reveal much to the earnest seeker who has undergone the first ordeal.

The ceremony of initiation described in AL I. 51 refers firstly to the ceremony of initiation of a Neophyte or man of Earth, but also to the grade of Lover of which it is the portal. The colour scheme of AL I. 60 is appropriate to this Grade and this ceremony, whilst that of AL II. 50 is appropriate to the Grade of Adept or Lover and its ceremony. This should not be taken primarily as a guide to temple furnishings, but to interior states and conditions.

Grade:	"man of Earth"	*	"Lover"
	or Probationer/Neophyte	*	or Adept
Spirit not seen			Purple
Fire Red			Red
Water Blue			Blue
Air Gold			Gold
Earth Black			Green

COMPLETE CONCORDANCE OF COLOUR REFERENCES IN THE CLASS A LITERATURE.

Twelve colours are referred to in Class A, but only one book gives all twelve. These colours are:

<u>WHITE = 79.</u> Associations: 9 = Moon, exalted in Taurus, White traditionally the colour of Kether, the first sphere. 79's numerations are too important and extensive to be given here, see Equinox VII passim.

<u>GREY = 63.</u> Associations: 3 = Saturn, Grey traditionally the colour of Chokmah the second sphere. 63 is also the numeration of VIRGO.

<u>BLACK = 45.</u> Associations: 5 = Mars, Black traditionally associated with Saturn and with Binah, the third sphere.

<u>BLUE = 64.</u> Associations: 4 = Jupiter, Blue traditionally associated with Jupiter and with Chesed the fourth sphere.

<u>RED = 63.</u> Associations: 3 = Saturn, Red = Mars and Geburah, the fifth sphere.

<u>GOLD = 26.</u> Associations: 6 = Sun. Gold = Sun, and is a purer form of the Yellow traditionally associated with Tiphereth the sixth sphere. The attribution here is more familiar in the grimoire and alchemical traditions than the G.'.D.'./Kabbalah.

<u>GREEN = 87.</u> Associations: 7 = Venus. Green traditionally the colour of Venus and of Netzach the seventh sphere.

<u>PURPLE = 108.</u> Associations: 8 = Mercury. The Key of Solomon gives the colours of Mercury as Purple or Mixed Colours. It is not certain whether mixed means only pied, chequered & such patterns connected with Magpies, Harlequins and other Mercurial symbols, or mixtures of colour such as orange, produced from red and yellow, and purple, derived from red and blue, especially as Mercury is also associated with alloys. However it may be Purple is traditionally associated with Mercury in the same traditions as dealt with under gold. Mercury is attributed to the Eighth sphere in the Qaballa.

<u>SILVER = 77.</u> Associations: 7 = Venus. It is noteworthy that the ancient Babylonians associated White, and accordingly Silver its higher analogue to their Goddess of the planet Venus, whose Lunar role was a later development. Traditionally (as under gold and purple) associated with the Moon. The Moon is traditionally associated with the ninth sphere in the Qaballa.

<u>BROWN = 56.</u> Associations: 6 = Sun. Brown as an Earthy colour may be taken to represent Malkuth, the tenth sphere. For 56 see Trigrammaton commentary and Equinox VII passim.

<u>SCARLET = 82.</u> Associations: 2 = Chokmah, specifically as a female force (see Equinox VII. No. 3). Scarlet is ALWAYS connected with the Scarlet Woman in Class A and is quite distinct from Red in context and significance.

<u>YELLOW = 54.</u> Associations: 4 = Jupiter. Yellow is usually associated with Tiphereth whose real colour is Gold. 54 = SET, but also FOUR, the number of Jupiter.

The Planetary Order of Liber VII.

"Liber Liberi Vel Lapidis Lazuli, Adumbratio Kabbalæ Ægyptiorum Sub Figura VII........the nature of this book is sufficiently described by its title. **Its seven chapters are referred to the seven planets in the following order: Mars, Saturn, Jupiter, Sol, Mercury, Luna, Venus.**" Adumbratio Kabbalæ Ægyptiorum translates approximately as "A fore-shadowing of the Egyptian Qaballa" - suggesting that this book is connected with the generation or development of a strictly Thelemic Qaballa, not necessarily identical with the gematria processes of E.Q., but concerned with theoretical or cosmological aspects of the system revealed thereby.

The planetary attribution most apparent in AL relies on the seven colours mentioned in AL - it thus refers to the seven traditional planets of astrology. This attribution is basically identical to that of the old Grimoires, whilst differing from the Golden Dawn attribution:

Saturn = Black
Jupiter = Blue or Azure
Mars = Red or Scarlet
Sun = Gold (Yellow not mentioned)
Venus = Green
Mercury = Purple
Moon = Silver (White mentioned in out of text note "Write this in whiter words").

<u>Key of Solomon ascription of the Planets to Colours and Metals.</u>
Saturn = Black and Lead.
Jupiter = Blue and Tin.
Mars = Red and Iron.
Sun = Yellow and Gold.
Venus = Green and Copper.
Mercury = Purple or Mixed Colours and Mercury.
Moon = White and Silver.

The careful student will notice that the metals all resemble the colours in some respect; copper oxide is green, rust is reddish orange and so on. Solomon gives further details thus: "Saturn ruleth over

Lead; Jupiter over Tin; Mars over Iron; the Sun over Gold; Venus over Copper; **Mercury over the mixture of Metals**; and the Moon over Silver.....unto Saturn the colour of Black is appropriated; Jupiter over Celestial Blue; Mars over Red; **the Sun over Gold, or the colour of Yellow or Citron**; Venus over Green; Mercury over Mixed Colours; **the Moon over Silver, or the colour of Argentine Earth.**"

Other, more esoteric attributions exist as will be shown.

Liber VII is the only Book in which all these colours appear. Since this book is involved with the planets it is meet to give a suggested zodiacal attribution, which while not infallible is at least suggestive.

Aries = Brown, mainly on the basis that Earth and Aries have the same numerical value. Gold would be appropriate as this is Sol's exaltation, but Leo has a prior claim as it were. Neither Red or Scarlet have the backing of gematria despite tradition: Brown at least can call on gematria (56) to remind us that Aries is the Sun's exaltation, and also has 5 as its first digit.

Taurus = Green, traditional, supported by gematria. Silver would also be appropriate as this is the sign of Luna's exaltation.

Gemini = Purple, traditional supported by gematria.

Cancer = White, traditional supported by gematria.

Leo = Gold, ditto.

Virgo = Black or Scarlet? Not totally satisfactory. Grey would suit the colour of the Hermit's robe (tarot attribution of Virgo traditionally) and also as noted GREY = 63 = VIRGO. Throughout the Class A Grey is spelt "Grey", save once in LXV, which has "gray", but this may be a proof-reader's error, especially as LXV was published in "The Blue Equinox", whilst Crowley was in America, whose spelling is not always consistent with English, and thus with the Class A.

Libra = Silver.

Scorpio = Scarlet. Black would be traditional and supported by gematria.

Sagittarius = Yellow.

Capricorn = Red, as the colour of Mars, whose exaltation this is, thus appropriate by gematria also.

Aquarius = Grey, via gematria. But Grey = 63 the number of Virgo.

Pisces = Blue, associated with Jupiter, as supported by gematria.

Rationalising these ideas a little we arrive at something like the following:

Sign.	Colour.	Rulership & Exaltation	Gematria Rulership.
Aries.	Brown.	Mars Sun.	56 = 6 = Sun.
Taurus.	Green.	Venus Moon.	87 = 7 = Venus.
Gemini.	Purple.	Mercury (Dragon's Head).	108 = 8 = Mercury.
Cancer.	White.	Moon Jupiter.	79 = 9 = Moon.
Leo.	Gold.	Sun (Uranus).	26 = 6 = Sun.
Virgo.	Grey.	Mercury Mercury.	63 = 3 = Saturn.
Libra.	Silver.	Venus Saturn.	77 = 7 = Venus.
Scorpio.	Black.	Mars (Pluto).	45 = 5 = Mars.
Sagittarius.	Yellow.	Jupiter (Dragon's Tail).	54 = 4 = Jupiter.
Capricorn.	Red.	Saturn Mars.	43 = 3 = Saturn.
Aquarius.	Scarlet.	Saturn (Neptune).	82 = 2 = Moon +.
Pisces.	Blue.	Jupiter Venus.	64 = 4 = Jupiter.

(Attributions in brackets are from The Book of Thoth, and are given mainly for completeness; they do give some understanding of the sign's nature, and are a better scheme than many modern attempts at co-rulership or reattribution of rulerships often proposed simply to do something, anything, with the "awkward" outer planets; see also Crowley's "Complete Astrological Writings".)

In LXV only ten of the colours are given, due perhaps to the fivefold structure of the book. They are the colours attributed to the Sephiroth earlier in this article - White = Kether through to Brown =

Malkuth; the colours omitted are the "more esoteric" Yellow and Scarlet. I should imagine that the Brown of Aries/Earth is intended to be a ruddy shade, and the Purple of Spirit/Mercury to be intended for ultra violet, so when used for artistic purposes, be it the making of talismans or whatever, it should accordingly be as vivid a shade as possible.

Libers Magi, Porta Lucis and Tau do not refer to the colours, for reasons connected with their structure and significance.

Liber Trigrammaton only mentions Black and this in connection with the Black Brothers. Considerations of Scorpio and Saturn are important in this book in other connections however, so this may not be entirely fortuitous.

Liber Stellæ Rubeæ names Black, Gold and Green; its nature is intimately involved with the Scorpio (Black) current as described in Equinox VII passim. Gold is the colour of the Sun, and of the Graal (NOT Silver as with ordinary chalices), its nature too is ruddy due to the connection of these ideas with blood; "red gold" is used in the oldest English poem "Boewulf" and throughout the sagas and elsewhere. Green is used in the expression "Twin images in green of the master" suggesting the twin serpents of the caduceus, and in AL green is used in describing Hadit as a snake. The tantric significance of these colours is appropriate here and in AL.

Liber Tzaddi gives the same colours; it is "an account of Initiation, and an indication as to those who are worthy of the same". I take this in a very technical sense, reminded of those "Certain Probationers (who) are admitted after six months or more to Ritual XXVIII" .."Liber Septem Regum Sanctorum....bestowed on certain selected probationers", the title of which document indicates Seven Rulers of the Sanctuary, the planets, or rather the chakras of the kundalini adept. I remind the reader of the emphasis placed on Liber HHH, and particularly its third section SSS concerned with Kundalini Yoga, throughout the A.'.A.'. syllabus; as set forth at length in "The Headless One", Equinox VII. No.6. The nature of the Initiation intended is Tantric, and its best candidates are to be found among the persons Tzaddi indicates. The significance of the colours in this book is then similar to their sense in LXVI (Stellae Rubeae), but green is not mentioned in connection with a snake but a hawk, and the shade or stone emerald is also mentioned; the significance of precious stones in Class A is not declared here, but Emerald has a significance apart from the galaxy of other stones mentioned in Class A, the symbolism of the Heart Girt with a Serpent, see "The Headless One" and elsewhere. Its "Black" is the Black of Earth, Saturn and so forth, the Northern Station in 0 = 0, which gives way to the Green of Venus. Gold appears only in the word "golden".

Liber Cheth, with its revelation of the Holy Grail, gives the Rosicrucian colours: Scarlet, Gold and White. It is the Book wherein Babalon is mentioned by name. The Scarlet Woman, Her Golden Cup, the Whiteness of the saints who pour their blood therein, the white and scarlet hue of the robes in the Abramelin operation, the colours of the Templar cloak and of the Grail knights, all this is most appropriate to the theme of this Book.

Liber CCXXXI mentions only black and white, as opposites, and gold in the word golden. Their significance is probably completely dependent on the context in which they appear. However it may be significant that the same colours, and those only, are named in DLXX, Liber Ararita.

Liber Capricorni Pneumatici gives only black, appropriate to Saturn, ruler of Capricorn, and Scorpio as ruler of the reproductive processes. Silver is given in the phrase "Silver Star" which Baphomet or Set, the deity whose word this book is, claims as His symbol. The association with Libra (Saturn's exaltation), whose significance is also tied up with the Scorpio complex is therefore appropriate. The whole sense of this book is concerned with practical magick, thus Libra-Scorpio, see Equinox VII. passim.

This analysis of colour in the Class A's is not intended to be exhaustive. The references each have a significance in their individual and original contexts; some may have in addition meaning in relation to the chapter in which they occur, for instance Yellow occurs only in Liber VII, in the Jupiter and Sun chapters. The Saturn chapter has Purple, Green, Black and Blue, reminiscent to a degree of the colour schemes used in rituals of the Fraternitas Saturni in Germany. Such attention to detail may be liable to mislead if followed merely for its own sake - but the equivalences are there nevertheless, and depict a universal harmony of symbol more subtle and sophisticated than any since the destruction of the library of Alexandria; indeed it seems to most investigators to be a unique phenomenon, more evolved than any previous cosmology.

CHAKRA PATTERN IN THREE GRADES.

The lower chakras in the normal spiritual physiogomy reflect the pattern of the magick circle with its four elemental stations; approximately the pattern may be traced as follows:

The groin area corresponds to Earth. The correspondences are confused in comparing oriental systems with western, for Malkuth generally represents the feet. There are euphemistic connections between various parts of the legs and the sexual organs in many cultures and symbolic schemes, so this will simply have to stand. The direction in the circle is generally the North, although many Thelemic rituals and allied traditions place Earth's quarter in the East.

The stomach area corresponds to Fire; this is the region of the Solar Plexus, and is concerned with digestion and energy production. This is not a particularly high form of fire, perhaps corresponding to alchemy's Green Lion and Vegetable Fire. Its region is to be found in the South in most traditions.

The heart corresponds to Water, its symbol is the Holy Graal. Accordingly its place is in the West, the direction of the Holy of Holies in the Solomonic temple, and not East as is vulgarly imagined, which is the direction of the Pillars at the entrance.

Air corresponds to the throat chakra. For detailed analysis of this schema see "The Headless One" Equinox VII, No. 6.

These elemental chakras in turn form part of the Tree of Life, or in E.Q. terms the Manifest Tree, see diagrams in Equinox VII No.'s 2 and 3. This is the system of the human body in ordinary terms, and corresponds to the "man of Earth" in the Grades scheme of the A.'.A.'..

The chakras of the Adept or Lover correspond to the central section of the Cipher of AL. II. 76, as the Manifest Tree corresponds to the latter ten numbers and letters, and the Unmanifest to the first ten. These eight spheres (the "middle eight" to borrow a term from contemporary music) have a combined numerical value of 93. They are dealt with at some length in the article which follows.

The chakras of the Hermit are similar in most respects to those of the man of Earth, save that the Spiritual chakras have been linked to the lower elemental, and the Earth and Air chakras have reversed, as shown in the Headless One.

All this might sound like the most arrant theosophical bilge, were it not confirmed by the independent experience, recorded and attested of those undergoing the ordeals. Of course the levels co-exist, and in exceptional persons the conditions attributed here to those in the Hermit or Lover phases of initiation (we say not of existence) may be "native" as say in the case of a great artist or genius.

We propose the idea that these processes of transformation are in fact totally natural, and form the basis of human evolution and achievement. Magick in this sense is almost a bio-chemical process, save only that it works with subtler energies that might not be best described as physical, but may well align at some points with organic processes controllable to some degree by will, exercise, diet or drugs, and most responsive to particular kinds of ritual processes linked to astrological cycles; particularly solar conjunctions with Venus, and it may be, other planets, such as Mars and even Mercury, whose orbits and gravitational fields are not too far distant from our own. That other imponderable factors may be at work the present author does not doubt, but I consider that the knowledge so far outlined is in any case a major practical and theoretical advance in an area that has hitherto remained obscure and unworkable.

(Notes on the "Old Letters" attributions of the colours in AL I. 60 and II. 50.

The colours mentioned in these verses may be cross-referenced via Liber 777 with the Hebrew Alphabet. The appropriate columns are II) Hebrew Names of Numbers and Letters and XVI) The Queen Scale of Colour (the scale from which the G.'.D.'. attribution to the Paths is derived). Here we will find that RED = P, BLACK = Th, BLUE = K and GOLD = R. These letters form a Temurah or Qaballistic anagram of the Word PRKTh - Paroketh meaning the Veil of the Sanctuary, which divides the Elemental Grades from the "Second Order" and of KPRTh the Mercy Seat. It also is equivalent by Hebrew Gematria to the name ShTh or Seth, see "The Headless One" in the previous issue of this Journal. The attributions in II.50 give LRPBM = 352 = AUR MA'aLH, the Exalted Light and ARK APIM "Long of Nose"; ie merciful; a title of the Supreme GOD. This number also gives us Hebrew words for "Lightning" and "an approach" as well as the name of the Enochian King of Fire. This suggests a change of level in these two attributions: one is below Tiphereth, the other approaches to the Supernals via Tiphereth, and "sees the Light". These ideas are wholly compatible with the ideas expressed earlier, save that the religious bias is missing from those former. It is also wholly appropriate to seek a qaballistic meaning behind these terms - as there is evidently some mystery attached to them, hence the use of the words "blind" and "secret" in the first of these verses, and the reference to "sight" in the second. The question of when such procedures are appropriate is difficult to determine satisfactorily, although Crowley gives some guidelines in "Equinox of the Gods" regarding the matter - but these are hardly likely to be wholly reliable in view of the fact that he did not possess the English Qaballa, a fact he fully recognises in the stated source.)

ASHARAT

QABALLISTIC MAGICK.

Qaballistic magick traditionally - by which we mean not the Golden Dawn variant but the original Hebrew practical qaballa - was chiefly concerned with obtaining access to various planes of being, of which the Sephiroth are by no means the chief example historically. The Gnostic ascent through the heavens has much in common with the original form of qaballistic magick and the "rising on the planes" practised by Crowley, Florence Farr et al. Crowley's exploration of the Thirty Æthyrs of the Enochian system approximates more to this kind of magick than do the various forms of "path-working" extant in modern occult circles. The visionary experiences undergone in these adventures of the spirit were attended by the most frightful psychic or (as we might say today with little if any amplification of meaning) psychological pressures. The unworthy or unsuitable experimenter with these methods was literally assaulted by armed angelic agencies, and some of the descriptions in "The Vision and the Voice" are remarkably similar to some of the old literature of the Hebrew kabbalah. When Crowley describes the efforts of the Angels to exclude him by force from experiences to which his degree of initiation did not entitle him, he could be quoting directly from the books of the Merkavah tradition of early kabbalism. The use of words of power and other keys to reduce or deflect these assaults is a common feature of these works. Similarly, in both the Gnostic and Kabbalistic world view, the initiate had to ascend through the planetary heavens before reaching more exalted levels of being, and finally suffering the experience of face to face intercourse with the King of Heaven.

All this may seem a long way off from the Book of the Law, but is this really so? The Qaballa of AL is intimately concerned not only with practical magick in the accepted sense of "results magick" but with the most exalted states of consciousness to which the initiate can aspire. Certainly the conception of deity contained in Liber AL is distinct from that of the Judaeo-Christian complex. Nevertheless, a qaballistic approach to the Book of the Law will inevitably lead to such visionary experiences, and dealings with various agencies on the thresholds of the sanctuaries of "Inner knowledge". These sanctuaries are guarded, as we seen, by the most potent forms of spiritual agency conceivable. Only a thorough mastery of the Qaballa will enable the initiate to pass within, and this will take many years to acquire. However, the proper performance of astrological magick, in the best sense - be it the therapeutic magick of Ficino, or the initiatory magick of the Sun-Venus - will be of enormous value in acquiring a sufficiently balanced nature to satisfy the guardians of these sanctuaries, and indeed to pass through the initial levels. In other words, astrological initiation is the equivalent of the passwords involved in the Gnostic ascent through the planetary heavens before approaching the deeper levels of the psyche (or of the cosmological model).

This might seem a little out of the way for many modern occultists, and perhaps offensive to their atheistic or rationalistic perspectives. All I can say in mitigation is that the world view of ancient Gnosticism and Kabbalah is the best approximation to the techniques and experiences involved with this system that I am able to find. Furthermore, since an enormous literature exists on the subject, with an advanced critical apparatus, I am not loath to make use of it.

The fact that magick does not adapt itself easily to modern scientific language, or to rationalistic psychological viewpoints, is not my concern. My efforts are directed towards making available a sophisticated modern magical methodology. The fact is that this system, if I may use such an ugly word, is similar in nature to some of the most evolved systems of the past, which have been largely neglected or misunderstood by contemporary occultists, and still more by contemporary psychologists and their ilk. Those who have made a deep study of the older systems may be able to appreciate the enormity of my undertaking. E.'.Q.'. is, in essence, a modern Gnostic system. It resumes the modus operandi and other elements of its ancient forebears, yet differs from them in one essential respect. Whereas the systems of the past are divided from us by a gulf of language, cultural perspective and religious outlook, the E.'.Q.'. is connected to us through the most significant text in modern magical history, uses our own language, and seeks to communicate with us in terms suited to our times.

This notwithstanding, the use of prayer in modern magick is not without its traducers. Since it has become increasingly fashionable to see the old gods as impersonal archetypal forces devoid of any life of their own outside our own consciousness, we must define our terms very carefully to avoid entering into futile debates over the nature of the forces behind AL. The finest definition available is that in Liber O: "In this book it is spoken of Sephiroth, and the Paths, of Spirits and Conjurations; of Gods, Spheres, Planes, and many other things which may or may not exist. It is immaterial whether they exist or not. By doing certain things certain results follow; students are most earnestly warned against attributing objective reality or philosophical validity to any of them." The prime example of such results is the Book of the Law itself, the direct result of a series of invocations performed in Cairo in 1904. That the Book itself contains sufficient data at a cursory glance (provided the frame of reference exists to understand it in its own terms) to prove itself beyond the means of normal consciousness to produce is indisputable. What is not beyond dispute - though the purpose of such dispute is questionable - is the means of transmission, granted that they were extraordinary. We might have to extend our definition of the collective consciousness of mankind to a mathematical and linguistic model capable of encoding and transmitting a qaballistic text through an individual consciousness under extreme conditions, and after much training. Certainly, if a strictly atheistic model is to be retained while accepting that a normal human consciousness is incapable of producing a text like AL within three hours, freehand, then some such idea would have to be accepted. It may be easier in the long run to say that an intelligence exterior to human consciousness was responsible for the Book of the Law.

Does this take us any further into the actual use of the Book as it appears to require? Here the answer has to be, not very much further. With or without having established the precise nature of the intelligence responsible for the writing of the Book of the Law, we are left with very few means of progress. Granted that our purpose is not literary criticism but philosophical enquiry, and perhaps a great deal more than that, then the obvious course is to follow much the same procedure as Crowley himself. Let us, then, establish two things. Firstly: what did Crowley do to attain the position of scribe? The answer here is simple enough; he undertook several years training: as a magician of the Golden Dawn; as a mystic in the Arab, Hindu and Buddhist traditions; and as a conventional western scholar of high academic standards (Bertrand Russell acknowledged him to have the best grasp of higher mathematics of any contemporary layman). Consequently, he was ideally suited to undertake such an adventure, having the mental apparatus to try and understand the process of transmission and retain some degree of detachment. This is to understate the case; for what was happening in the writer's chair depended on his mystical and psychological training for success. Crowley had at his disposal a deep knowledge and experience of transcendental psychology via his Buddhist studies, and a wide range of magical and mystical techniques, culled from a dozen cultural perspectives and reduced to a science by his able hand. In some way Crowley understood what was happening, and so may we. When we speak of magical techniques, we are not concerned with objective results necessarily. What we are speaking of, in the context of this discussion so far, is the scientific fact that certain techniques produce alterations in consciousness, and with luck and training, access particular areas of consciousness. There is nothing very contentious here. The Eight High Trances of Buddhism are as capable of scientific verification as any less dignified psychological or psychic state. The psychological knowledge of the followers of the Dhamma is known to be of a very high standard. What is contentious is the implication that such methodology, used in an unorthodox fashion - be it legitimate to some school or strictly experimental or even accidental - is capable of throwing a consciousness not too dissimilar to the average westerner's into a state where an intelligence - be it part of his own or entirely distinct - called "Aiwass, the minister of Hoor-paar-kraat", could dictate a book as significant in human history as the Bible, yet in a cultural context where such things are either not credited, or are thought to have conveniently ceased in a bygone era. Certainly Crowley did not stagger down from one of his many mountaineering expeditions clutching vitrified stone tablets engraved in letters of heavenly fire. What he did do is scarcely less problematical. Indeed, the difficulties are of considerably greater scope. Had he produced a "Book from Eternity" in the fashion of Moses, then only the gullible would have been impressed. Such things are, after all, within the capability of a man possessing rudimentary skills with a power tool and the gift of the gab. To produce a book possessed of such startling mathematical structures, armed only with a fountain pen, is quite another matter.

So, returning to our purpose, we have to obtain a similar degree of familiarity with ecstatic and mystical states and techniques as Crowley, and a philosophical frame of reference such as he possessed. This is what fitted him to be scribe, and will serve us in interpretation. The second point we need to establish is the nature of the relationship between qaballist and text. Let us examine the procedures of the ancient kabbalists and learn from them what such a relationship entails. This we cannot learn from Crowley or his peers in the Golden Dawn, for their claim to possess any significant portion of the kabbalah is extremely suspect.

At this point, it is amusing to dilate upon the subject of "authority" in kabbalistic matters a little: "From the brilliant misunderstandings and misrepresentations of.....Eliphas Levi, to the highly coloured humbug of Aleister Crowley and his followers, the most eccentric and fantastic statements have been produced purporting to be legitimate interpretations of Kabbalism." Gershom G.Scholem in "Major Trends in Jewish Mysticism", to which he adds in a footnote: "No words need to be wasted on the subject of Crowley's 'Kabbalistic' writings in his books on what he was pleased to term 'Magick', and in his journal, The Equinox." It is worthy of note that Scholem also avoids mentioning the vast majority of Renaissance "Christian Kabbalists", in whose tradition Crowley and the Golden Dawn possessed more legitimacy. Crowley was not exactly complimentary about the Hebrew system either: "The Qabalah, that is the Jewish Tradition concerning the initiated interpretation of their Scriptures, is mostly either unintelligible or nonsense." ("Little Essays Towards Truth.") Crowley's argument is reasonable enough in context, but once we examine his other works on Qabalah we find inconsistencies, for while here he is lauding the Tree of Life as an analytic tool in transcendental philosophy, elsewhere he leaps into the "unintelligible nonsense" in a big way, particularly via gematria, apparently operating a double standard; on rare occasions he even uses "colel", surely the most notorious fudge in the repertoire of Hebrew, and, for that matter, Greek kabbalists. Our understanding of the relationship of kabbalist with text is not going to be advanced much by Crowley, since that tradition was virtually a closed book to him.

The modus operandi of traditional qaballism is ascertainable from such works as Scholem's and also those of Kaplan (see Reviews in Equinox/BJT 7 and 8). Although the former authority is explicitly uncharitable to the work of non-Jewish kabbalists, and the latter implicitly, this is perhaps readily excused on the grounds of both the cultural heritage and scholastic background of these two authors. Disregarding their evident bias, we should look closely into their works for a picture of traditional kabbalism of greater lucidity than was available in Crowley's day. The main feature that emerges is extreme immersion in the written word of the Torah, coupled with intense prayer and meditation. The magical apparatus surrounding the method is one familiar to all students of the Book of the Dead and the Books of the Gnosis. This consists of the use of Words of Power to access the various divisions of the underworld or cosmos. In this, we can readily see how the E.'.Q.'. can be of very direct assistance. The Tables of A.M.E.N. will be very readily adapted for such purposes, extracting the appropriate Names and using them to invoke the various levels of the Thelemic Cosmo-conception.

The Tables of A.M.E.N.

These tables are designed to facilitate the construction of rituals on qaballistic lines, and have been used with great success by several groups and individuals for some years. The cosmology implicit in this schema originated with empirical work with E.'.Q.'. and astrological ritual. It is important to bear in mind that this model is part of a greater system, and that the system in question has a "slant" or emphasis on particular regions of experience. While the general symbolism is essentially similar to astrology and even pre-existent qaballistic models, the resemblance is superficial. Accordingly, we find such apparent anomalies as PLUTO = 76 = TAURUS, ARIES = 66 = URANUS = EARTH, and CANCER = 78 = FIRE. In the region in which E.'.Q.'. lives and moves and has its being, these "anomalies" become potent arcanum.

The foregoing remarks must serve as sufficient warning that this attribution concerns realms distinct from or tangential to those the conventional astrologer or ceremonialist is concerned with. In a word, E.'.Q.'. has "attitude". The emphasis is - to most practical intents - on the movement of the planets and luminaries through four signs of the zodiac. Where other signs are concerned, they must be understood in terms of this emphasis. Accordingly, while astrological expertise is a definite advantage, astrological dogma may be entirely counterproductive. E.'.Q.'. does not much care that Aries begins the year, or that Cancer is associated with the home or parents. It is concerned with forms of initiation and experience outside of the conventional occultism of virtually any era; a truly "New Aeon" system, of "new symbols". The first of these symbols, of course is ONE, (since Zero or NONE "precedes the beginning") and in E.'.Q.'. ONE has the value 46. Of all the words in AL with this value, the most significant and fundamental idea is WOMAN. But of Her we do not speak - which plays a part in the construction of the Tables of A.M.E.N..

The tables which follow divide the universe into Four Worlds - a conventional pattern so far. (There is another sense in which it appears that Thelemic qaballism posits Three Worlds, but that need not concern us here.) The Four Scales of Number representing these Worlds are, for recondite reasons, given as headings the four letters of the Word or Name AMEN. The first of these scales represents the "Infinite" or highest expression of the idea concerned; in the case of ideas classified under 5, the highest or infinite expression is taken to be 58 (using 8 for Infinity), for 10, 108, and so on. So Names corresponding to these values have been placed in the columns as appropriate on numerical grounds. The second such scale represents a more materialised or extended form of the original idea. Now the number is spelt, so that 5 = FIVE = 76, and so this column consists of Names equivalent to the gematrias of the numbers. The third column, corresponding to Vau or the Son in Hebrew symbolism, is a combination of the two preceding, its father and mother as it were. Staying with the number five as our example, this means that in the third column the Name will be equivalent to 5 + FIVE which is 81, the value of KHEPHRA among other Names, which will be found accordingly in that place in the Table. The fourth column represents the formal symbol in the macrocosm of the number in question. Although other forms of symbolism are entirely possible here, the beginner is warned against any personalised attribution, for should these be incompatible with the true nature of the force the results will be at best disappointing and at worst catastrophic. The best course is to use the conventional planets and elements, bearing in mind the nature of the system itself in relation to those symbols. To E.'.Q.'., Fire is a symbol of the Goddess, since FIRE = 78 = NUIT. So whilst it is conventional to attribute both Venus and Fire to the number Seven (Hebrew Netzach, representing the Elemental grade of Fire and the Planet Venus), it is worthy of particular note that in E.'.Q.'. VENUS = 71 and FIRE = 78, as if to ram some special point home.

One further point before turning to the Tables themselves: it might appear logical from the view of mathematics that the series should start with ONE, but in practice, which is the whole purpose of these Tables, the number ONE as a symbol of WOMAN is concealed - "Let them not speak of Thee as One" - so the series begins with the number twelve in the place of one, and continues through to eleven. This arrangement has proved far more satisfactory in all ways than the first option, and is undoubtedly the correct form.

THE TABLES OF A.M.E.N.

KEY	INFINITE	VALUE	SERPENT	SYMBOL
TWELVE	128= BAPHOMET	89= NU+HAD+IT	101= MENTU	76(PLUTO) = HERU-RA-HA
TWO	28= ANKH	34= AL OAI ABRA	36= AIWAZ AMN	145(NEPTUNE) = ASI + NEPTHI
THREE	38= AIWASS YAMA	90= TYPHON	93= TAHUTI	73(SATURN) = RA-HOOR-KHU
FOUR	48= ASAR + ISA	54= SET BUDDHA	58= HADIT	143(JUPITER) = SOL INVICTUS
FIVE	58= HERU	76= HERU-RA-HA	81= KHEPHRA TA-NECH	39(MARS) = AUM
SIX	68= JESUS	50= BES COPH	56= ISIS KHONSU	36(SUN) = AIWAZ
SEVEN	78= NUIT	79= ABRAHADABRA	86= TITAN	71(VENUS) = IO PAN
EIGHT	88= COPH NIA	87= FALUTLI	95= AORMUZDI	115(MERCURY) = NU % HAD*
NINE	98= QADOSH ISIS	76= IACCHUS	85= SHOSINEL O NUIT	49(MOON) = MARY EROS
TEN	108= HOOR-APEP ISIS-HATHOR	63= MAUT	73= BACCHUS AOUIE	66(EARTH) = FIAT
ELEVEN	118= ANKH-AF- -NA-KHONSU	101= MENTU TUTULU	112= PAN IO PAN	66(URANUS) = FIAT

* These two Names must be "counted well" to obtain this value. See previous issues of this Journal for details of this technique, which has proved time and again to be of value in ritual, whilst apparently being an obscure qaballistic technique. It is for this reason that it is described "longhand" in our earlier issues, despite the fact that a quicker and simpler method exists.

The vast majority of these Names are from Class A. One or two are combinations, and in the case of SOL INVICTUS the form was simply too apt to ignore. The Name SHOSINEL is an anagram of the word Holiness, the literal meaning of QADOSH. Of the combined Names, it is worth remarking that ISIS-HATHOR is named with reverence in Liber 418, whilst HOOR-APEP is a principal form in Pyramidos and elsewhere. The point to be borne in mind is that it is the number rather than the letters which give this table its chief efficacy; in theory one could construct completely synthetic names to match these values, but theory isn't enough - these Names have additional potency from their association with the Holy Books of Thelema. What should be carefully avoided is thinking of, say, Nuit as a Spirit of Fire, or of Iacchus as a Moon-God. Whilst some such associations are valid within limits - such as Jesus' association with the Sun in "Christian" qaballa - the tendency if unchecked would wreck the system rather than access it fully. The important thing is that these Names have POWER and through their numerical values that power may be used to control or to access the energies of the Universe. That this is literally true may come as somewhat of a shock, and the reader may choose to disbelieve it. In the context of an astrologically timed tantric ritual, however, every word and action is significant - it is important in such circumstances to say and do only what you intend. The effect of such words and actions in the context of such a ritual are enormously increased compared to the day-to-day effect of willed/unwilled and half-intentional words and actions, given the confused and uncertain manner in which human interaction with the environment is generally conducted.

Proceeding with the Table in the Sphere of the Elements, the ritualist alters the fourth column in lines 6 through to 10 as follows;

(6) 68. 50. 56. **113/SPIRIT = RA-HRUMACHIS.**
(7) 78. 79. 86..**78/FIRE = APEP.**
(8) 88. 87. 95. **65/WATER = BABALON.**
(9) 98. 76. 85. **36/AIR = AIWAZ.**
(10) 108. 63. 73. **66/EARTH = FIAT.**

These Names are used to formulate the Pentagrams or AL sigils in the Four Quarters in the Pentagram rites etc. in use by the groups and individuals mentioned earlier. The form of this ritual is as follows.

RITUAL OF THE PENTAGRAM.

Begin in the centre of the circle, facing East. Formulate a brilliant sphere of light clearly above the head, radiant and powerful. Feel love and reverence for this sphere of light. Raising the right hand to it, say:

O GLORY BE; dropping the hand to the genitals, say: UNTO THEE; retracing the line to the centre of the chest then touching the right shoulder, say: THROUGH ALL TIME; tracing back across the chest, touch the left shoulder and say: AND THROUGH ALL SPACE. Touching the centre of this Cross of Light, say again: GLORY; folding the arms one over the other in the position of Osiris Risen, say as the right hand rests on the left shoulder: AND GLORY and as the left crosses it and rests on the right shoulder: UPON GLORY; resting in this position conclude: EVERLASTINGLY, AMEN & AMEN & AMEN. Conclude with the Sign of Silence, imagining the godform to be of vast size and feeling the footstep of the god shaking the earth as you advance your foot.

Go now to the East and draw the Banishing Pentagram of Earth, vibrating FIAT. Tracing the circle round to the South draw the Banishing Pentagram of Fire, vibrating APEP. Continue to the West, and draw the Banishing Pentagram of Water, vibrating BABALON; trace the line on to the North, draw the Banishing Pentagram of Air and vibrate AIWAZ. Complete the line back to the East and return to the centre, face East, spread your arms in the posture of Osiris Slain and say aloud, as if in the presence of powerful and benign gods:

BEFORE ME MATTER, BEHIND ME MOTION;
ON MY RIGHT HAND, TIME,
ON MY LEFT HAND, SPACE -
FOR ABOUT ME BLAZE THE PENTAGRAMS
AND IN THE COLUMN STANDS THE SIX RAYED STAR.

This last line refers to an AL sigil above and below, which, while not consciously drawn, are implicit by virtue of your magical actions in this rite; they may therefore appear quite spontaneously, but if not they should be formulated clearly in the same way as the pentagrams, but without being traced.

In conclusion, repeat the Qaballistic Cross as in the beginning.

Another form of this ritual exists, using the Invoking Pentagrams of the Elements in the order as above, but the Pentagrams are charged with the Highest Name of the force invoked then the Enochian sigil of the Element is drawn in the centre and charged with the Names given above, thus:

Earth Pentagram HOOR-APEP or ISIS-HATHOR, Sigil FIAT.
Fire Pentagram NUIT, Sigil APEP.
Water Pentagram COPH NIA, Sigil BABALON.
Air Pentagram   QADOSH-ISIS, Sigil AIWAZ.

Once the Circle has been completed in the East, the ritualist faces WEST across the Altar in the Sign of the Enterer (the posture of the central figure in "The Lovers" in the Thoth pack) and says aloud and with intense solemnity and resonance:

```
THE WORDS AGAINST THE SON OF NIGHT,
TAHUTI SPEAKETH IN THE LIGHT.
KNOWLEDGE AND POWER, TWIN WARRIORS, SHAKE
THE INVISIBLE, THEY ROLL ASUNDER THE DARKNESS.
MATTER SHINES, A SNAKE.
SEBEK IS SMITTEN BY THE THUNDER.
THE LIGHT BREAKS FORTH FROM UNDER.
```

The palms of the hands must be directly above the altar vertically, face down.

(The Magician who understands the nature of the Ark, or of its counterparts, Dee's table and that described in the Leyden papyrus, may make certain additional gestures, blessing the altar after this part of the ceremony with the appropriate signs, and the Name RA HRUMACHIS = 113 = SPIRIT.)

The ritual then continues thus: go clockwise to the West and face East, seeing the figure of the Hermit in the Sign of the Enterer in the Eastern quarter just vacated. Continue the ritual as above "Before me Matter...." etc. The Sigils, Pentagrams, fiery circle and AL Sigils above and beneath must be maintained in the mind's eye throughout. This ritual is much more potent than the first, and may be used as a formal Temple opening in E.'.Q.'. related work. On no account should it be performed frivolously or without full knowledge of the signs and symbols used; nor without full preparation, robed and burning Abramelin or other holy perfume etc. etc. Conclude as before with the Qaballistic Cross.

The rule to remember in the use of Pentagrams is that in invoking, the Infinite Name is used to charge the Pentagram and the Symbol Name to charge the sigil, whereas in banishing, only the Symbol Name and appropriate Pentagram is used. This is in accordance with the tradition that in consecration the highest symbol or Name of the force invoked is used, i.e. the *Infinite* expression of the idea.

In Hexagram rituals, much the same rules apply. Pentagrams are used to invoke the quarters and/or elements, Hexagrams are used to invoke the planets, e.g.: invoking Venus: draw Hexagram of Venus, vibrating the Name from the Infinite scale, NUIT; draw sigil (either the planetary sigil or the appropriate Enochian sigil) vibrating the Name from the Symbol scale, IO PAN. The Hymn to Pan may well be incorporated in the ritual both for its use of the invokatory phrase IO PAN, and for the effectiveness of this particular incantation in its own right, which will be found to be appropriate to the nature of many operations of Venus in any case.

It has not been found worthwhile to invoke the signs as agencies. They serve rather the role of containers of the planetary forces, and if they are represented in the ritual it is in terms of Temple decor, and their influence will be as a modifier of the basic planetary energy.

It is important to bear in mind with these tables that there can be no final version of the Names used. It appears to matter comparatively little, for example, in rituals of Jupiter, whether one uses ASAR + ISA for 48 or, equally valid numerically, LASTADZA, or even devises a new word, either by combining letters by addition to the required sum or taking a pre-existing word of the desired value and rearranging the letters to form a barbarous name. This said, there are many cases in which the Names themselves impart information concerning the principle invoked. The yardstick of pure number in the use of invocations ensures that the practitioner will not stray from the path of truth, which might very easily occur in using names of various ancient cultures which are not fully understood. In the Tables of A.M.E.N. the mathematical relations between the planetary forces and the numbers are readily assimilated and will not serve you false. The importance of this is hard to over emphasise, since these forces, which we gaily refer to as Planetary, are in fact only so on the mundane level (the fourth column, what Crowley would refer to as Mundane Chakras) - on the higher levels they are little less than, and perhaps a good deal more than, divine forces. We are dealing here with agencies akin to or identical with the "Angelic" authors of the Enochian system or of AL itself. These forces are extremely potent; they are capable of initiating the magician by the most direct means, including drastic alterations in his or her mental, psychic and bio-chemical constitution.

God's Holy Mysteries - a user's guide.

Let me reiterate that in these processes we are dealing with what in Dee's time would have been called God's Holy Mysteries. In our own day, we are accustomed to speak of archetypes, of constructs, egregores, cones of power or simply "synthetic spirits". The idea that the Universe is run by (not simply created by) some kind of deity is not terribly fashionable, and "does not compute" with our modern scientific viewpoint, not even for the average layman, let alone the hard-headed physicist. The use of the word "God" or even "god" is likely to be extremely contentious - nor am I fool enough or dogmatic enough to promote an **unquestioning** belief in superhuman intelligence. It has become almost an article of faith for Thelemites to believe in extraterrestial intelligence, due to Aleister Crowley and Kenneth Grant et al insisting that communication with such intelligences is of supreme importance in magical work. This is certainly not my attitude - it may be extremely important at some stage for such communication to develop; the question is at which? In the initial stages of magical work, I believe it is important not to seek such apocalyptic goals. As if having another chapter of Liber AL dictated to us would serve any purpose when we don't understand the first three sufficiently well to agree on first principles! What is important, obviously enough, is to train your various faculties, psychic, physical and mental to the highest possible degree. To accustom yourself to the terminology and methodology of the best occult traditions, and to investigate for yourself their various claims. This must be done in the most thoroughgoing manner possible, with or without an occult order or teacher to assist you. Train yourself to the highest possible degree of skill and understanding which is within your capability.

It is then that such adventures as the Knowledge and Conversation of the Holy Guardian Angel (whatever that may mean) become possible, and meaningful, not before. But even so, what of these Holy Mysteries, and what of God? The answer is, as intimated earlier, that the Qaballa demonstrates that the Book of the Law could not have been produced by any human intelligence - in the terms we understand - or by any means which science can as yet begin to comprehend. The mathematical and philosophical complexities revealed by a simple letter-number substitution technique, in which the "cheats" which are possible with such alphabets as Hebrew are simply not present or possible, make it inconceivable that Crowley or any other occultist of his calibre - let alone someone of lesser ability - could have written it.

The Qaballa reveals a good deal more besides, of an esoteric nature, and on a level so advanced that the training above described is almost essential to even appreciate a portion of it. It is true that processes such as invocation and astrological timing are comparatively simple to put into effect. What is not simple is dealing with the Book on its own level, and following the chains of ideas and number symbolism to their ultimate goal. This requires not only considerable intellectual gifts, but also -dare I say it - moral qualities rarely found in twentieth century culture. The very simplest of rules in traditional magick assume phenomenal importance in this area. The Book of the Law simply does not envisage, and consequently cannot accomodate, any individual who is not possessed of the traditional qualities of a magician becoming involved with it. Of primary importance, considering the very nature of a book, is the ability to keep one's word, for one's word to mean what it says. Even with this, there are no guarantees of success in approaching the sovereign sanctuaries which its structure reveals and conceals. This indeed is the great secret of its construction, that the elements which reveal its meaning for initiates are the same mechanisms that conceal its secrets from the profane. The last words of the Book of the Law are: "The Book of the Law is Written and Concealed." Elsewhere it says: "it is revealed by Aiwass", and the words CONCEALED and REVEALED have the same numerical value; and this, like each and every turn of phrase and choice of words in the Book, is no accident. "Now let the light devour men and eat them up with blindness" is no idle threat, it is fact; the light, which enables us to see, is the very instrument by which AL blinds us to its truths, blinds us, that is, until or unless we are ready. We must approach AL with great courage and determination, this much it tells us itself; we must also approach it with knowledge and humility, with great sincerity and humanity - that much it simply assumes, for it was not written for persons devoid of these qualities. Such individuals it will puff up with pride and lead to their destruction. Modern fairy tales such as "Raiders of the Lost Ark" portray extremely graphically the consequences of seeking to pervert the energies of such "sacred" power sources. There is no question of such consequences being "unfair", nor of calling the sanctity of the Book into question on the basis of such events. It would be most unwise to make such judgements. It has been said that magical energy is neutral, and that it is men who turn it to one end or another, in a similar manner to electricity. This analogy is only partially helpful here. Certainly, those who tap these energies without due preparation have only themselves to blame for undesirable results, but the energy is not neutral; it has a viewpoint, it has a purpose, and it is the attempt to manipulate it or deal with it in terms alien to its nature which produces such dire results. AL makes it quite clear that these consequences exist, and that attempts to use it without understanding are dangerous. It is unfortunate if these warnings go unheeded, but it is not "unfair".

What then is the purpose of the Book? The answer here is simple, in that it can be expressed in one word, and complex, in that this word involves imponderables beyond human comprehension. The purpose is, in one word: Initiation. Initiation of the individual, of the collective and of the human species. The individual is the primary concern of the Book at this time. This is because the individual is the logical beginning for the entire process. Logical in AL's own terms of reference. That the ultimate purpose of AL is to initiate a new phase in human evolution is, perhaps, a commonplace; nevertheless, a discussion of this kind cannot omit to mention it.

The immediate form of initiation which the Qaballa of AL has made possible is through the Sun-Venus Pentagram. This is initiation by ordeal, the Ordeal X described cryptically in the Book of the Law. This Ordeal separates the chaff from the wheat, the fit from the unfit. What it does not do is make silk purses out of sows' ears. This said, there is abundant evidence that the Ordeal initiates persons possessing basic human qualities, regardless of their supposed intelligence or knowledge, or any other supposedly desirable quality. To clarify this, I must resort to biography.

A simple man, a man of no special intelligence, but having real skills in mechanics, such as welding and car maintenance, became involved with a magical order. After a period of time in which he underwent the initiation rituals associated with the Sun-Venus, triggering the Ordeal X, a transformation occurred in his make-up. His former skills were not lessened; indeed if anything they were greatly enhanced, and he made some of the most impressive ritual weapons it has been my privilege to see. Yet this was not the most striking transformation. The same individual became an extremely competent astrologer - not in itself that remarkable in an astrologically oriented group, had he not also developed excellent skills as a counsellor, a rare gift, especially with no formal training. This was by no means all; the same individual, within a period of about three years, had acquired all these abilities, undergone a major personality transformation (a clear out of conditioning inherited from society) and without any peer-group pressure whatsoever (as might be inferred in the case of astrological skills) had developed remarkable psychometric gifts, with a degree of sensitivity usually associated with women of an otherwise frail constitution and unworldly temperament. These transformations in his personality and make-up, involving such varied skills and abilities, were all accomplished without his "losing the common touch". His abilities with metals were obviously not diminished, nor was his ability to mix and work with the same social group he always had previously, but nor was he out of his depth among the initiates of the Order. Of course, this man was not a "sow's ear" to begin with, else he would never have been involved with this group in the first place, and supposing he had, would have been swiftly ejected from the system by the mechanical processes of the Ordeal itself. This case history has a particular point to it, in terms of the almost religious nature of the Qaballistic path - it indicates that the Ordeal X and the system of magical initiation associated with it possess a moral dimension; that, as a great magician of another tradition once remarked, a handful of moral qualities are worth a hundred magical powers.

As a qaballist I would say this is true, but also that these same qualities **are** great magical powers. If we take a look at the names of the Sephiroth they seem archaic and alien. If however we look more closely, reminding ourselves what these titles mean in our own language we become aware of something we might not have noted consciously before. Let us do as I suggest, and examine these titles in English, not as gematria values, but as simple words: The Crown; Wisdom; Understanding; Knowledge; Mercy or Glory; Justice or Power; Beauty, Harmony or Compassion; Victory; Splendour; The Foundation, and finally, The Kingdom. These are moral powers, human qualities and and ideals. If we imagine for a moment that the Hebrew kabbalah and indeed all previous systems are abrogate, that the magick of the future retains the essence but not the outward forms - then the Tree of Life in our times might have other qualities, of a similar nature, rather than this list. If we look back to the origins of the Kabbalah, we find that such lists have existed before. The kabbalist and sage Rav, of the third century A.D., said: "Ten are the qualities with which the world has been created: Wisdom, Insight, Knowledge, Force, Appeal, Power, Justice, Right, Love and Compassion." In our own times, it might be that the Universe is interpreted in terms of the qualities of Liberty, Truth, Justice, Courage, Integrity, Love, Reverence, Strength, Conscience, Pleasure and Serenity, or any number of similar qualities. This idea might become the centre of an important meditative practice. Another important point that arises is the difficulty we have seeing what is under our noses. Many students of the kabbalah fail to see clearly that the Sephiroth are moral powers; they see the exotic titles rather than the meaning, nor is this entirely their own fault. If nothing else, E.'.Q.'. brings home to its devotees the interior world of the qaballa. To the Hebrews these old titles were not exotic, the words struck home to them just as the word freedom sounds in the ear of an oppressed person in the land of a tyrant, or love in the ear of a young girl. In the same way, the English Qaballa brings us the power and potency of the ancient magick in a form comprehensible to the aspirants and adepts of today.

To return to our theme, of course the ability to produce wonderful effects is what we **expect** from a magician, or indeed from ourselves as magicians - at least once in a while. This is only too **understandable** - as we are all children after all in many ways - but we know too that the ability to love, to understand or to behave honourably is also miraculous, and is worthy of a magician, or even a saint. These are all magical powers, and will move mountains as effectively as any lightning bolts from the fingertips, or ectoplasmic strands from the mouth and nostrils. When we speak of Archetypal forces, what are we really talking about? Not some strange dreamlike character such as the Jungian Animus, nor any god, spirit or hobgoblin. An Archetypal force is a human or universal quality such as Justice, and any person who **personifies** such a force **possesses** magical power. This reminds me of the Golden Dawn motto, "Strive to become more than human"; this is altogether too ridiculous, for without at least one or two of these qualities, dormant or half-forgotten, in our hearts or minds, we are not even human, let alone more than human! Possessing one of these powers is not easy. We are the most dangerous enemies of our own principles; we alone can betray them, though every other person in the world attempts to cause us to do so, we alone have the power to say yea or nay. There, I've done it, I've bitten the bullet and talked as straight as I can on the single most important aspect of Initiation, the candidate and their ordeal. Of course, this will leave you none the wiser should you undertake the adventure, for Initiation is never what you expect, or it would not be Initiation. I have risked making myself ridiculous, by pontificating at such extravagant length, and it is time to turn to magical procedures, to meditation, to practical qaballa; but do not lose sight of what has passed between us in these few pages. Magical power is real, more real than any other form of power, and yet more subtle and illusive.

Qaballistic Meditation

Qaballistic meditation is an important aspect of this system, and many assumptions are based on its results - making much incomprehensible without personal experience; the precise nature of the technique is detailed below. The bare bones are not dissimilar to the Middle Pillar exercise of Israel Regardie, but the similarity is superficial, as will emerge in the course of this section. The Middle Pillar Exercise, for those who are unacquainted with it, is a series of practical instructions expanded from the papers of the Golden Dawn. The Exercise has much in common with certain tantric practices, indeed Regardie draws attention to a work entitled "The Secret of the Golden Flower" which shows this relationship quite clearly. The shortcomings of the technique as it stands are a) its brevity, b) its variants, some of which are far less germane to our purpose than others, while useful in other spheres - the method performed standing up is useful in the context of the Pentagram Ritual for instance - and c) its lack of the true automatic quality necessary to breach the gates of the Astral Plane. The strength of the technique lies in its compatibility with the Pentagram, Vibration of God-Names et al, and its sound qaballistic structure.

Those who are familiar with the Middle Pillar Exercise and with the pranayama exercises of Crowley's Liber E will readily assimilate the ideas I am about to outline. In order more readily to integrate these ideas and the technique into the framework of this work, and to enable the student unfamiliar with the method to understand what is to follow, I will first discuss some details.

1/. Before undertaking this work, it is essential that the operator is already familiar with the English Qaballa and with AL, and perhaps the other Class A writings. Besides this, a degree of preparation with ritual exercises is called for, so that the Pentagram ritual described earlier will be performed daily, twice at the least. The effect of this is to balance and integrate the "Elemental" forces in the magician's make-up. As well as this, it is a good idea to become extremely familiar with the Bornless Rite. This is especially the case if the meditation is to form part of a Magical Retirement as described under heading no.7 below. In this case, the operator will perform the Bornless Ritual daily, at dawn, noon, sundown and midnight, in his physical body at first, later in the mental body, and as proficiency in the technique described is attained, in the astral body.

2/. Liber E contains, among other things, a programme of pranayama exercises similar in most respects to the standard yogic techniques, with one essential distinction. This new element is an example of Crowley's genius, and cannot be understood except by reference to various passages of his records and other snippets which were never properly systemised, or by thorough understanding of the automation of the physical processes in yoga and kindred methods, not generally known in the West. Essentially, the difference consists of the use of a watch to measure the breath cycles, rather than the traditional use of counting heartbeats or simply counting off seconds. The problem with these latter methods is that the heart and mind are subject to fluctuation, so that the rhythm of breath is in fact subject to irregularities beyond the practitioner's ability to control or even detect. The use of a watch removes this imperfection and truly automates the process, with the result that the exercises are very much more effective in terms of time and effort. Unfortunately, the cycles Crowley advocates are far too strenuous to allow for the other essential feature of this technique, which is utter relaxation.

3/. The relaxation methods described in Regardie's book "The Middle Pillar" are excellent, and should be used. Briefly they consist of laying down and tensing the whole body. This tension is then relaxed, the idea being that you cannot tell how unrelaxed you are until you consciously tense up and relax. This principle is applied in detail, so that for instance, starting with the toes, one tenses and relaxes them, then the feet, then the ankles, lower legs, thighs and so forth. The difference here between Regardie's method and this is that due to the presence of a watch the practitioner must have their head supported by pillows, so that the relaxing of the neck becomes more critical than might otherwise be the case. Since many westerners have problems with the throat chakra regardless of the nature of the techniques in use there is a good case to be made for "ritualising" this problem in this manner anyway.

4/. The meditation proper begins with the visualisation of a sphere of white brilliance above the head. Once this is achieved, the practitioner commences to vibrate the Divine Names appropriate to the sphere. This is accompanied with the cultivation of feelings of love and reverence towards the sphere, which represents Kether in the Hebrew schema.

5/. The practitioner goes on to add the other spheres of the Middle Pillar, including Da'ath, all in white light, all with their appropriate Divine Names absorbed and vibrated with the breath cycle.

6/. The breath cycle itself should be simple, and consists of four parts: exhalation, holding out, inhalation, holding in. The rhythm to a large extent depends on the psychic constitution of the operator. As a general rule, this may be worked out astrologically, Earth and Water signs using a cycle based on two and its multiples, Fire and Air signs a cycle based on three and its multiples. E.g.: Earth and Water 4 out, 2 hold, 4 in, 2 hold - which may be intensified as the operator gains proficiency to 8 out, 4 hold, 8 in, 4 hold. In the case of Fire and Air signs this will be 6-3-6-3 and 9-6-9-6. This rule may not hold universally, but the nature of the cycle best suited to the individual may be worked out by a close examination of the natal chart, weighing active and passive factors to obtain the required picture.

7/. The various methods of circulating light described in Regardie's book may be employed if desired; however, the student may well find that things take their own course along similar lines. The important thing is to seek to extend the period of practice as far as possible. It should be done daily, at the same time, and the student should realise that one hour is scarcely sufficient. What is sufficient? This is imponderable, but as a general rule the student should be aiming at a period of three hours per session. Obviously, this makes for great difficulties in day to day life, so that simpler and less extended versions of the exercise are desirable; but at some point in your career as a magician, and the sooner the better, for reasons of health, vitality and enthusiasm, you should undertake a "Magical Retirement" with this technique as the basis, along the lines of the Abramelin operation. While a certain degree of emotional and mental maturity is desirable with this methodology, it is also essential that the student's health and vigour be at its peak, so that preferably the operator will be between 25 and 45 years of age.

8/. The method of concentration employed in this technique is controlled association. By this is meant that the student will restrict their thoughts to the correspondences, symbolic and numerical, appropriate to the Sphere on which they are working. Thus when "Kether" is being cultivated, the range of thoughts will be restricted to its symbols, and to the words and phrases which are numerically associated with it. This gives great freedom of movement, while at the same time retaining a single idea, and similarly for the other spheres. At later stages of the exercise, once the Middle Pillar itself is firmly established, the student may go on to use the appropriate colours for the various spheres, and to add the side pillars in their appropriate colours. These should preferably be taken from the astrological and chakra references in "The Equinox - BJT", which derive from AL rather than quasi-Hebrew systems.

9/. Having mastered these phases of the technique, and fully accomplished the extension of the technique in time to the full period of three hours, or at the very least one and a half hours, the student may go on to perform rituals in the spheres. Whereas the meditation has been worked from top to bottom, the rituals must be worked from "Malkuth" up. This entails a correspondence between the sections of the ritual(s) and the levels of the Middle Pillar (and only the Middle Pillar is to be employed). For the Pentagram Ritual and the "Elemental" quarters of the Bornless Rite the correspondences are as follows: East = Malkuth. South = Yesod. West = Tiphereth. North = Da'ath. The student should not concern themself at this point with the appropriateness or otherwise of these correspondences, but simply work with the rituals in these spheres, vibrating the various Names, and forming the various sigils, signs and lineal figures (pentagrams etc.) in the appropriate chakras. The raison d'etre will become plain with practice. With the last two phases of the Bornless Rite the correspondences will be: Spirit Active = Ajna Chakra or "third eye" (roughly "Kether" as the cranial suture). Spirit Passive = Sahasrara Chakra or above the head (roughly Ain Soph or "Kether" above the head; these equations are approximate, and as said above are not the practitioners concern at this stage.)

The preliminary phases of the ritual, such as the Purifications and Consecrations, should be worked in the Middle Pillar likewise. The Purifications consist of visualising a chalice above the head pouring water down; or alternatively a simple blue downwards pointing equilateral triangle above the head, descending through the Middle Pillar. Whichever is employed, the water or triangle (or both, since both methods should be practised and may well coincide) descends to the heart chakra. The appropriate verse of AL is recited at the same time. The Consecrations are performed in a similar manner, so that the flame or red upright equilateral triangle ascends from the groin to the heart, where it interlocks with the water triangle; again the appropriate verse from AL is recited internally. This exercise obviously will precede the Pentagram Ritual which in turn precedes the Bornless Rite.

10/. If at any time in the course of performing these exercises the operator feels themself tensing up or losing concentration then the entire process should commence anew, beginning with the tensing and relaxing phase. This tendency should be overcome before attempting to perform rituals in the Middle Pillar.

11/. Once the student has acquired these abilities, they will find their accustomed magical procedures much enhanced, and may undertake these exercises without such great preparations. At this point in their career, they will be able to perform very sophisticated rituals in their Astral Body, whilst walking in the country or sitting in their armchairs. The effects of rituals performed in the physical body will also be greatly enhanced, to the point at which, for instance, other persons present, as in group rituals, will be aware of the changes in the Temple when they perform Banishing Rituals and so forth, and the effects of invocations will be enhanced to the point at which inducing states of possession in the Priestess will be a relatively minor matter.

This is all in the future, however. The course of this initiation may well take some few years, despite the results of a six month preliminary retirement, which will be in themselves a substantial step forward. The reasons for this delay are difficult to establish. The most obvious reason is that the pressures induced by the operation set in motion the destruction of some major complexes and disorders in the student's make-up. The resolution of these takes some little time. This may be interpreted, rightly or wrongly, as a period of recovery from the Ordeal itself. It may also be seen as a period in which you rebuild your life after the obstacles in your environment, some of which may be extremely dear to you, have been removed.

The time at which the Ordeal and Retirement is undertaken should be astrologically determined, preferably coinciding with aspects for mystical achievement (Neptune/Pluto), and the period of resolution will of course depend on the transits and progressions of your natal chart. Difficulties encountered will almost certainly relate to the natal, and the quality of results, and their duration will also depend on astrological factors. Talented astrological magicians will find ways of off-setting some of these difficulties, and of lessening others, particularly once the Ordeal is over. The main stumbling block then is the degree to which your natal chart involves the possibility of this experience being available to you in the first place. The presence of bad aspects does not exclude the possibility of mystical and magical experience, but may well present difficulties; such is the nature of Ordeals in any case. The presence of aspects involving such experiences is essential.

Having shown how meditation and ritual can be effectively combined - lest any think ritual too frivolous an affair for a "mystic" - it is time now to turn our attention to ritual magick once more, and to continue this exploration of its concealed depths.

Ritual Construction

The basis of most rituals is a seven-fold structure, consisting of: preliminary banishings, purifications with water, consecrations with fire (either incense or oil, preferably the latter), the statement of intent (frequently represented graphically in the form of a talisman, but equally well stated verbally), the invocations, the charge to the spirit (similar in most respects to the statement of intent) and the license to depart with the final banishings. This skeletonic structure can be developed in a number of ways, of which the best - outside of improvisation on the spot with minimal preparation, which only the experienced magician should attempt - is simply to cut and paste from source books and rites, adding special flourishes and so on as appropriate. This method can be supplemented with sections of one's own composition, either qaballistically composed or poetical etc.

1). The Banishings: a pentagram ritual devised specifically for use with this material was given earlier in this essay. Banishings should also include the preparation of the magician and the place of working, e.g. the bathing of the body and the dismissal of other concerns from the mind in the case of the operator, and the exclusion of unnecessary symbols and paraphernalia from the work-place. As well as this there is the banishing of unwanted influences from any new materials to be used in the ritual, which may well take the form of a sub-ritual performed in advance.

2). The Purifications: the traditional Thelemic purification is performed in conjunction with a quote from the Book of the Law: "For pure will, unassuaged of purpose, delivered from the lust of result, is every way perfect." This is best extended into a libation with the cup in each quarter, with continual sprinkling between each quarter, saying as you go about the circle "Azure Lidded Woman", each word can be accompanied with a lifting of the cup in salute to the quarter. In the centre or the east after completing this circuit one can then perform a final salute, raising the cup three times with the words from AL:

"For pure will, unassuaged of purpose..." lifting the cup aloft,
delivered from the lust of result...." raising the cup on high again,
is every way perfect..." final raising of the cup.

3). The Consecrations: a similar process can be followed in the case of an incense consecration, substituting the censer for the cup and the phrase "I am uplifted in thine heart / and the kisses of the stars / rain hard upon thy body." for that given above. In the case of oil being used, the primary thing to observe is the consecration of those participating, as all else follows from there. In this case simply go clockwise about the circle in the case of a group ritual and anoint each brow with the Holy Oil (Abramelin oil is obviously the first choice for most operations, particularly qaballistic rituals such as those under consideration), saying "Burn upon their brows, o splendrous serpent!" as you draw the appropriate symbol. The best for general use is the sigil of NOX which is an X in a circle. In the case of a particular consecration, e.g. of an item created as the basis of the ritual, the anointings are more elaborate. Either one draws the highest symbol of the force invoked (which can obviously be a divine name) on the item concerned, or in the case of a talisman or sigil draws the names and symbols in oil over their inked or engraved counterparts. This operation may be done with the finger, but if the operator possesses a small bone wand (a badger's penis bone is good) this can be used as a pen for the oil.

The opening of the Temple from Liber Pyramidos is an excellent ritual, combining these three preliminary stages, although it may be as well to retain a separate banishing ritual. This rite is frequently misunderstood, due in part to the subtlety and humour of its composer, Aleister Crowley, blessed be He. Essentially, the ritual consists of preparation of the operator in various ways, **symbolised** by the chain, the scourge and the dagger. These items need not be used, or even be present in the ceremony, they simply represent silence or control in thought, word and deed. The physical shock which their use accords may be given by the water and oil; a worthwhile action, since the shock is useful in clearing the mind. What shock? you ask, correctly, for I have not yet told you. The answer is simple; rather than stabbing, scourging and binding yourself, take your cupped hands, dip them in your wide brimmed cup and douse your head with the contents of the cup of flesh thus formed saying:

"The lustral water smite thy flood, through me, lymph, marrow and blood."

Then take the oil, smear some on your finger (the choice of finger I leave to the operator's ingeniuum) and draw the sigil of NOX on your brow, saying:

"The fire informing let the oil, balance, assain, assoil."

The shock from the rush of cold water over the head and down your spine and the heat of the Abramelin oil burning a hole in your forehead is quite adequate, and will leave fewer questions to answer at your next medical than the multiple lacerations and stab wounds resulting from too literal a reading of the text as handed down to us.

Obviously, in the use of such methods it is best to either work naked or wearing the simplest of robes, open at the front and as loose fitting as possible without slipping off the shoulders. Over elaborate dress and headgear is best avoided, since large amounts of saline water is likely to ruin your coiffure, let alone masonic silks!

4). The Statement of Intention. If possible, this should contain the appropriate Divine Names and/or sections of E.'.Q.'. "cut-up" harmonious to the ritual intent. These should be incorporated into a clear and concise statement of the purpose of the ritual. It may well be advisable to incorporate some means of establishing your authority in the matter, for instance giving the signs and words of your grade and those preceding it. If this is not applicable, then some indication of the necessity of the ritual can be made instead, such as pointing out that it is necessary to your spiritual advancement (particularly as an adjunct to the obtaining of Knowledge and Conversation of your Holy Guardian Angel). The use of a talisman may be appropriate here, or alternatively in the Charge to the Spirit.

5). The Invocations. It is almost invariably the case that the best commencement to the invocations is the so-called "Preliminary Invocation of the Goetia", or, as it is colloquially known, The Bornless Rite. This ritual is so important that I have dedicated an entire article to it in Equinox/B.J.T. 6. The reasons for its pre-eminence are manifold, not least being that it gets you "tuned-up" for ritual work, and thoroughly tones up the esoteric muscles. Following on from this invocation come the appropriate chapters from the Treasure House of Images and/or other spells, such as the E.'.Q.'. "cut-ups" and so forth. This subject is too involved for thorough analysis here, but it is worth observing that of the many invocations Crowley undertook, the most interesting in many respects are those that involved either a human being as the material basis or utilised a seer or seeress.

6). The Charge to the Spirit. Whether or not the operation involves a strictly defined summoning of a spirit, angel or intelligence etc., the Charge is a necessary adjunct to any ritual. It may well take the form of a talisman, or alternatively a sigil. In this case, obviously, the talisman is an indication in precise terms of what you require from the ceremony. In which case, you ask, why include it, having done pretty much that in the initial statement of intent? The answer, so well as I can frame it, is this: the statement said why you were going to perform this ritual in the first place - it is essentially a passive phase of the rite itself. The Charge is the focus of the active phase of the ritual. The word "Charge" actually implies rather neatly the very function of this phase of the ceremony. To charge something is to endow it with power (charging a battery, laying an explosive charge), or to apply power (charging with your cavalry) - alternatively to charge is to demand payment. All these associations are apt. We endow things with power in order that they can serve us, as we desire this spirit or invoked energy to do. We lay an explosive charge in order to remove something that impedes us or creates problems in other ways, as we wish the result of this ceremony to do. To charge the enemy is to dispose of them (ideally), in much the same way as an explosive charge does. To charge for something is to exact compensation for a service, which is also apt for our analogy, for the incense and whatever else employed in the ritual has been largely for the benefit of "the gods" or spirits, who presumably asked us to behave in this manner originally. We have done so, now we want something from them in return. All considered the term is appropriate **whether or not we actually summon a spirit**, for the energy raised by the rite is now to be turned to a purpose, and that purpose needs stating now, as it did at the beginning, in order to balance the ritual and to produce an effect.

7). The final Banishings. This will include a licence to depart in the case of a full invocation or even simply an implied invitation to a spirit. The best form for general use is: "Depart in peace unto thine habitations and be there ever peace between thee and me evermore, and be thou ever ready to come when thou art called, either by a word, or by a will, or by these sacred rites of magick." Alternatively, if no spirit was invoked, or just for variety, we might say: "I hereby bid to depart all spirits which may have been entrapped by the performance of these rites, and be there....(etc. as before)". This precedes the final banishings.

With the Sun-Venus and other rites of a peculiarly holy nature, it is not desirable to banish, either before or after the ritual. In the case of the preliminary banishings, if it is deemed necessary to prepare the place we will do so in advance; the full celebration of the Liber Yod "Megabanishing" might be the best course, and afterwards leave the Temple for a day or two. In any case we will enter the temple shortly before the rite begins and light incense, both to dispel the smell of camphor if Yod was performed, and also to set the tone for the rite. Anyway, this preliminary censing is not a bad idea as it avoids asphyxiating the celebrants and interfering with the use of the voice. This is especially the case if any of your group or yourself are of the large class of asthmatic occultists. The use of incense during the ritual will be fairly sparse, and depending on the nature of the rite quite possibly will not include actual burning of ingredients, simply warming of essential oils. In rituals where a concrete result is called for, it may be that actual burning is necessary; in this case it is well to be prepared for the fumes that will ensue. Water for the throat (as well as the possibility of fire - precautions are best taken before rather than after - be warned, ecstatic priestesses really cannot see candles, and on occasion exalted priests don't know their robes are on fire!) should be on hand, likewise asthma inhalers and so on should they be needful. Do not be concerned that these things will detract from the atmosphere of the ritual. It is more likely that the atmosphere will detract from the ritual if these precautions are omitted!

The idea of balance is inherent in this structure from the word go. We begin and end with a banishing, and we precede and conclude the invocations with the Statement of Intent and its complement the Charge. The whole pattern of the ritual can be laid out in a diagram. The appropriate geometric figures representing each stage are as follows. Banishing by a pentagram for obvious reasons. Purifying by a downwards pointing triangle, the symbol of water. Consecrating by an upwards pointing triangle, the symbol of fire. The statement of intent by a square or rectangle, the shape of a piece of paper, for this section of the rite is usually a written document (not a pact, but a document nevertheless), for as we said earlier, the ritual must be necessary, and as such subject to law, and thus to the idea of contracts etc. The Invocations by a Hexagram, both because the use of Hexagrams is synonymous with the act of invoking a particular force (the Hexagram of Venus is used in an invocation of Venus etc.) and because it represents the meeting of the higher and lower worlds. The Charge by a square or rectangle, in that it is essentially like the Statement on another level. The License to depart and final banishings by another pentagram. These symbols have collectively thirty points, which in Hebrew Qabalah àla Golden Dawn represents the idea of Justice and thus of Balance. In English

Qaballa thirty is the number of WILL, the English meaning of Thelema.

This "balanced will" is the best structure for nearly every purpose, but there are exceptions. We have mentioned the Sun-Venus; now let us look at its structure.

The Sun-Venus Ritual

The celebrants enter the temple, which is prepared well in advance in accordance with certain general requirements. It is banished, purified and consecrated before the actual ceremony, since to imply that the Goddess invoked was not present already, and that whether She was or not She needed a good wash and brush up is hardly polite, let alone appropriate. Accordingly we enter the temple, which is sweet scented, warm to stifling in temperature and very comfortable - cushions etc. litter the floor in the area to be occupied by the celebrants, and a throne is positioned in either the South or West. In the South if the ritual is intended to be initiatory (this is more appropriate in theory to a Sun-Mars, but theory and practice are two different things: the Sun-Venus creates the cult into which we are initiated, and is a less painful approach to the group than the pressures of the Sun-Mars), and West if it is intended as an act of worship (and heaven help those who avoid the idea of worship due to some cock-a-mamey pseudo-intellectual objection to religiosity). So far, so good, the ritual is devoid of **integral** banishings, purifications and consecrations. Where does it start then if not with our supposed sections one, two and three? The answer of course is with the Book of the Law: "Let the rituals be rightly performed with joy and beauty!" declares the high priest, and the rite is underway.

Having opened thus unconventionally, we leap to stage four, the statement of intent, which in this case should be extraordinarily simple. "We, the sisters and brothers of the .... Temple of the .... are come hither to celebrate the conjunction of our Lord the Sun and Our Lady Venus". There, wasn't that easy? So what next? Straight to section five, the Bornless Rite. Do we then proceed with the other invocations? No, we do not, the whole outlined above breaks down here as well as at the beginning. At this point, the Priest concludes his Invocation and the High Priestess stands. (It may be that the Priest has asked: "Is any Sister willing to offer her body as the vehicle of the Goddess?" it may be otherwise.) She advances to the throne and performs the Ceremony of the Opening of the Vault of the Adepti. In a nutshell, that is, she performs the essential part of the hexagram ritual "I.N.R.I...." etc. up to and including the Opening of the Veil; she then takes her seat in the throne, and closes the veil behind her. Of course there is no physical veil; that would seriously interfere with what is to follow. Incidentally, it is considered bad form in E.'.Q.'. Lodges to use the Hebrew forms of the letters I.N.R.I., and there are slightly different forms of this ceremony in such places as "Secret Rituals of the O.T.O." if you want to dig about. It is not considered bad form (by the powerful ruling oligarchy anyway!) to use the initials INRI or indeed on occasion the name of Christ. If anyone objects to this minor deviancy, which I am not disposed to justify at length, then allow me to point out that while the name "Jehovah" does not appear openly anywhere in the Class A, Jesus and Mary most certainly do, and that is enough authority for me. Besides which, the ultimate secret of (O.T.O.) sex-magick is intimately bound up with the idea of the Christian Trinity, so I am told, so let's not quibble. If you want to interpret INRI as standing for something other than Jesus of Nazareth King of the Jews, that is fine, but do not interfere with the essential shape of the ritual.

I shall now return to the analysis of this pre-eminent ritual. We omitted (or rather sneaked in) the first three sections of our skeletonic structure; we then went to stage four and half way into five, and the pattern broke down. What next? Back to part five, the adoration of the enthroned Priestess and the Invocation of the Goddess into her body. What the Priestess has done is to dedicate her body to this purpose. Any resemblance to the Gnostic Mass is coincidental, simply showing that even born-again Freemasons can't be wrong all the time! The invocations are best kept rhythmic and "nonsensical". By nonsensical I do not mean actual gobbledy-gook, but something "full of sound and fury, signifying nothing"; the best and most appropriate script for this stage of the rite is to be found in Liber 963, the Treasure House of Images. Use the sections appropriate to the Signs occupied by the Sun, Venus and any other planets involved if there are any. The Ascendant at the start of the ritual (generally either Cancer, Libra or Taurus, although an excellent case could be made for Pisces) can be commemorated by the appropriate chapter, and finally the 169 Cries of Adoration. These may be read by the priest and any other person present. If the Priestess herself wishes to read one, then don't try and stop her, so long as she does it first, and leaves the 169 to someone else.

The next stage, annoyingly enough, may well overlap with the one just discussed. It consists of the High Priest invoking from scratch, not memorised and certainly not read from paper, simply from the heart. This is in line with an injunction from Liber AL: "Invoking me with a pure heart and the serpent flame therein." It is also good psychology, in many respects, since to read aloud to an incarnate Goddess does not show much ingenuity, and also interferes with the prime directive of the entire rite once the Priestess is on the throne no-one, **but no-one,** takes their eyes off her. Eye to eye contact is preferable, but if she is looking at someone else, you still keep looking at her! This injunction of course does not mean that the Chapters of the Treasure House of Images need to be committed to memory in their entirety, the reader is allowed to look at the page! However, once the UN chant has begun, and the readings are over the eye to eye contact is essential for all, including the invocant, in fact him in particular.

So, we have dealt with the various stages of the ritual from the banishings through to the invocation. What of the Charge to the Spirit? That is largely in the hands of the Invoking Priest. He will know where the ritual is intended to go, and if he is right (for the Goddess and/or the ritual may have ideas of their own) then the Charge will generally take the form of that intention being actualised. By this we mean, for example, that if he intends the Priestess to visit some particular region of the Astral Plane then he will take her there; and if he has some intention, having got her there, then that too will be actualised. In other cases, such as ritual union, the Charge will take the form of a change of mantra from UN to YES.

There will be no final banishing in this ritual; the concluding words will be simply: "The ending of the words is the Word Abrahadabra."

So in this case, the sevenfold structure of what we may call a "general ritual" is not sufficient, although there is little deviation from the pattern. What deviation there is is enough to show that such a structure is not fixed; it is there to be useful, not to present us with obstacles. For a comprehensive guide to these various stages of ritual, we direct the reader's attention to Crowley's master work "Magick".

The magical ideas presented in this section, particularly the remarks concerning Liber Pyramidos, should be carefully compared with the ideas mentioned in the section on Qaballistic meditation. The ability to perform these rituals at least partly in the Astral Body, in and out of group contexts, is of the very first importance.

To give an idea of how this ritual structure works out in practice, I give an example of such a rite broken down into these seven sections. This ritual is rather a tour-de-force, involving several different strands; it was performed early in 1991, and was very effective both in terms of its performance and the result.

Invocation of Venus and Jupiter.

Preliminaries: The Banishings were performed by means of the Pentagram ritual starting: "O Glory be unto Thee...." as above. The Purifications were performed by the Azure Lidded Woman ritual with the words "For pure will..." by the Officer of the West, governing the works of Water. The Consecrations were performed with the oil; there being four officers present, each took a quarter and was marked upon the brow, with the words: "Azure Lidded Woman", then the officer retired to the centre for the words: "I am uplifted...".

Here followed an amended form of the Mark of the Beast Ritual, as follows:

I. The Elevenfold Seal.

Standing in the centre of the Temple, facing East; a gong is sounded, thus: 1-3-3-3-1.

The Vertical Component: with the right thumb between the first and second fingers, the fist closed, make these gestures with the "point" of the thumb:

1. A circle about the head, crying **NUITI**

2. Drawing thumb down to groin (Muladhara), crying **HADITI**

3. Retracing to breast, crying **RA-HOOR-KHUITI**

The Horizontal Component: using full-span of the outstretched hand:

1. Touching forehead, mouth and larynx, crying **AIWAZI**

2. Tracing thumb from right to left across face at level of nostrils.

3. Touching centre of breast and solar plexus, crying **FIATI**

4. Tracing thumb from left to right across breast at sternum level.

5. Touch Svaddisthana and Muladhara, crying **BABALONI**

6. Trace thumb from right to left across abdomen at hip level.

The Asseveration of Spells: clasp hands upon wand with fingers and thumbs interlaced, crying:

THE BEAST! BAPHOMET! BES-NA-MAUT! FIVE WOUNDS! SCARLET WOMAN!

Strike the gong 3-5-3.

II. The Enchantment

During circumambulations, pause every time a planetary position is passed, giving the Sign of the Enterer - right foot advanced, both arms reaching forwards, with fingers and thumbs pointing forwards - towards the planet, in this instance Venus and Jupiter.

1. Advance to circumference of circle.

2. Turn left and circumambulate anti-clockwise until the direction of the first fixed sign is reached. (The position in the circle which most closely approximates to the position of the sign at the time of the ritual.)

3. Perform the appropriate elemental pentagram etc. (see below) for the sign.

4. Continue circumambulation three quarter circle and perform appropriate actions.

5. Continue circumambulation three quarter circle and perform appropriate actions.

6. Continue circumambulation three quarter circle and perform appropriate actions as above. (These are: for Taurus, the invoking Pentagram of Earth, the Name FIAT, and the Sign Vir; for Leo, the invoking Pentagram of Fire, the Name APEP, the Sign Puer; for Scorpio, the invoking Pentagram of Water, the Name BABALON and the Sign Mulier, and for Aquarius, the invoking Pentagram of Air, the Name AIWAZ and the sign Puella. These signs are to be invoked in the order in which they are reached; i.e., if the rite is done with Libra rising (East), the first of these four to be reached travelling anticlockwise from the East will be Leo, then Taurus, then Aquarius and finally Scorpio.)

7. Spiral anticlockwise into centre*, spinning clockwise on one's own axis. Halt facing the position of the fastest moving planet in the configuration (Venus in this case). * Since in the case of a group rite this would lead to collisions, and in any case not all could occupy the centre, it is suggested that in group ritual the spiral be replaced by a circle dance anticlockwise whilst spinning clockwise.

8. Raising wand, trace Unicursal Hexagram overhead.

9. Give the Sign of Mater Triumphans (feet together, left arm across breast as if supporting a child, with right hand pinching left nipple), then strike the ground with the wand (or hand), crying out whatever E.'.Q.'. spell is most appropriate to the intention and nature of the rite.

10. Here perform whatever ritual actions are appropriate to the planets and intention.

(8 to 10. The celebrants of our example rite ended their spiral dance, striking the ground and crying "BALANCED POWER AND JOY!" The officer responsible for the Mark of the Beast - the one making the gestures and Pentagrams et al - formulated the Hexagram, all gave the sign. This part of the ritual corresponds to our "Statement of Intent". Its effect is to "fix" the power of the planets invoked, creating a Universe in which the conditions required exist. The statement then may be very brief, and if possible should consist of a qaballistically generated phrase. BALANCED POWER AND JOY has the value 214 = VENUS + JUPITER, also interestingly enough, 2 x 107; = SUN + VENUS, see also SOL INVICTUS = 143 = JUPITER.

11. If only one magician is present, dance clockwise, spinning anticlockwise back out to the East.

The invocations were inserted at the accomplishment of this stage of the Mark of the Beast. Two Priests were involved with this, one to recite the E.'.Q.'. spell composed of words and phrases having the four values attributed to Venus (the fastest moving planet) in the Tables of A.M.E.N., the other to make the Hexagrams of Jupiter and Venus in the quarters with the Names from the Tables of A.M.E.N., i.e. for Jupiter: East = ASAR+ISA; South = SET; West = HADIT; North = SOL INVICTUS. For Venus: East NUIT; South = ABRAHADABRA; West = TITAN; North = IO PAN.

> "By the Fire of APEP and the Lion Roar of His voice!
> I invoke Thee NUIT - ye are my star, all power to it!
> I invoke Thee by ASAR & ISA & HOOR!
> I invoke Thee, lithe fantasy, all power to Thee!
> I shall behold all power in Her display!
> I see all power in Her display!
>
> Thou art heaven - the white yonder - seven thou art of roses and signs, seven in song, ritual, and some higher ritual. ABRAHADABRA!
>
> I invoke Thee by the seal of the bride - by the scents and the words and the cubic throne of the images!
>
> I invoke Thee TITAN thou breath of scents, I invoke Thee that knowest thou art Lord Khem - myself no more - IO PAN!
>
> I invoke Thee Lady Maat by the Pillars and the Tower, by the sheer pearls of naught about the limbs of Venus, her glamour slaying hearts!"

In order to allow sufficient time for the Hexagrams to be drawn in the four quarters, this spell was said twice; no other attempt at synchronisation is necessary.

This invocation was followed by The Hymn to Pan, accompanied by the sound of spears clashing ("MUSIC OF MY SPEARS" = 214 = VENUS + JUPITER). This produced a splendid ritualistic atmosphere, the metal of the spear heads, and the wood of the shafts producing an "ethnic cum industrial music" sound which seemed very conducive to the ritual. This idea, of generating ritual **actions** from the gematrias has frequently produced startling effects, and is well worth the attention of the ritualist using E.'.Q.'..

Another E.'.Q.'. spell followed here, composed of phrases with the value 214. This was the first part of the Charge to the Spirit. The second part consisted of all four participants assuming the Death Posture and visualising a sigil composed of the combined runes of O and H, the letters of Venus and Jupiter (7 & 4 in E.'.Q.'.)

The cue for the end of the rite consisted of the final words from the Mass of the Phoenix: "I entered in with woe, with mirth and with thanksgiving I now go forth, to do my pleasure on the earth among the legions of the living."

Then came the conclusion of the Mark of the Beast:

12. Step into the centre, and once again perform the Elevenfold Seal, omitting the statement of ritual intention, and adding cymbal or bell chimes 3-5-3, and the word **ABRAHADABRA!** (Taking the place of the phrase "The ending of the words is the word Abrahadabra!")

This outline shows how a simple skeletonic structure can be used to generate a ritual of great sophistication and power. The end result here was not only "classical" but great fun to perform. The principle of "Energised Enthusiasm" is hard to improve on! There is more to ritual than mere structure. The ritual should be appropriate to the force invoked, either in symbol or in mood or both. There is no point invoking the god of generosity in a temple which is freezing and frugally furnished. Equally, there is no point invoking the Goddess of Love if you don't feel in the least romantic or at least cheerful and well disposed towards the opposite sex! If these appropriate feelings are absent, learn to feel how you want to feel or need to feel. Of course, if the ritual is conducive to generating or encouraging these feelings, all the better!

There are important considerations which lift magick to the level of an Art. This is the alchemical aspect of ritual, and should not be neglected. When one invokes the benefics - with or without a luminary, and preferably in conjunction - you should preserve something of the ritual. This occasion is one when the powers are well-disposed towards you, so of course it is reasonable that you want to keep a chunk of all that well being about the place. Having realised this, it is a logical next step to think, why not accumulate something from one ritual to the next, continually, keeping the essence of ritual after ritual. A talisman, of course, perpetuates the energy of a particular rite, and if reconsecrated accumulates energy from one rite to the next, but only rituals of similar character, for a talisman is a passive participant in the ritual. In order to accumulate the energy of - for example - **all** aspects of the benefics & luminaries, the "vessel" needs to actively participate in the rite. As we are talking alchemy here, it is as well to come out and say what I think is the best idea, as so few alchemists do. Briefly, there should be a sacrament of wine, if not of food as well, at each such ritual. In these rites it is customary for the Priestess to consume the last of the wine in the chalice. So how do you keep some of it if she has consumed the last drop? Easily! A phial, dipped in the wine as it goes round, after it has been consecrated, and then firmly stoppered until the next rite when the benefics are invoked. Then, you empty the phial into the wine at the same point in the proceedings, and refill it at the same time. In this way, the lodge consumes the essence of the rites that have preceded this one, and renew the accumulated force of the sacrament that is retained. A very powerful elixir is thus kept in constant renewal, but losing nothing of the aspects it has been consecrated at previously. If one compares the theory of homeopathic medicine it will be seen instantly that this is the case; though the dose that remains from previous rites is minute compared to the quantity of the new wine in which it has been diluted, it is nevertheless "omnipresent". The principle of homeopathy was expressed to me as "the smallest possible particle obsessing the entire medium" - whoso gives one particle of dust? This feature of the ritual is so important that I am at a loss to emphasise it enough. Remember that Nuit is the "Continuous one"; this is the real distinction between Astrological Magick and haphazard sorcery - the continuity of the rituals, the alchemical quality of the entire process, and the elasticity of the hierarchy of the planets. All astrological magick is worship of NUIT by its very nature. Try and understand these points, and realise quite how much magick depends on these elements to become organic and continuous, rather than, as is so often the case, an uphill skating race.

JSK.

INTRODUCING THE WAKANABA KAMEA EXTRAPOLATOR!

The following material is the result of the author's anal retentive involvement with magick squares, barbarous tongues and other peculiarities of the Grimoire Tradition. The results are spectacular in many ways, not least being the ease of pronunciation of the barbarous language which results from the technique, and the inexhaustible quantity of "custom derived" words, and indeed entire incantations, which may be obtained with the minimum of industry by the magician or sorcerer who is stumped for a really mean and utterly original incantation for every conceivable occasion.

The Wakanaba Kamea Extrapolator is a refinement on the magick squares derived from the "Counting Well" technique (see EQUINOX-BJT passim), designed to turn each sub-square into a syllable, and combining these into lines of incantation; then proceeding to apply the same technique to the value of each column to provide the second "verse" of the incantation, and the value of the entire square into a Grand Word or Name which is placed at the end of each verse.

The method is as follows: every number in a magick square represents either a letter in the range 1 to 26, or, in the case of higher numbers, a combination of letters. These letters are then rendered pronounceable by the simple device of supplying every consonant but L with a vowel, on the following pattern:

    W K N B receive an A, (thus "WAKANABA")
    H V Y M receive an O,
    S G J X receive an U,
    D R F T receive an I,
    Z C Q P receive an E.

Whenever a number equivalent to a vowel occurs (i.e. 7 = O etc.) it is given an L, thus O = OL. When the number 2 appears (either by itself, or as part of a number higher than 26) it becomes LA. Double numbers are halved, i.e. 44 becomes HO not HO-HO; this may not hold good for the column values which as we will see produce altogether different words, though retaining the virtue of easy pronunciation. The final rule is that zero when it appears in numbers higher than 26 is treated as if a 7, for fairly obvious reasons.

An example of the entire technique follows, from a square published in an earlier issue of this Journal. The square was derived from the words BLACK/STONE counted well together. The use to which this may be put is determined in this case by the numerical value 600, interpreted as extending the Law (LAW = 6) into the Three Worlds (three digit number). So having ascertained the purpose of the rite, we can go on from the talismanic square to the qaballistic incantation:

```
25  44  27  34  45 = EL HE LE WA-HO HO-SU
 7  26   9  16  27 = OL PE KA JU LO
 6  25   8  15  26 = DI EL ZE YU PE
18  37  20  27  38 = FI WO BA LO WAZE
14  33  16  23  34 = NA WA JU IL WA-HO.
```

70 165 80 115 170 gives us OLOL ALDISU ZE-OL ALALSU ALOLOL.

600 provides us with the Great Word: DIOL-OL.

Rationalising these expressions to personal taste, we would end up with an incantation as follows:

a) ELHOLO WAHO HOSU, OLPEKA JULO, DI ELZE YUPEI FI-WO BALOWAZE; NAWA JUILWA-HOI - DIOL-OLI

b) OL-OL ALDISU ZE-OL ALALSU ALOL-OL: DIOL-OL!

                                                                                                                TAU MAGNUS

THE CIPHER OF AL.

AL.II.76. "4 6 3 8 ABK 2 4 ALGMOR 3 Y X (24) (89) RPSTOVAL. What meaneth this, o prophet? Thou knowest not; nor shalt thou know ever. There cometh one to follow thee: he shall expound it. But remember, o chosen one, to be me; to follow the love of Nu in the star-lit heaven; to look forth upon men, to tell them this glad word."

The solution of the cipher of II.76 has been a perennial problem of Thelemic Qaballism ever since AL was dictated to Aleister Crowley by Aiwass in 1904. To put this in perspective, let us quote from some of Crowley's various commentaries on this enigmatic verse: "A final revelation. The revealer to come is perhaps the one mentioned in I.55. and III.47. The verse goes on to urge the prophet to identify himself with Hadit, to practice the union with Nu, and to proclaim this joyful revelation unto men."

"Verse 76 appears to be a Qabalistic test (on the regular pattern) of any person who may claim to be the magical heir of the Beast. Be ye well assured all, that the solution, when it is found will be unquestionable. It will be marked by the most sublime simplicity, and carry immediate conviction".

Of first importance are the qualifiers: "perhaps" and "appears to be". Certainly AL mentions a "child of thy bowels", "his child and that strangely" and "one to follow thee", and other cryptic references of like sort. In what sense this individual could be said to be Crowley's successor is rather a moot point. Indeed, are we justified in assuming these references relate to one individual?

There is then the question of "a Qabalistic test (on the regular pattern)". What is the regular pattern? Or rather what, if anything, did Crowley suppose it to be? There is no such pattern blazingly apparent in the G.'.D.'. tradition, for example, which has to be considered Crowley's main "influence" in such matters. The only outstanding example of a cipher in the G.'.D.'. tradition is the rather crude "Cipher MS" from which their rites and Anna Sprengel's address were allegedly translated. This cipher is of such a transparently simplistic nature as to exclude serious comparison with II.76. The analogy drawn between II.76 and the rim of the Sigillum Aemeth elsewhere in this issue might be just, but the methods employed in relation to the Seal are not "marked by the most sublime simplicity". The "Bacon cipher" style manipulations involved in extrapolating the Names of the Great Elemental Kings, or the Sigils of the Vast and Mighty Overseer Angels, from the Enochian Watchtowers and the Seal of Truth can hardly be said to "carry immediate conviction" to most sane persons.

The only such "regular patterns" which are truly comparable are to be found in Graves' "White Goddess". In this work Graves portrays the complex and jumbled clues to the nature of various ritual alphabets of antiquity. (That some of his work is pseudo-historical is not germane here.) The riddling alphabetical mysteries he describes do not resemble II.76 much either. However, the legendary characters who have solved such riddles have achieved religious status of one sort or another, and the nature of their solutions might very well be taken as indicative of II.76's significance. Whatever Crowley may have meant by a "Qabalistic test (on the regular pattern)", it seems to me the only useful attitude to take is that the test is not of a person, but of a potential "English Qaballa". If there can be found to be a close relationship between the structure of the qaballistic alphabet and II.76, then the test's primary conditions will have been met. Here the comparison with "The Song of Amergin" riddle, described by Graves, becomes more appropriate, since in that story whoever unjumbles the verses and explains the ambiguities discovers <u>the order of the alphabet</u>.

It seems obvious to me that no solution whatsoever will be self-evident to all. Imagine two Thelemites agreeing on any matter of even half the apparent significance of this verse! Add to this difficulty the fact that the person whose solution is deemed to be correct is "entitled" to the "dignity" of being recognised as Crowley's successor and the scope for contention is magnified not twice but a thousandfold. Crowley believed at least for a time that the child was Frater Achad, who discovered not the English Qaballa, but a significant key word which produced some intriguing results when applied to some of AL's puzzles. This word was AL, from which the Book of the Law (formerly "L") takes its present technical name. It is my belief that this keyword was more significant than Achad or Crowley realised, being in fact "the key of it all" or rather "the key of it: AL". The problem was that the key was not placed in the lock, the lock being the ordinary order of the English Alphabet.

We turn now to the discovery of E.'.Q.'. and its relationship to certain frameworks found in the manuscript of AL itself. The "order & value" was discovered by an esoteric Order in the U.K. who had magically sought it out. They ritualised their intention to discover it and set to work to do so. First they came up with ABC = 1 2 3 etc. and various other dead ends. These they ritually burnt, and soon after one of them noted that counting eleven letters from A we obtain L, thus AL. This process was continued until the order ALWHSDOZKVGRCNYJUFQBMXITEP was "obtained". So far, so good; next they turned to the mysterious grid on sheet 16 of AL III. In the manuscript of AL. There are two ways of writing the alphabet on this grid, down or across. If we go across we get:

```
A B C D E F G H
I J K L M N O P
Q R S T U V W X
Y Z A B C D E F
G H I J K L M N
O P Q R S T U V
W X Y Z A B C D
E F G H I J K L
M N O P Q R S T
U V W X Y Z A B
```

The diagonals give an order well known to numerologists:

```
1 2 3 4 5 6 7 8 9
A B C D E F G H I
J K L M N O P Q R
S T U V W X Y Z
```

This order and value does not produce any particularly useful or interesting results when applied to AL, but it is curious that the grid should produce such a recognisable pattern. Now look at what happens when we write the alphabet down the grid:

```
A K U E O Y I S
B L V F P Z J T
C M W G Q A K U
D N X H R B L V
E O Y I S C M W
F P Z J T D N X
G Q A K U E O Y
H R B L V F P Z
I S C M W G Q A
J T D N X H R B
```

The diagonals give ALWHSDOZKVGRCNYJUFQBMXITEP. Note that diagonals ascending from the left side of the grid give the AJS order, and that the other grid gives ALW in alternate diagonal squares upwards.

More curious still, there are 2 geometrical stars of 26 points which convert ABC into ALW and vice versa, and two stars that produce AJS and vice versa, and a fifth that creates and uncreates a third order, AFK. The AJS is a ninefold progression, the ALW an elevenfold and the AFK a fivefold progression. The AFK order requires "knight's moves" to be formed on the grid as it exists in AL. Unfortunately, I do not know for certain where or why the AJS order originates in "traditional" numerology, although Regardie and/or the G.'.D.'. have been credited with it. I have seen work with a grid one line shorter than this, which creates 3, 5, 7 and 9 fold sequences of letters, but since only the grid on sheet 16 creates the elevenfold order, since it possesses many curious properties and since this is the form used in AL, these "alternatives" remain at best curiosities.

While there may be some significance to these other orders, they are significant only by relation to the elevenfold order. An example of this shared significance is the fact that all such "cipher alphabets" give the same numerical value to the name ISIS. There has been a certain amount of work done by various parties with these alternative orders, but none has produced results as significant as the ALW order. This is to some extent the fault of the experimenters, who have flawed their findings by using their pseudo-ciphers on words which are a) outside AL and the Holy Books, and b) outside the English Language! Such words as Yesod and Aleph hardly require an English Qaballa for amplification. If there is any significance to these ciphers it remains to be shown. Whereas, at the very least, the elevenfold order has reconstructed the ancient art of magical astrology. The exposition includes some details so well hidden in the past that they formed the basis of some of the most esoteric practices - and the methodology and even the names of the most hidden occult societies - in known history!

So much for the nature and structure of the cipher, the alphabet and the matter of the grid of sheet sixteen of Chapter III. in the manuscript of AL. It falls to me now to describe the relations between II.76 and E.'.Q.'..

Applying E.'.Q.'. to II.76 we obtain the total value of 351. This number has some interesting entries in Crowley's Hebrew "Sepher Sephiroth" which we will leave to the reader to seek out. What is more significant for our purposes (for I dislike comparisons between Qaballas, even in cases as fundamental as this) is the fact that 351 is the sum of the numbers 1 to 26, the number of letters in the English Alphabet, and consequently of the values attributed to the letters. Thus is established a close connection between II.76 and E.'.Q.'. by simple addition.

If we consult the manuscript of AL and examine II.76 we find that the cipher is in two lines, thus:

4 6 3 8 ABK 2 4 ALGMOR 3 Y

X (24) (89) RPSTOVAL.

The first line consists of seventeen numbers and letters, the second of eleven. If we multiply 17 by 11, as suggested perhaps by the x at the beginning of line two, we obtain 187. This is the value of the phrase ENGLISH ALPHABET (from AL II.55), and also of the words FOUR ONE EIGHT. This is indeed significant, since by the first method, addition, we obtained the value of the series 1 to 26, and here, by a curious "coincidence", we obtain by multiplication the name of the series.

The cipher demonstrates mathematically the veracity of English Qaballa. However, there are other curious properties of this string of numbers and "words", as will be demonstrated below. The more abstruse development of this material is not "marked by the most sublime simplicity", it may not "carry immediate conviction", but it has shown itself to be of remarkable value, and may yet prove to be the most important aspect of E.'.Q.'..

Let's begin with some simple gematria. Crowley's commentary to II.76 includes the preceding verse II.75: "Aye, listen to the numbers & the words." LISTEN = 93, whilst NUMBERS & THE WORDS = 200. The verse in its entirety adds to 418. This, as we have seen elsewhere, is the number of LIBRA + SCORPIO + SAGITTARIUS + CAPRICORN. It is also, in Thelemic Tradition, the number of the Great Work, as well as the value of ABRAHADABRA when spelt with Hebrew letters by Crowley, and of ABRA % HADABRA in E.'.Q.'., and as seen above, the words FOUR ONE EIGHT are equivalent by gematria to the phrase ENGLISH ALPHABET. For now let us simply bear in mind the numbers 93 and 200 in relation to the astrological factors Libra and Scorpio.

$4 + 6 + 3 + 8 + A + B + K + 2 + 4 + A = 58$ = LIBRA, HADIT, etc.

$L + G + M + O + R + 3 + Y + X = 93$ = SCORPIO, DIVIDE, TIME, TAHUTI, etc.

$(24) + (89) + R + P + S + T + O + V + A + L = 200$ = MANIFESTATION.

What we have here is two sets of ten, one balanced (LIBRA) and unmanifest (HADIT), the other manifested (MANIFESTATION) in the realm of duality (200). These two are divided (DIVIDE) by 93. The Name TAHUTI in this context is more than a little reminiscent of the G.'.D.'. documents (echoed in Pyramidos and Israfel) entitled "The General and Particular Exordium". Before turning to these, it is worth remembering where Tahuti's name occurs in the Class A, AL.II.39: "A feast for Tahuti and the child of the Prophet - secret, O Prophet." This, of course, is a reference to the "one to follow thee." Now let us turn to the G.'.D.'. documents aforementioned; which I shall quote in their entirety. The passages of special relevance are in bold type.

<u>The General Exordium</u>

"The Speech in the Silence:
The Words against the Son of Night;
The Voice of Thoth before the Universe in the presence of the eternal Gods;
The Formulas of Knowledge;
The Wisdom of Breath;
The Radix of Vibration;
The Shaking of the Invisible;
The Rolling Asunder of the Darkness;
The Becoming Visible of Matter;
The Piercing of the Coils of the Stooping Dragon;

153

The Breaking forth of the Light;
All these are in the Knowledge of Tho-oth."

The Particular Exordium

"At the Ending of the Night,
At the Limits of the Light,
Tho-oth stood before the Unborn Ones of Time!
Then was formulated the Universe;
Then came forth the Gods thereof,
The Aeons of the Bornless Beyond;
Then was the Voice vibrated;
Then was the Name declared.

At the Threshold of the Entrance,
Between the Universe and the Infinite,
In the Sign of the Enterer, stood Tho-oth,
As before him were the Aeons proclaimed.
In Breath did he vibrate them;
In Symbols did he record them;

For betwixt the Light and the Darkness did he stand."

It is perhaps unnecessary to remark that Thoth/Tho-oth is identical with Tahuti. These documents form the basis of the G.'.D.'.'s cosmogony and "creation myth", so that it is quite startling to find II.76, an apparently meaningless string of letters and numbers, echoing them quite so forcibly.

The Universe is of course represented by 200 = MANIFESTATION, whilst the Infinite is Fifty-**Eight**. II.76 accordingly represents Two "Trees" separated by 93. The first Tree is the Unmanifest World, perfect, balanced and "Bornless". The second Tree is the "Tree of Life" as we generally understand the term. This is quite in accord with old Kabbalistic tradition, since before Malkuth came into being Da'ath was an actual Sephiroth. It is the falling of Da'ath that creates Malkuth. The Lodge of the A.'.A.'. responsible for the discovery of E.'.Q.'. went a great deal further than this in their exegesis of II.76. In order to understand what is to follow, the student will need to be wide awake, and possessed of considerable qaballistic "savvy". Rather than try and explain the hermeneutic processes used, I will simply give the material as it stands. As said above, this material is by no means self-explanatory. I shall simply have to presume that enough material of interest has been laid before the reader to convince you that the effort of coming to grips with what is to follow is effort well spent.

If we have to LISTEN (=93) to the numbers and the words, how are we going to go about it? Mumbling this string of letters and numbers as a mantra is not particularly productive, so what else can we do? The rationale of the qaballists who first discovered E.'.Q.'., and set to work on the by no means enviable task of clarifying II.76, seems to have been: since some mathematical process is certainly implied by this "Qabalistic test (on the regular pattern)", we can add 93 = LISTEN to the various numbers and letters. Whilst the results are not immediately self-explanatory, they do have a certain internal consistency. By this I mean that the values thus obtained recur in our study of the Class A texts with E.'.Q.'. in places of critical importance, so that we are more ready to admit the importance of their discoveries, even if - separated in time and understanding as we are - we do not altogether understand how these calculations and decisions came to be made in the first place. As the historian of the birth of a Qaballistic system, my task is, like theirs, unenviable. It is also, one concedes, a unique and indeed a privileged position. But I digress.

So: applying E.'.Q.'. to II.76 we get:

```
4 6 3 8 ABK 2 4 A / LGMOR 3 YX / (24) (89) RPSTOVAL
58 LIBRA           93 SCORPIO    200 MANIFESTATION
```

As the reader will know from our previous references to 93, this number represents the menstrual flux in woman, SCORPIO; the whole formula being LIBRA SCORPIO SAGITTARIUS CAPRICORN = 418. A table explaining how this formula works out on various levels concludes this article, it was first published in The New Equinox, Vol.6 No.1. 93 is of course the value of the word Thelema in Greek, and this is the Word of the Law. If II.76 represents a universal formula, which is to say "the creation of the world", then the word LISTEN applied to the NUMBERS & THE WORDS (= 200 i.e. MANIFESTATION) seems to mean that we are to subject MANIFESTATION to the Law of Thelema.

Adding 93 to each number in the "Manifestation" part of II.76 we get:

(1.- 2.- 3.- 4.-5.- 6.- 7.- 8.-9.-10)
117-182-105-119-98-117-100-103-94-95.

These numbers are then taken as the key numbers of the Sephiroth (see numbers in brackets for Sephirothic correspondences). Applying the same rule to the Libra section of the Cipher we obtain:

(1 2 3 4 5 6 7 8 9 10)
97-99-96-101-94-113-102-95-97-94.

The number 58 = HADIT = LIBRA. In AL, Hadit says: "I am perfect, being (= 93) Not;" Libra is the sign of The Balance. The LIBRA/HADIT Tree is perfect, so the tenth sphere is in the "Da'ath" position to give the perfect and original form of the Tree.

The number 200 = MANIFESTATION or duality (2). Nuit, who is None and Two says, AL I.29: "I am divided for love's sake". In the next verse, we find the "PAIN OF DIVISION" = 200 = MANIFESTATION. The means by which Zero manifests is the Tree of Life, therefore we have the "trees of Eternity" (AL I.59) divided by 93. As will be seen by the qaballistically inclined Thelemic magician, this schema follows AL in its interpretation of manifestation. Consider the "Creation Myth" of AL in I.28 (28 = WORD):

NONE BREATHED THE LIGHT FAINT AND FAERY OF THE STARS.....
 60   117   117   80   71

On the Tree of Manifestation, Kether and Tiphereth have the same numeration (God the Father = God the Son, to use the language of the Old Aeon), which is 117 = HOOR PAAR KRAAT. Consider this proposition: if NONE, i.e. Zero, is the Qaballistic Ain Soph, the next word must indicate the number 1 or Kether, and 117 is the value arrived at for Kether by the process outlined above. None is Nothing, and NOTHING = 97 = RA HOOR KHUT, the top and bottom of the unmanifest Tree, which begins and ends in NOTHING, logically enough. Strictly, however, NONE = 60 = DEATH, which relates to Scorpio (93), equated with the House of Death in Astrology. This is too complex a subject to enter into here, where we are already in way over most folk's heads, including mine! The NONE = DEATH aspect of this formula applies to the Grade of Magister Templi, whereas this essay is written primarily for Adeptus Minors or those aspiring to that Grade.

It will be seen that various spheres involved in this exposition have the same numerical value, and there may just be a co-relation here with some of Grant's ideas concerning a Two Tree system - but this is not an analogy I wish to push too far. Whether or not these numerations indicate a particular affinity between these spheres is a fascinating area for speculation and experiment (see article by Tau Asellus in this issue), but it should be borne in mind that the Two Trees are Divided by 93, and the interrelations between them depend to some degree on particular stellar configurations. When these aspects or positions occur, the 93 Current is activated and energy flows out of Manifestation to the Perfect Tree and vice versa. If this did not occur then Destiny would be fixed, and astrology would work uninterrupted on a race of automatons, such as Adam and Eve appear to have been before the intervention of the Serpent of Genesis. Indeed, things could be even worse than this; but they are not. Destiny so-called can be aborted, magical effects can be created, and Change can and does occur. In the case of a single Tree, such as is vulgarly imagined by uninitiated "kabbalists", Life itself would be virtually impossible. Nothing could occur in the realm of manifestation beyond the creation of unicellular organisms - this is logical if you think about it, since a Tree going from Zero to manifestation could only produce this at best without periodic interference from outside the system. This is why the deities of Initiation possess dual characteristics, such as Baphomet, the twin-sexed DOUBLE-POWERED deity of the Magicians.

Having said that the work of Kenneth Grant bears some vague resemblance to elements of E.'.Q.'., it is worth tracing briefly where these distinct paths overlap, and where they diverge. Grant's focus on the role of the Priestess in magical work finds parallels in our own, but so do Culling and Bardon. Grant is by his own admission incapable of bringing this important aspect of magical work into being. The Two Trees are the closest point of contact between Grant's system and the E.'.Q.'., but there are ample traces of such a schema in the older Qaballistic texts, in AL itself and elsewhere. The extreme point of divergence between Grant's work and that of the English Qaballists is in actual practice. Grant's work is unmistakably on the extreme borders of occultism, with no safeguards to prevent delusion. E.'.Q.'. and its magical methods have the yardstick of pure number to avoid the pitfalls (colloquially known as Choronzon) of the 93 Current. There is a limit to how much accurate information can be obtained from Astral work alone, due to the nature of the thing itself. Only pure number can reveal the truth, and it is part of the Thelemic tradition that astral visions should ALWAYS be checked by pure number to ensure validity. It is against the background of pure number that the Class A material must be examined to avoid similar pitfalls.

At the end of the second chapter of AL it is said: "They shall worship thy name, foursquare, mystic, wonderful, the number of the man; and the name of thy house 418." THY HOUSE = 101, MYSTIC = 101. This suggests that the House in question is the House of the dual one, for 1 + 0 + 1 = 2, while 101 is the value of various double symbols such as ELEVEN, PILLAR + WORLD, DOUBLE WAND, and WANDED ONE (from the expression Double Wanded One); also SOLVE COAGULA, the double formula which is found engraved on images of Baphomet. The dual one is of course this same BAPHOMET (= 128 = THE BEAST, SCARLET WOMAN, SUN AND VENUS and ORDEAL X) expressed in the Zodiac as CAPRICORN = 121 = balanced duality.

The importance of Capricorn is as the final stage in the Libra-Scorpio-Sagittarius-Capricorn cycle. During the Sun's transit through these signs, the candidate in the Ordeal X experiences and resolves the conflicts or dualities in their nature, to emerge in Capricorn as a child - or even a manifestation - of Baphomet. This is the meaning of the title applied to Baphomet in old literature, the frequently misunderstood REX MUNDI or Lord of the Earth. The triumphant and revitalised initiate, the CROWNED CHILD = 128.

JAKE STRATTON-KENT

SIGN / SUBJECT	LIBRA	SCORPIO	SAGITTARIUS	CAPRICORN
Sun-Venus Magician	Candidate	The Ordeal X	Integration	Thelemite
Woman	Unfertilised Seed	Menstrual Flux	Rest	Renewed Woman
Christ	Judgement	Crucifixion (N.B. "Mysteries of the Crucifixion" = 418)	Mysterious Three Days	Resurrection
Christian	Sin versus Self	Repentance	Redemption	Christian
Nature	Harvest	Apparent Death of Nature	Rest	Green Man (potential for renewal)
Mind	World/Ego conflict	Neurosis	Breakdown. Upsurge of Unconscious Forces	Catharsis
Existence	Life	Death	Rest	Rebirth
Evolution	Evolutionary Stasis	Conversion of Species	Consolidation of Adaptation	New Variety
Science	Problem	Intense Study	Rest	Solution
Nations	Conflict	War (negotiations)	Armistice (agreement)	Peace
Health	Disease	Treatment	Rest	Renewal
Day	Activity	Onset of Sleep	Rest	Renewal
Mystic	Illumination	Dark Night of the Soul	Realisation	Prophet
Thelemite	Names Enemy in Libra-Scorpio	Enemy cast into "93"	Silence	Free of Enemy
Minor Adept	Names all the things he does not want - enemies	Enemies are destroyed, leaving vacuum in experience and consciousness	Vacuum is filled by "what the enemies are not", i.e. that considered advantageous to the Magician's Will.	Will of Magician fulfilled

AL.II.76 AND THE LUNAR MANSIONS.

The core of the Book of the Law is the 76th verse of Chapter Two containing the cryptic series of numbers and letters: "4 6 3 8 ABK 2 4 ALGMOR 3 YX 24 89 RPSTOVAL." We have shown how the numerical value of this cipher is the same as the sum of the numbers 1 to 26, representing the letters of the English Alphabet. "Two seventy-six", as the cipher is known among English Qaballists, is not only mathematically equivalent to the "Order and Value of the English Alphabet" (A = 1, L = 2, W = 3..etc.) - it is its counterpart or double. It has almost a symbiotic relationship with the alphabet, so that work with English gematria becomes a commentary on II.76. With the aid of astrological attributions, and ritual structures from the text itself, the outlines of a sophisticated cosmology emerges from the triad of AL, II.76 and English Qaballa. The experimental nature of this process makes it a dangerous path which tests one's integrity to the limit - but at the same time, an awareness is there from the beginning that the work is not one of devising, but of delineating a pre-existent but unexplored structure.

There have been many aspects of traditional occultism which have laid dormant throughout the supposed occult revival. Periodically, serious students come up against a brick wall of information deprivation. The Golden Dawn synthesis and most schools which have followed in their wake, even those of oriental origins, remain virtually silent on the magical application of the following: the 28 Lunar Mansions, the North and South Nodes of the Moon (Dragon's Head and Tail), the Part of Fortune etc. etc., to say nothing of the question of astrological timing in general - a situation which has been to an extent remedied by the appearance of this Journal. A recent survey of "Chaos Magicians" showed 90% were now using some species of "astrological" timing. Though it must be borne in mind that this is less significant than it sounds, as addressing Necronomicon spells to Yuggoth leaves a little to be desired in terms of comprehension and discrimination! It is appropriate, therefore, that the next step in reaching this comprehension, of supplying the blanks, should appear - as so often before - in this Journal.

The Lunar Mansions are traditionally 28 in number, and form as it were a larger zodiac, seemingly commencing with Aries as does the Tropical Zodiac, but with many links to the true constellations, in common with so called Sidereal Astrology. Since the Mansions combine Lunar energies, readily accessible to the magician on a day-to-day level, with Stellar energies, generally considered unsuitable terrain for all but the highest initiates (9 = 2 in conventional language, referring to Chokmah - the Sphere of the Fixed Stars - and Yesod, the Sphere of the Moon; as does the grade of 2 = 9 in another manner), it is evident that a great and potent system could be buried behind the dust and debris of the medieval sources. Other considerations pile up before we get started on a solution. 28 days is the average length of the menstrual cycle. The so called Lunar phases map this time in simplistic form, so might not the Lunar Mansions reveal rather more about the unwritten truth: "There is no Goddess but Woman"? The secrets of female initiation are among the largest deficiencies in the occult revival; might this not be one of the very keys to that sanctum?

That is about as far as I got in turning this problem over and over for a decade and a half. I knew in the back of my mind that this was something big, I knew too that there were 28 numbers and letters in II.76. For some reason I never compared the two; I assumed that would be too obvious, that nothing would result except a confused mass of data. However, as so often in this system, other minds were working on the same lines. It came to pass, as they say, that I heard from the Past Grand Master of the Order I currently represent. A chance reference to AL.II.76 and the Lunar Mansions passed his lips, and I was onto the question again like a devil unleashed. I did what I wish I had done several years ago: wrote out the cipher alongside the titles of the Mansions. As I did so, a feeling of awe and reverence stole over me like the shadow of an enormous winged creature overhead. This was clearly the work of a god! The positioning of the constellations and their subdivisions form a fantastic commentary on the magical system obtained from E.'.Q.'., including a great deal which the Editors past and present and their various colleagues have always considered too sacred for publication.

It was already apparent, of course, that the supposed powers or virtues of the Mansions according to the ancients were full of blinds and outmoded considerations, such as the retrieval of runaway slaves. What no-one could have anticipated was that the curious structure of II.76 as interpreted by the Order's Qaballists - i.e., as a structure consisting of an unmanifest or perfect Tree of 10 spheres, a "middle 8" having the value of 93, associated with Scorpio, and a final manifest Tree of 10 spheres - would be mirrored and amplified by the Mansions and their correspondences. Which is precisely what the reader wants to see right now, I imagine, so without further ado:

4.	0° Aries	]Horns of Aries
6.	13° Aries	]Belly of Aries
3.	26° Aries	]Pleiades
8.	9° Taurus	]Eye or Head of Taurus
A.	21° Taurus	]Orion's Head
B.	4° Gemini	]Little Star of Great Light, 3 stars in Orion's shoulder. Contains Algol at 26°
K.	17° Gemini	]Arm of Gemini
2.	0° Cancer	]Misty or Cloudy
4.	13° Cancer	]Eye of the Lion. Contains Sirius at 13° 57'
A.	26° Cancer	]Neck or Forehead of the Lion
L.	9° Leo	]Mane. Contains the Aselli 8° 35'
G.	21° Leo	]Tail. Contains Regulus 29° 41'
M.	4° Virgo	]Wings of Virgo or Dog Stars
O.	17° Virgo	]Spike of Virgo or Flying Spike
R.	0° Libra	]Covered or Covered Flying
3.	13° Libra	]Horns of Scorpio. Contains Spica 23° & Arcturus 24°
V.	26° Libra	]Crown of Scorpio
X.	9° Scorpio	]Heart of Scorpio
24.	21° Scorpio	]Tail of Scorpio. Contains Serpentis 19°
89.	4° Sagittarius	]A Beam
R.	17° Sagittarius	]A Desert
P.	0° Capricorn	]Head of Capricorn - a Pastor
S.	13° Capricorn	]Swallowing. Contains Deneb 19° & Vega 15°
T.	26° Capricorn	]Star of Fortune
O.	9° Aquarius	]A butterfly or Spreading Forth
V.	21° Aquarius	]1st Drawing
A.	4° Pisces	]2nd Drawing
L.	17° Pisces	]Pisces

There is too much material contained in this table to comment upon adequately, but of particular interest is the 93 section, commencing within a degree with the Aselli or Asses, sacred to Typhon and to Jesus simultaneously! The Lion symbolism implicit in the Word of the Aeon (i.e. LEO = 34 = ABRA) is subsumed here, and we are reminded also of a Virgin pulling a Lion's tail in earlier periods of aeonic succession. VIRGIN, of course, has the value of 93. But most important of all, we find that "The Burning Way" - 15° Libra to 15° Scorpio - is here placed before the appearance of the manifest Universe. Creation in fact originates within the 93 section, and the Tree emerges from X, the deepest part of the Scorpion, and emerges under the auspices of Scorpio still, and the star Serpentis of ominous repute. In effect, this means that the manifest universe is the result of the menstruation of the Goddess.

There are various ways of examining the correspondences of the characters from II.76 with the Lunar Mansions; one particularly interesting example, which ties together many diverse threads, involves Aries. Aries is a significant point for commencing occult work, outside of the context of "Seasonal Rituals" as popularly understood; there is something distinctly esoteric about this sign, in which the Sun is exalted, and the sign following, in which the Moon is exalted. Whereas however both Sun and Moon either are or represent principles in the act of creation, Aries and Taurus are simply stages in the unfolding of some aspect of that action. Both Abramelin and the Alchemical Great Work involve working with the principles of Creation, and both processes are commenced on or around the Vernal Equinox, according to tradition. This indeed has become part of the stock in trade of the more esoteric doctrines. "The Sun in the Belly of the Ram" is almost an alchemical cliche - but look at our table: the second line gives us 6, the number of the Sun, "in" the Mansion entitled the Belly of Aries. Some glimmerings of all this may be followed up in Dr. Dee's "Hieroglyphic Monad", but a more fruitful line of research is via E.Q. - for we should remember that while Dee was skirting round heliocentricity he lived before Uranus, Neptune and Pluto were discovered. This is relevant to our theme, as you might suspect, for ARIES = 66 = URANUS, whilst TAURUS = 76 = PLUTO. These outer planet references might well remind us of the "Three Principles" of the Monad, the Supernals of the Kabbalists (exemplified by the Outer Planets) exerting their influence on the "Process" of the Year through the "exaltation" of their vice-regents, the Sun and Moon.

The insights available with this "new" knowledge are quite breathtaking - and Dee and all the rest are rendered virtually superfluous save for purposes of illustration. The Two Trees model first published in TNE/BJM Vol.6. No.1. is clearly an authentic advance on all previous Kabbalistic models. This pill may seem hard to swallow, but the medicine is well overdue; Dr. Dee, commending his "London Seal of Hermes" (a curious title, for it - i.e. the Heiroglyphic Monad - was published in Antwerp, and dedicated to a foriegn potentate) is most specific in his prescription: "grammarians...will change their concepts. Arithmeticians will develop a new notion of number...geometers will find the principles of their art insufficiently established.....**After studying the treatise, the cabalists will recognise that their art is universal and not, as had been thought, confined to the Hebrew language; this new cabala, exemplified by the Monas Hieroglyphica, will reveal the secrets of the entire creation through new arts and methods"**. (Quoted from Peter J. French in his biography "John Dee".

It is evident to many that the work of Dee was a precursor of Thelema. "...For in the book Tarot was preserved all of the wisdom (for the Tarot was called the Book of Thoth) of the Aeon that is passed. And in the Book of Enoch was first given the wisdom of the new Aeon. And it was hidden for three hundred years, because it was wrested untimely from the Tree of Life by the hand of a desperate magician. For it was the Master of that Magician who overthrew the power of the Christian church; but the pupil rebelled against the master, for he foresaw that the New (i.e., the Protestant) would be worse than the Old. But he understood not the purpose of his Master, and that was, to prepare the way for the overthrowing of the Aeon." (Cry of the 6th Aethyr, MAZ.) It is evident too that Enochian was intended to transcend the Hebrew Kabbalah, and even the scriptures; Casaubon speculates that Dee's "received" books were intended to eclipse the Bible. If so then this passage becomes clear, for three hundred years before the reception of AL is the date of the legendary discovery of the Tomb of Christian Rosy Cross (1904 - 300 = 1604); curiously enough too, the dictation to Dee and Kelley - by the spirit Nalvage - of the Enochian "Holy Book" began three hundred and twenty years **- to the day -** before the reception of the third and last chapter of AL, i.e. 10th April 1584.

The trouble is that to many people the technical side of this work seems awesomely complex, or even ludicrous. This is by no means due entirely to the relative novelty of applying qaballistic techniques to the Book of the Law; what is novel to many is the process itself. Where can one turn for analogies to this process? The answer is not difficult to find, but some justification will be necessary. Many readers will be acquainted with some version of the Enochian system. Various examples exist, such as the Golden Dawn system, the closely related Crowley variant, and the Schueler and DuQuette/Hyatt derivations of these on the one hand, with "purist" versions returning to the Dee and Kelley materials to extrapolate anew, such as Robert Turner and some Caliphate afficiendoes of the system. One should not forget either the work of Pat Zalewski, demonstrating a strong investigative bent in unearthing rare Golden Dawn Enochiana. Whatever the merits of any of these, and some of them are considerable, we seldom get a feel of the work of Dee and Kelley themselves, who, suddenly landed as it were with the outlines of a vast and original system from praeter-human intelligences, had to explore it tentatively and with great daring, whilst manipulating abstract mathematico-linguistic structures (or ciphers if you prefer) with great care and precision - although accidents certainly occurred in their "holy laboratory". If one examines some of Dee's records from which the modern versions are derived, an unfamiliar territory opens up.

The derivation of names and sigils of subsections of the system from the apparently meaningless jumble of letters and numbers on the rim of the Sigillum Aemeth bears a curious resemblance to the work of English Qaballists with II.76 and the numerical superstructure of the text of AL itself. The rim of the Sigillum Aemeth bears more than a superficial resemblance to II.76. These processes are seemingly haphazard or are at least based upon an unknown logic. But from them arise majestic and coherent structures which - taken by themselves - are so neat and well formed as to bear no relation to the crazed handwritten text of "A True and Faithful Relation of what paffed for many Yeers Between Dr. John Dee and Some Spirits", or indeed the equations and formulae which have appeared in the pages of this Journal. This analogy, between the experimental and exploratory nature of Dee's work and that of English Qaballa, is apt on other levels also, of which perhaps some readers may have an inkling. It suffices for our purpose that we feel no justification is necessary for the manner of presentation employed in our Journals!

And so, indifferent to incomprehension, I append still another curiously derived table to accompany those which have gone before, and those which will doubtless appear in future:

GOD-NAMES OF THE LUNAR MANSIONS.

4 + FIVE (number of Mars, ruler of Aries) = 80 = ANUBIS
6 + FIVE = 82 = PAN-PAN
3 + FIVE = 79 = ABRAHADABRA (This Mansion ends in Taurus, and 79 = SEVEN = Venus, Ruler of Taurus.)
8 + SEVEN = 87 = FALUTLI
A + SEVEN = 80 = ANUBIS
B + EIGHT = 107 = HOOR KHUIT
K + EIGHT = 98 = QADOSH-ISIS (Note that this Mansion ends in Cancer, and 98 is 9 the Moon, in the infinite series.)
2 + NINE = 78 = APEP or NUIT. (Note that 78 is the value of Cancer.)
4 + NINE = 80 = ANUBIS
A + NINE = 77 = KHUIT or AMMON-RA
L + SIX = 52 = ADONAI or HAT-HOR
G + SIX = 61 = AMEN
M + EIGHT = 108 = HOOR-APEP or ISIS-HATHOR
O + EIGHT = 95 = AORMUZDI
R + SEVEN = 91 = NU-AHATHOOR or IAO MARSYAS
3 + SEVEN = 82 = PAN-PAN
V + SEVEN = 94 = NEFER
X + FIVE = 98 = QADOSH-ISIS, also ITEP
24 + FIVE = 100 = HRUMACHIS
89 + FOUR = 143 = SOL INVICTUS (Note that 143 = JUPITER, Ruler of Sagittarius, of which this is the first Mansion.)
R + FOUR = 66 = FIAT
P + THREE = 116 = ANKH-F-N-KHONSU
S + THREE = 95 = AORMUZDI
T + THREE = 114 = ADONAI-ABRASAX (Note that 114 = 71 x 2, accordingly IO PAN IO PAN might apply here.)
O + THREE = 120 = RA HOOR KHUIT
V + THREE = 100 = HRUMACHIS
A + FOUR = 55 = APIS
L + FOUR = 56 = ISIS

As with the Tables of A.M.E.N., these Names should not be considered to be the Names of the Spirits of the Mansions, so much as mathemagical formulae for controlling and understanding such regions and species. In conjunction with the Tables of A.M.E.N., this table might very well be used as *the N or Symbol Column in a ritual of the Mansion, for example,*

A.M.E.N. Names for Invocation of the First Mansion, "Horns of Aries":
A Name = 58 = HERU
M Name = 76 = HERU RA HA
E Name = 81 = KHEPHRA (As this is a Lunar working, TANECH might be preferred.)
N Name = 80 = ANUBIS

A.M.E.N. Names for Invocation of the 23rd Mansion, "Swallowing":
A Name = AIWASS
M Name = TYPHON
E Name = TAHUTI
N Name = AORMUZDI

TAU MAGNUS

Review: Mein Kampf. Hitler, A.

Those readers who managed to read the article on Empirical Pragmatic Idealism will enjoy this book. Unfortunately most editions are copiously footnoted by unappreciative woolly-minded liberals. This apart the book is quite excellent, particularly on the subject of propoganda. Few other signs of Hitler's occult activities are visible, but the discerning student will see here the first foreshadowing of mass-media mind-manipulation.

Saatchi and Saatchi, the Priory of Zion (sic) and the C.I.A. keep this essential manual next to the bed.

The military capers are straight out of "Boy's Own" and have an atmosphere of Victorian Imperialism at its most naive and idealistic.

The personal details are, to say the least, obscure, or at most dishonest, but then what politician, let alone National Messiah, would have it any other way? Available at all vegetarian bookshops. Read it.

MAGNUS DICTUS.

Review: The Magical Record of the Scarlet Woman - 1924 (Leah Hirsig) Publ: TOPY.

A valuable insight into Thelema through the eyes of a woman, who understood more than anyone near Crowley at the time (see her notes in Crowley's diaries). There is a marked resemblance to Dee's records of the Angelic Conversations. T.O.P.Y. are to be congratulated on making this book available.

ANTON K. JETTSTRAKE.

Review: The Dimensions of Paradise (John Michell) Publ: Thames & Hudson

The author is respected by all students of the Qabalah. This work, his magnum opus, encapsulates the author's vision of a Universal Harmony concealed in number within the Hermetic, Gnostic and Christian sciptures and expressed in the geometry of the Temple, be it Solomon's or English Heritage's.

His gentle scholarship ranks with Frazer or Graves, and the implications are no less epoch-making (how d'ye like it so far John? Ed).

Of particular interest to Thelemites will be the correspondences of the number 666 and its relationship with 1080 in Greek Qabalah. With Crowley and other qabalists he shows that The Beast is an aspect of The Lamb, the Scarlet Woman an aspect of the Bride of Heaven, and Babalon identical with the New Jerusalem.

To echo the editors of 'AGAPE' many moons ago, "it comes as somewhat of a surprise to learn that an Aeon that ended so badly should have begun so nobly".

SOPHIE ZUMM.

Strange sounds of inspiration & of expiration; some peculiar people are expressing the same current in musick (the flux and reflux of oc-cultural energies) as E.Q., cut ups and sigils express in lines and letters. Three family networks at work in this field are:

BETTER DAYS: with the OROONIES, ULLULATORS, OZRIC TENTACLES and other bands this current is very much a live one! Info from: B.D.D. 1, Woodmans Hill, Berkley, Frome, Somerset. BA11 5JJ.

GAIA RECORDS: ROYAL FAMILY & THE POOR, strange vibes from a complete fanatic! Its wonderful! Write to GAIA records. PO Box 134 Liverpool L69 8BP.

TEMPLE RECORDS: Psychic TV, the Angels of Light and other weird and wonderful sounds including ritual music from various oc-cultures. B.M. TOPY LONDON WC1 3XX.

All the above will send you details if you send them an SAE. We accept no responsibility for the state of your mind afterwards!

PENISIS O' GORRIDGE.

THE BOOK OF THE LAW. Dining and drinking copies, very well produced without any errors whatsoever. Also extremely cheap, 50p for one or four for a pound, evangelists take heed! We bought 20 straight away! Available from the OTO BM Box 3338. LONDON. WC1N 3XX.

A.K. JETTSTRAKE

AUSTIN OSMAN SPARE'S "BOOK OF SATYRS" - an individually numbered limited edition of quality postcard reproductions of all 13 illustrations is available from M.Goss PO Box 338, London E15 2QL

MAITRE RAKOCZI

STOP PRESS REVIEW!!! EUPHONICS: A Poet's Dictionary of Sounds.
By John Michell. Illust. Merrily Harpur. Published by Frontier publishing.
This book's usefulness will readily be apparent to poets, dramatists, orators, advertisers, magi, occultists and all who require to choose words and sounds for their powers of invocation. The combination of certain emotive sounds for purposes of enchantment and poetic invocation is a basic technique of magic. The mystical overtones to this subject have placed it beyond the academic pale; professors of linguistics prefer other approaches to the mysteries of language. What do they know?! A doctor's chair is a poor price for soul and integrity! As the author possesses these in abundance, allied with profound learning and humour, we can only recommend that you BUY THIS BOOK!

WORDS MADE FLESH. Ramsey Dukes. £6.00, available from TMTS. Wharf Mill, Winchester, Hants, SO23 9NJ.
The magician's approach to an "Information Universe" (as opposed to a spiritual or materialistic universe y'know) is to enter "**vivid**"-ly the context of his operations without quibbling about "right" & "wrong" or "true or false". In my vocabulary a magician is necessarily "**obsessed**", in R.D.'s he has a "**vivid**" imagination, either way THE MAGICKAL PROCESS MANIFESTS THE IDEA. Clever ol' Ramsey shows the hyper rationalist occultists why they have chaossified. Older readers will note that Ramsey's literary talents have reached new peaks in this latest work, which deserves to be huge!

Fu Ming.

Thundersqueak has also been reprinted with a new preface (by Ramsey Dukes). 'Sfunny, when I first heard of "the author of Thundersqueak" I thought someone was taking the piss out of "the author of Psychonaut", I was wrong, in fact it's another classic from The Mouse That Spins.

Lolet Carper.

SEXUAL MAGICK. by Katon Shual. £4.00, from Mandrake, PO. Box 250, Oxford, OX1 1AP.
We were going to review this, but "Basketcase" lent it to a sweetheart, so we still haven't seen it! Anyway it's mainly Katon's articles from **NUIT-ISIS**, which are excellent. I particularly liked "Must we love de Sade" (not included) which compares de Sade's "120 Days of Sodom" with Anger's "Pleasure Dome" & the Abbeys of Rabelais and Crowley. "In another dimension with voyeuristic intention - well secluded, I see all," as my sweet sister said.

Mr. R. Raff.

How the hell do you review all the occult magazines you've read recently, when a) their tastes, our tastes & the reader's tastes converge or clash seemingly at random; b) we don't carry adverts as this implies...well never mind what it implies; c) there's war in heaven? Also (in our Period of Silence) we weren't reading occult magazines anyway. How indeed? Here's one possible solution:

Key:

♪ Contains OTO histories and/or other historical/biographical material.

☼ Editorial content &/or house writer's articles of high standard.

☻ Lovecraftian horrors &/or other Gothic stuff (expletive deleted).

☺ Ideologically sound; "don't try and reason with me, I'm a fanatic!", without getting dogmatic about it!

♂ Contains material of practical use to occultists who aren't messing around.

‼ Contains material that in itself may truly be called a unique and original contribution to occultism.

CHAOS INTERNATIONAL:	☼ ☻ ♂
KAOZ:	☼ ☻
NOX:	☼ ☻ ☺ ♂
NUIT-ISIS:	♪ ☼ ☻ ☺ ♂
PAGAN NEWS:	☼ ♂
STARFIRE:	♪ ☼ ☻ ☻ ☺
THE EQUINOX:	☼ ☺ ♂ ‼
T.O.P.Y. BULLETIN:	♪ ☼ ☻ ☺ ♂
TWO THOUSAND A.D.:	♪ ☼ ☻ ☺ ♂
(Slaine's comin' to fix the fish-men!)	

Prices and availability vary considerably, & things change, enquiries to the editors with SAE for any information. Critics of my review can "kiss my axe".

ANTON. K. JETTSTRAKE.

SKEAT'S: A REVIEW

Indo-European languages may be assumed to carry a similar, if not identical, cultural ethos. The etymological roots as given in Skeat's are the "barbarous words" that lie behind our language. What is significant about this now is that although in the West our Tradition is emerging from a decline, the same cultural tradition has thrived for centuries in India. What we Westerners know in a skeletonic form in Theory (and experiment admittedly is not entirely extinct) lives there in everyday experience. The archetypes are developed in a manner suited to their exotic environment but the processes of energised enthusiasm adapt readily enough. This involves putting Flesh on the Bones of our Tradition. If we examine Skeat's list of roots of words in "English" usage we find that the Sacred language of India is our remote "Aryan" ancestor. The English Qaballa is (as it were) a reincarnation of the cultural matrix of we "barbarians", once expressed in Runes and Oghams, the true ancestors of our alphabet. (We leave aside considerations of the Julian cipher +19/-7.)

Crowley certainly used Skeat's in reconstructing the Names of the Bornless Rite, a ritual which is pure Western Shamanism. The operator "assumes" beast forms & "vibrates" the Names along a phallic shaft of will, "Unto the ends of the Universe", i.e. up the spine to the brain, the body "visualised" as immense in size; each series of words relates, in ascending order, to the "chakras", viz: Air*=Groin, Fire=Solar Plexus, Water=Heart, Earth*=Throat, Spirit Active=Pineal Gland, Spirit Passive=Above Head. Why are the elements in this order? Surely it would make more sense to have Genitals as Earth & Throat as Air? Yes, it would; indeed the elemental attributions to the quarters in, say, the Star Ruby are arranged exactly like that. But! As Crowley emphasised, the Holy Guardian Angel ritual is different from and even the reverse of usual procedures.

The Bornless Rite was originally called the "Headless Rite", and magicians who use the Bornless Rite, and analogous yogic and tantric processes, find the Da'ath Chakra or larynx is or feels "blocked". Qabalistically this is the Abyss. Remember all the sword and neck symbolism?

Liber VII, ch. 5. vs. 47. "He shall await the sword of the Beloved, and bare his throat for the stroke."

Throat=Pentacle (or Platter), Genitals=Dagger (or Sword). Solve et Coagula, or "fixing the volatile & making volatile that which is fixed", is, so to speak, turning Air into Earth and vice versa. Thus the ascending kundalini passes the Da'ath centre when the "Flaming Sword" cuts off the head. Unfortunately for the Golden Dawn methodology the "divine white brilliance" only descends when it's good and ready; it is the "ascending mode" which is important initially, not only throughout yogic tradition but in other living traditions such as Voodoo.

(Not to mention alternative medicine; an unzipping gesture down the front of the body &/or a lateral gesture across it, as in the Qabalistic Cross, would be seen as negative, even harmful, by some exponents of this most practical branch of the "physiological gnosis".)

The whole science and art of magickal gestures cannot be rectified without stepping outside (once & for all) the purported synthesis of the Western Tradition known as the Golden Dawn.

When language becomes symbol, sex becomes language.

The Book of the Law (& the processes it describes) are not in Sanskrit, and the processes of producing an hieratic text in English involves truly bizarre extensions of what even psycholinguistics professors know about language. But these are the very processes involved in reanimating the corpse of Western Shamanism.

The Un-Rite, with its roots in AL ch.I, vss.62,63 as described in the Five Pointed Star article (Equinox VII. no.2.) is a feast of the Thelemic Tradition which has put Flesh on the Bones. Living Magick, neither theory nor faith but the living embodiment of the Unwritten QAB-AL-LA or "Oral Tradition".

What a brilliant dictionary! Spelling is defunct!

Barnaby Wilde.

Since most supposed books on occultism are published by vested interests, for consumer markets, occult magazines should contain the real state of the art material. To a certain extent this is true; we might instance the article on Goetia in NOX 6, or similar articles which appear from time to time in other "underground" occult magazines. Yet more and more the occult press is dominated by material that is either retrospective or "arty". A certain amount of historical material is acceptable, even interesting, but when there seems to be a danger of such fare becoming our staple diet one must draw the line. To be fair, however, it must be remarked that some portion of the readership seem to need courting by such means simply to meet the costs of the publisher. Yet since many such magazines are partly financed either by advertising or by mail order companies this is hardly sufficient excuse. The main objection to such material is that it is retrospective. It sometimes seems as if Magickal activity consists of admiration societies for some of the less commercial eccentrics of the last hundred years. We might expect Qabalah, Astrology and Alchemy but all too often what we get is some views on Crowley, Spare, and Lovecraft, and then more bloody Lovecraft.

However, let's get on with the reviews.

BRITISH MAGAZINES

Chaos International. BM SOL, London, WC1N 3XX. £2.70. Now more than ever the "House" magazine of the I.O.T. (who?), not entirely free of Thelemic material, nor of fish worship. Carries much practical material.

DOOR. Directory of Occult Resources. Spiral Publications, 8 King Street, Glastonbury, Somerset, BA6 9JY. £2.50. No Fish! Masses of information on where to find people, places and things, also articles by Vee Van Dam, letters and reviews. (Channelled communications from Solar devas!?)

The Equinox - British Journal of Thelema. Thelema, Magick, NO FISH. The Editors are satisfied that "Chaos" Magick/Science/Maths are expressions of the 93 Current, and they should know. Probably the best magickal magazine in the world.

NOX. 15 Oxford Street, Mexborough, S.Yorks. £3.00. Plenty of fish worship, with good critiques of occult pershonalitiesh and useful practical material.

Nuit Isis. PO Box 250, Oxford, OX1 1AP. £2.00. Glossy Thelemic magazine. Articles of general interest, with some directly magickal material including some excellent serialised articles in the back issues, two major ones just ended, so changes probably afoot. Fish worshippers catered for.

Pagan News. Box 175, 52 Call Lane, Leeds, LS1 6DT. 30p a shot. An occult monthly newspaper carrying some practical material, plus reviews (GRR SNARL), ads and other material of some interest. One could be forgiven for thinking that occultism started and ended in Leeds when one reads this, but that's par for the course oop North. "Unless of course you know better."

Starfire. BCM Starfire, London, WC1N 3XX. The fishiest of them all; latest enlarged edition £5.00. Similar to the sadly defunct SOTHIS in format, excellent production job. Latest edition carries practical material of great interest as well as the - in my opinion - wholly gratuitous sludge stuff.

TOPY Bulletin. Temple Press, c/o PO Box 23, Brighton, BN2 4AU. (£6.50 annual sub.) Carries good articles and useful information, ie ritual music, dream machine plans and so on all covered. Traces of fish discernable. Latest edition carries an excellent article regarding the mythology of Venus devouring the Sun - particularly interesting to Thelemic astrologers. Generally speaking, when a planet is conjunct the Sun the planet is 'combust', its power overshadowed by the Sun, but at Sun conjunct Venus the situation is the reverse. Damned good magazine! Badly printed by Kiblah Publishing!

U.S. MAGAZINES

BAHLASTI PAPERS. Kali Lodge OTO, Box 15038, New Orleans, LA 70115, USA. $2.00 per issue, $24.00 per year. Lively monthly magazine reflecting a very active OTO Lodge in New Orleans, fun and fast moving, the model of what a newsletter type magazine could and should be and seldom is, at least in this benighted country!

IN THE CONTINUUM. P.O. Box 415, Oroville, CA. 95965. Features rare or unpublished Crowley works of high interest. Basic instructional material valuable to all Thelemites. Astrology, Qabalah, Tarot, Magick and Ritual and such historical materials as Crowley's correspondence with Jane Wolfe, and her diaries. All back numbers continually in print, 10 numbers of Vol.I. 12 of Vol.II, 10 of Vol.III and 4 of Vol.IV. to date, 5 dollars each including postage. Published by **THE COLLEGE OF THELEMA**, write to Phyllis Seckler at the address shown, and make cheques payable to her. This grand old lady has been a servant of A.'.A.'. for 50 years, and valuable service it is. Highly recommended.

SOCIETE. Technicians of the Sacred, Suite 310. 1317 N San Fernando Blvd., Burbank, Ca. 91504. USA. Of particular interest to exponents of OBEAH (that's Voodoo to the uninitiated). Well printed magazine, articles vary considerably, from the learned to the sociable. Carries plenty of contact and supply data, and runs an efficient network service of its own. Links with Michael Bertiaux but independent of his organisations. Subscription rate for overseas customers $10.00 for two issues.

GNOSIS. Is available in the UK from Cthonios Books, 7 Tamarisk Steps, Hastings, TN34 3DN. £2.95. PO BOX 14217. San Francisco. CA 94114-0217. USA. $4.00 each or $15.00 annual subscription. Glossy quarterly, not exactly an underground occult magazine, but high quality, deserves support for its high profile, which has attracted the usual Christian hysteria.

Also seen: **Magical Link** (Caliphate OTO) and **Thelema Lodge Newsletter** (Caliphate OTO), internal documents of the Caliphate; the latter carries a continuous research file on the Enochian materials, of considerable interest, the former carries updates on Order publications, including the real organ of the Caliphate **"The Oriflamme"**. Current issue carries ALL Jack Parson's works, projected next issue contains complete Abuldiz and Amalantrah materials.

P.S. I wish we got decent reviews as well as all the appreciative mail, most of the above don't acknowledge our existence in print, I wonder why!? We acknowledge theirs after all, and you the reader want to know these things, or so you tell us anyway. PLEASE GISSA REVIEW, flattery would be nice of course but just straight information would not go amiss! For those who do mention/describe us to their readers, our heartfelt thanks. To the rest, get your act together.

A NOTE FROM THE EDITORS

What a curious thing history is, take the history of the Equinox title! First Crowley used it on behalf of the A.'.A.'. to expose the G.'.D.'., which involved Mathers taking him to court. Then Crowley produced another one on behalf of the O.T.O.. Then Crowley died and Motta tried printing one, not a bad effort in places either. But Motta took someone else to court for calling themselves the OTO, meanwhile Motta called himself head of the OTO and A.'.A.'.. That takes us to volume five (no even numbers) then the someone else produced more of volume three.

Back in England there was a New Equinox which was around so long in the absence of any Equinoxes it decided to change to the Equinox and confuse everybody by being Volume Seven (after 6 TNEs not ONE THREE and FIVE Equinoxes). If anyone wants to produce Volume Five (or is it Nine, I got lost a little way back there) with entirely new material of immense significance go ahead. Just so long as you know what you are getting into.

THUNDERSQUEAK by Angerford & Lea. ISBN 0-904311-07-4. £6.95 from TMTS, Wharf Mill, Winchester, S023 9NJ. Having given this book a brief plug in EQUINOX VII.4, we feel it deserves a more detailed review, so here it is. An unusual collection of purportedly nihilist/anarchist essays, bearing the library classification of MAGIC/POLITICS. This book carefully examines and demolishes the ethical (UNethical) priorities and magickal methods currently used by various factors in our society, addressing the respective natures of our civil service, law agencies, education, economics, technology and morality.

As the prevalent media tricks used by those responsible for engineering our consciousness become increasingly obvious to the discriminating observer, books like this become essential reading, revealing the "new wave" of inspired subversion techniques available to all sides in the "mind-war".

To quote the editorial afterword, "If you think of this book as a book of failed ideas, then you will be free from being enslaved by it". Keep it next to your copy of "Mein Kampf".
ALAN M TURING

TANTRIC ASTROLOGY by Mike Magee. ISBN 1-86992-806-7. £4.95 from Mandrake, PO Box 250, Oxford, OX1 1AP. This is a book on natal astrology, with progressions and transits - based on the Indian Sidereal zodiac rather than the Western Tropical zodiac. It is not, unfortunately, a book on the timing of tantric ritual. Much of the material will be familiar to those who read Magee's earlier pamphlet "Shri Yantra and Sidereal Astrology", but there is much clarification and extension of those ideas, such as the planetary pairs of Cyril Fagan. We must point out though that in our opinion the true magickal astrology died out in the East before the West, and furthermore, that the position of the sidereal Zodiac is dependent upon an arbitrarily fixed datum. Inexperienced tropical astrologers should beware of confusing definitions, as identical terms are used in both tropical and sidereal astrology with quite different meanings. This might be dangerous in magical astrology, as a tropical "square" is a hard aspect whereas a sidereal "square" (ie between navamsashas, or ninths) is a soft aspect. This said, the author of this book finds useful material in modern western studies (Fagan, Gaugelin, Reich) at the risk of upsetting those purists to whom the East is the source of all wisdom.
BATRAXOPHRENOBOO KOSMO MACHIA

LIBER MCCLXIV by Aleister Crowley et al. from Albion Lodge OTO, BM Thelema, London WC1N 3XX. "A Complete dictionary of all sacred and important words and phrases given in the Books of the Gnosis and other important writings both in the Greek and the Coptic". Well, that's what Crowley said about it; now the Caliphate OTO have published it in a miniscule limited edition of about 30 at a tenner and about 8 at £25.00 (deluxe edition). As Crowley was going to publish this in an Equinox that failed to materialise, we recommend it to all **REALLY** SERIOUS qaballists.
ALTHOTASH

VOUDON GNOSTIC WORKBOOK, by Michael Bertiaux. Magickal Childe @ $29.95 (619pp).

A truly formidable work in many ways. It requires an effort of suspension of disbelief - the more acute since the author is a past master of what the magicians of darkest Yorkshire call "solipsism". There are some leg pulls, there are some dashed peculiar notions, unfamiliar and bizarre terms abound as well as more familiar terms in unfamiliar contexts. This apart the book is quite excellent; the pseudo intellectual brand of solipsism that creates such nausea in fuddy duddies like myself is conspicuous by its absence. Bertiaux calmly takes for granted what so many cultists waffle about until you are sick of hearing it. For this author spirits are real, it is our terms of reference which are subjective. Consequently mythology, science fiction and pseudo-science, as well as intuitive perception of reality, supply means with which to cope with these forces.

Other delights for the more erudite among you include a gematria scheme using five dice, generating values A=5 through to Z=30, identical in most respects to a scheme once proposed by Gerald Suster. There is also an emphasis on the Moon in Scorpio Current among other arcane delights. Besides this, there are some other wonderful aspects to his approach. Not for MB are the tiresome speeches of the Key of Solomon or the Golden Dawn; he is more likely to conjure the spirits with "I LOVE YOU" than "ANAREXICK CAAMANDO NIFE etc.". His remarks concerning Aiwass and other Thelemic matters may be unsuited to the ardent fundamentalist like myself, but there is much in his approach which is commendable and workable. A unique style, at times reminiscent of "The Green Book" in Arthur Machen's tale "The White People", at others like "Le Poule Noire" and similar works. It may not be what the anthropologist calls Voodoo, it may not be what the scholastic dodo calls occultism, but it is a wonderful read and involves some startling voyages in imagination and much excellent magickal material, a sorcerer's handbook written with wit and insight. One question though, why were the sigils left out? Answer, they are available in Societé magazine, Volume 2 #1, and I've suggested that Temple Press stock up on them, so try them. Any more questions? Good.
JAKE STRATTON-KENT

GOLDEN DAWN ENOCHIAN MAGIC, by Pat Zalewski. Llewellyn @ $12.95 (190pp).

This book is another example of the vitality of G.'.D.'. traditions derived from Dr. Felkin's Lodge in New Zealand. Much that remained obscure or was omitted in Regardie's "Complete Golden Dawn System of

Magic" is here expounded, expanded and elaborated.

Of particular interest is the Tabula Collecta material which is one of the most essentially practical parts of the Enochian system. Purists may complain that some of the material used is not Dee's but Dr. Rudd's, but since the Golden Dawn's elaborations aren't Dee's either this complaint is hardly relevant. There are some other points which historians might query, but I shan't worry about them.

The author is collaborating whole heartedly with Llewellyn on TWENTY or so other G.'.D.'. books from the rich vein of N.Z. magic - including the awesomely titled "Sex Magic of the Golden Dawn", some hint of which may have been intuited by students of the "Secret Inner Order Rituals" book. What I hope to see is a book on the "Astrological Magic of the Golden Dawn", for there are tantalising hints in this,and other books from N.Z. that horary and electional rules were observed by some of the Inner Order Adepti.

In closing, let me add that this is not a rehash of well known material, but an extension of Enochian studies by a competent and informed Enochian magician in the Golden Dawn tradition. His remarks on the significance of the Moon in Enochian magic and the readily discernible emphasis on Venus in the Tabula Collecta material are also worthy of note. He that has ears let him hear.

JAKE STRATTON-KENT

THE COMPLETE BOOK OF ASTROLOGICAL GEOMANCY, by Priscilla Schwei & Ralph Pestka. Llewellyn @ $14.95 (425 pp).

Hmm. It gives deserved credit to Agrippa, the main source of geomantic materials. In case you don't know, Agrippa gives more than one scheme of attributions (see 4th Book of Cornelius Agrippa) and this book uses one of the less well known variants to attribute the geomantic symbols to the signs of the Zodiac - and a more familiar scheme to attribute them to the planets - with some odd and even unhelpful results. The book claims that Geomancy relates to Horary Astrology, so far so good, but claims that astrology is incomplete without geomancy (eh?). It sayeth: "through the horary chart we perceive that which is orderly, cyclical and obvious". Not if Via Combusta is rising we don't, chum! Nor if the Moon is therein, or Mercury is retrograde, or Saturn is in the Seventh or a dozen or so other conditions which prevent the chart being "radical". So much for: "In the usual horary reading the querent asks a question and the astrologer gives an answer". Then they say: "the addition of symbolical manipulation brings in chance. This takes astrological geomancy one step beyond the usual horary astrology. Physicists now understand that chance and chaos are a basic part of existence; even chance and chaos show predictable patterns". Yes indeed, but these patterns break down! Chaos sets limits to predictability, as does Horary Astrology. And Horary Astrology shaped the form of Geomancy. In traditional Geomancy for instance, the symbol Rubeus (usually attributed to Scorpio) in the First House invalidates the chart, which is identical to the horary rule that V.C. rising renders the chart non-radical and unreadable, i.e. predictability breaks down! The attributions in this book, and the interpretations derived from them cause this element to vanish. This alone undermines their basic premise.

On the credit side however they do recommend combining Astrology with Geomancy, and at least mention Horary Astrology. Unfortunately, the recommended method is to ignore the astrological houses - a method they mistakenly attribute to Mundane Astrology - and simply see what signs the planets are in and relate them to the geomantic figure. Mundane Astrology, of course, does not ignore the Houses, quite the contrary. Possibly the authors have misunderstood the old (and in my opinion spurious) <u>Mundane Aspects</u> - which take planets apparently three houses (ignoring interceptions etc.) rather than genuinely 90' apart as being in Mundane Square. But a mistake like that would take some making.

What I'd like to see is a decent study of a) the various geomantic schemes described in the 4th Book; b) the three known types of African oracle related to Geomancy (Ifa etc.) and c) some hints at the origins of Geomancy in Babylon or Sumeria. This book fails on all these counts, and while it raises some interesting questions it does not do them justice. As we are in the business of providing information, and even - gawd 'elp us - advice, let me rectify at least one deficiency of this book: when using divinatory methods <u>of whatever kind</u> ensure that the Moon is not in Via Combusta, and that V.C. is not rising. In fact, a Horary figure erected for each such operation would not go amiss. Use Horary alongside Geomancy, or any divinatory technique soever, and you won't go far wrong. Inter-disciplinary work can only broaden your horizons and improve your results.

JAKE STRATTON-KENT

HORARY ASTROLOGY - The History and Practice of Astro-Divination, by Anthony Louis. LLewellyn @ $18.95 (557pp).

Yes, it's big, and yes, it's good. It already has a subtitle, but another one could have been "The Encyclopedia of Horary Astrology". I am thoroughly impressed. If you already have a couple of decent books on Horary, say either/or De Luce or Appleby, don't think this book is superfluous, because it isn't. If you have no books on Horary and are just about to go get one, put this one at the top of the list (but don't forget De Luce and Appleby either, they are a more handy size for most things). As Horary is a pet subject of the editors and their more compos mentis readers, you can assume that this book is good because we say it is. As I have never read a bad book on Horary Astrology (mind you, I haven't read everything in this guy's bibliography either), to say this may be the best yet, is praise indeed. There is so much information in this book. It quotes some of my greatest heroes, like Guido Bonatti (otherwise Bonatus), who aren't that well known in the U.K. but are accorded great respect by American astrologers (not the sugary pill brigade, there is much more going on in U.S. astrology than a trip to a Glastonbury bookstore might suggest!) who are doing so much to promote this much maligned branch of the Art. Maligned by whom? Some rather tepid occultists who don't know any better, and the nineteeth century's scientists, and the seventeenth century's humanist priests! Brilliant occultists of the past, like Bonatti and Lilly were streets ahead of the game, and this book deserves a place next to them on the shelf of every thinking occultist and astrologer. Horary is easily the most important branch of astrology to an occultist, so the sooner you chuck Linda Goodman's Sunsigns out the window and study the subject properly the better, and there is no better place to start than with this book (unless you can handle translating or transcribing Bonatti and Lilly, who, great as they were, are rather old fashioned).

JAKE STRATTON-KENT

THE FULCANELLI PHENOMENON, by Kenneth Rayner Johnson. Neville Spearman @ £8.50 (323p).

Although published in 1980 we got a review copy anyway! OK, so it's not new, but then neither am I. It is pretty interesting though. Neville Spearman are a curious company; their material is frequently on the verge of the "lunatic fringe" but rarely if ever falls over the edge. This book is a case in point; it is weird and wonderful, but well documented and interesting. Fulcanelli is one of those dodgy characters who haunt historians, an alchemical adept whom no-one can track down (and the fledgling C.I.A. had a good go at the end of W.W.II). He seemed to know how to build an atomic pile before Uncle Sam's boys got round to it. Not only that, but like the Compte de Saint Germaine he seems to be a bit of an immortal adept! Not bad for the twentieth century, and he wasn't dreamed up by the author either, the plot is a lot thicker than that. Well, you can read it and find out for yourself. The guy is actually at the centre of a literary genre - a kind of one man Rennes le Chateau mystery. There are some other interesting bits in this book: a potted history of alchemy, a bio' of Saint Germaine (you ought to look into these immortal adept guys, they are too interesting to be written off as phonies, considering where they were and what they did, rather than whether they lived for ever), and some intriguing hints about a Cabala of argot. This is a kind of "twilight language" derived from Sufi and alchemical sources, and the etymology of "cabala" is not the Hebrew one usually quoted but from "caballo" a horse, from whence chivalry and cavalier derive. Not intrigued? Well, try this quote: "The fact that these are the phonetics of English words should not surprise us. English has replaced Latin as the world language - a fact that would have been forseen by a truly illuminated man of recent centuries, looking into our own times." Link the ideas of the book mentioned in the previous review and you wonder quite how far this E.'.Q.'. stuff reaches back into the ancient past, as well as into the future. Alchemy is an important and largely ignored part of the esoteric tradition, as significant, in some respects, as astrology and qaballa. So watch this space, we will return to this subject anon!

JAKE STRATTON-KENT

THE TRUTH ABOUT THE TAROT, by Gerald Suster. Skoob Esoterica @ £4.99 (108pp).

Those who know Gerald's work won't need much encouragement from me. This book is described quite adequately by its title, but a few more words of description won't go amiss. The first part of the book is pretty straightforward, traditional interpretations, descriptions of the cards, a resumé of the astrological and qabalistic attributions of the cards, etc. All that needs saying about this part of the book is that it is easier to follow and work with than the Book of Thoth. The second part of the book is a delight - life, consciousness and the modern world as seen through the eyes of a Tarot adept, and what a crystal clear vision it is. How about a quotation, but where to start? Dipping in at random we find: "Our intellect, though sharp as a razor, must not be allowed to get in the way. It is a splendid servant but a bad master. This is one of many meanings of the Path which leads from Hod to Tiphereth, XV The Devil. This experience involves the realisation, nobly expressed by William Blake, that "everything that lives is holy". We must fully accept our own sexuality and that of the Universe for, as the artist and magician Austin Osman Spare wrote: "All things fornicate all the time." We must accept that many truths about the Universe are shocking to the average ego. And we must face what has been called the Dweller on the Threshold."

Another point - on which alone this book should be commended above all the catchpenny handbooks which clutter up the crystal caves and fortune teller's emporiums - is the "Royal Game of Human Life: Or Celestial Snakes and Ladders" chapter which presents a splendid game involving the Tarot attributions to the Tree of Life, whereby each player gets to build his own "stairway to heaven", while simultaneously sabotaging his opponents' similar efforts, dropping them down various routes to lower and lower spheres. I know two Probationers to A.'.A.'. who learnt their attributions in two days flat with the aid of this game, and thoroughly enjoyed themselves in the process.

Er, there is also a mention of English Qaballa in the appendix by the cover artist (RAG) - which considering Gerald's previous criticisms of this system he hadn't seen is rather a pleasant gesture.

What else can I say? BUY IT!

JAKE STRATTON-KENT

WHO OWNS STONEHENGE, by Christopher Chippindale, Paul Devereux, Peter Fowler, Rhys Jones and Tim Sebastian. Batsford @ £12.99 (176pp).

Profusely illustrated, with a list of contributors as distinguished as it is long, this book serves not only to in inform the reader on various views regarding the origin and significance of this important and often controversial site, but also to explain and describe the custodial feelings of its many diverse enthusiasts. In this task it succeeds very well. Views from the archaeological establishment and the earth mystery experts and a particularly intriguing contemporary bardic view that uses the poetic form of historical dialogue - the language of myth - to illuminate the present as well as the past.

JAKE STRATTON-KENT
(Qaballistic English Druids)

PRACTICAL SIGIL MAGIC, by Frater U.'.D.'.. Llewellyn @ $8.95 (134pp).

Everything you wanted to know about sigil magic but were afraid to ask! The author systemises material from A.O.Spare, Pete Carroll & Ray Sherwin on the one hand, and Cornelius Agrippa, Francis Barrett and the G.'.D.'. on the other. In many ways his book is more useful, on this subject at least, than any of the aforesaid.

Frater U.'.D.'. (alias Ralph Tegtmeier) also manages to squeeze in some fine distinctions regarding two schools of occultism: the Pragmatic School (the Chaos good guys) and the Dogmatic School (the OTO bad guys). His thesis is that Crowley was originally a precursor of the Pragmatic School, throwing out medieval junk and getting down to what worked or what would work just as well if not better. He maintains that Crowley then backslid into a Dogmatic position, holding up the Book of the Law and dragging every one off to the Non-stick Mass every Sunday. Spare, on the other hand, he sees as the great white hope of Pragmatism, who (while being prior to the period in which these terms apply) founded no dogmatic school nor put forward any final versions of the truth. I confess this is the first time I've read Fra. U.'.D.'. and yet his use of words like Empirical and Pragmatic sound rather reminiscent of my first book - which you may recall was compared to Snell and Carroll's work! Yet here I am maintaining that the Book of the Law is the focus of an Empirical-Pragmatic-Idealistic system, and that Crowley's lapses into pseudo-masonic schemes and dreams are not the "mantras and spells" promised in AL. How can this be? Well, look at this book and its ilk and meet the Big Three or Prime Movers of Magick Arte. What do we find? a) we find Physiological processes - be they mental, sexual, emotional or whatever, they relate back to the human organism; b) we find astrological symbolism (and perhaps even astrological timing, even if it be of the rather naff "Days and Hours of the Planets" variety, or the rather more useful Lunar Phases and Tides etc.); c) we find Numbers and/or Letters which are largely synonymous in any case). Physiological-Astrological-Numerical or in other words P.A.N.. Those who approach the Book of the Law and/or magick "each for himself", with these three measures as his yardstick, will be no more hidebound by dogma than, say, Pete Carroll!

So, to sum up, this book is a must for Chaos Magicians on the one hand, and for enthusiasts of Practical Qaballa (English Qaballa that is) on the other. Or are these hands one hand, and are they clapping? All I know is that I constantly fall between two stools; my sympathy for the pragmatic approach alarms many Thelemites, while my adherence to P.A.N. in my reading of AL confuses the Chaotics! Returning to Sigils (remember sigils?). This book covers Austin Osman Spare and his theory of Sigils: the "Word" method; the "Pictorial" method; the "Mantrical Spell" method and trance and activation of sigils. It then moves on to the Alphabet of Desire, first as a structuring principle, namely a method of categorisation via symbols in a quasi-qabalistic method à la Carroll's Liber Null. Secondly, as a Mirror of the Psyche created by chains of association where sigils or components for incorporation in sigils are recorded in a dictionary for combination as necessary. This method is my own preference since it grows and expands organically - and as U.'.D.'. shows, the dictionary itself is a useful guide to your motives, mentality and progress when you go through it after a period of compilation and use and see what you have included. You can then see what your sigils and symbolic language tell you about yourself; are there several dozen symbols for wealth in it, and only one for love? Have you been wiping out politicians left, right and centre while imagining yourself as a calm, apolitical and intensely spiritual being? Some other interesting material emerges in this chapter; quote: "Spare [stated] that the Alphabet of Desire is part of a special proto-language of man's own unconscious". Sound familiar? There is then a chapter on Atavisms which covers some weird and wonderful ground which will delight and astonish those who wish to "explore the river of the soul" or discover "from whence do ye come?" I shan't spoil your fun by giving details, but this chapter will open doors of experience which will pluck the strings of many an occultist's heart.

Next...(yes, there's more folks!) a word about theory, covering models: Sherwin's model (also claimed by Mike Jamieson, "Art's fine but plagiarism's quicker!") and some of his own including one adapted from Theosophy! This chapter concludes with a timely reminder that "who has the how is careless of the why". Chapter Nine involves traditional magic squares and planetary sigils and is not to my taste, but at least shows U.'.D.'. hasn't chucked out the baby with the bathwater as so many Chaos types do (or try to do). This quality sets U.'.D.'. apart time and time again throughout the book. The book is then nicely rounded off with a handy glossary and notes on various points from the main text, plus a bilingual bibliography of German and Anglo-American works relating to his dealings with the subject.

Well, I'm impressed! Not only did I read and re-read it, I also begged a copy of Liber Null from a friend (you know who you are) and re-read that. My advice to you is to do the same... I may beg to differ on many points with the Chaos crew, but - and this is a big but - they have done more to bring magick into the 20th Century than anyone else since Crowley and Spare, until me, that is.

MAGNUS DICTUS

SEEDS OF MAGICK, by Catherine Summers and Julian Vayne. Foulsham @ £7.95 (188pp).

Well, this is quite a book, I like reviewing books like this! There is virtually nothing negative to say about it from my point of view. There seem to be some negative things to say about it from other points of view, although perhaps that's because it tells the truth in little throwaway lines, so they have to criticise other parts of the book to make themselves feel better about the irreproachable bits they don't like! For instance, look up hereditary witches in the index and you will find a page reference leading to a mention of children of first generation occultists being the GENUINE hereditary witches! Not guaranteed to please the "more pagan than thou" brigade. So what is it about? Briefly, it is a multi-purpose book, its subtitle was not chosen by the authors, but might tell you a little: "An exposé of Modern Occult Practices". The blurb on the back tells us two things, that this book is designed to DEFEND occultism from the Fundamentalists, and that Foulsham are not among the publishers crapping themselves in the face of the Christian hysteria about "Shaytanishm". Inside the book there are no apologetics such as are usually associated with such a defence. Far from it; we are presented with a Thelemic/Maatian/Wiccan fusion of great depth and power, calculated to include everything from menstruation to the Great Rite without getting tacky. It also deals with the kinds of difficulties that groups might encounter, and here I really got to identify with the writers! If you want to set up a group on intelligent lines, with stuff your budding members can relate too and derive benefit from, this book is the best thing since Huson's "Mastering Witchcraft" or the Farrars' various books. It is also of much wider scope, whereas those books were purely Wiccan (whatever that means!). These folk have put together something which combines all the best and most readily planted and watered seeds. Thelemites who consider themselves above Wicca should a) wonder why Crowley-Poley went to such lengths to promote it by co-writing the Book of Shadows and trying to find someone to establish a Wiccan religion (he tried Achad before Gardner), and b) wonder why their own efforts so frequently correspond to the seeds falling on rocky ground of the Christian parable. Personally, having done outdoor rituals unrelated to Wicca for several years, I have found that the Wiccan thing comes along of its own accord just because I'm working in the English countryside. We are talking about a tradition capable of sustaining itself as an organic self-perpetuating entity, and that is BIG stuff! Suck it and see, girls and boys, and participate in the future.

JAKE STRATTON-KENT

PLANETARY MAGIC, by Denning and Phillips. Llewellyn @ £20.95 (400pp).

This book is not concerned with the planets of astrology but with archetypes existing simultaneously within the "Divine Mind" and human consciousness. Consequently, we may disregard the remark on the flyleaf about the book revealing "knowledge and wisdom which has hitherto been obscured in the splitting of Astrology and Magick as different studies." In fact, the approach put forward is nothing new; the strong point of the book is that it is a concise guide to correspondences based ritual in one book. The correspondences constitute a major portion of the text, and include some items of interest, such as the attribution of the Greek Vowels to the Seven Planets, although no source is given for this attribution, which has evaded some capable qaballists. "The optimum time" to invoke the "planetary" archetypes, we are informed, is the planetary hour of the archetype in question, although we are also to consider the Season of the Year and the Moon's phase. The gap between "astral magic" and astrological magic is no narrower for this book than it was before. This division originates the conflict between the christian doctrine of free will and the astrological idea of predestination; "christian" magicians replaced the planets with angels whose place in the divine hierarchy "corresponded" to the planets, but involved no timing element. Instead, the "doctrine of signatures" was reinterpreted to indicate the handiwork of these angels in God's creation, leaving us with the anachronistic profusion of astrological symbols in occult books devoid of astrology, a situation which has lasted 500 years. Until the Equinox Volume VII in fact!

JAKE STRATTON-KENT

FIRE AND ICE, by S Edred Flowers. Llewellyn @ £8.95 (215pp).

If I say anything more about Llewellyn's books you will all think I'm a shareholder; but they do do some good books. "Fire and Ice" is a handy compendium of Fraternitas Saturni material. It includes some half a dozen rituals, with a pretty goetic feel to them - lots of sigils traced in the air accompanied by barbarous names, sex and blood sacrifice. Add a chunk of Luciferian Gnostic philosophy, some odd-ball astrosophical lore and some historical stuff about Crowley and Gregor Gregorius and you have it. It's rather an intriguing book, by the same author as the "Futhark" book on Rune Magic - the best I've seen on the subject, with its authentic Runic numerology and guide to the use of English as a "Ritual Language". Runes were part of the curriculum of the Saturni's so you may find the two go rather well together.

JAKE STRATTON-KENT

LIBER CYBER, by Charles Brewster. Personally published papers @ £7.00 (100pp).

Charlie has done his time as a founder member of Stoke Newington Sorcerers and its magickal childe the I.O.T., as well as in and out of Thelemic groups. If you thought Astrology was outside the brief of Chaos Magick then Charles is the guy to put you right. This book presents a series of his ever popular lectures, and a list of titles might whet the appetite of our more scientifically or theoretically inclined brethren and cistern: "So-Called Magic or Fraud or Bullshit - Does it Matter?"; "Paganism and Heresy in the Christian Era"; "History and Development of Secret Societies"; "Pythagorus and the Mathesis of Chaos"; "Chaos and Gaia"; "Chaos and Cosmos"; "Astrology - A Rational Chao/Dynamic Appraisal"; "Eclipses". Cover art by...RAG! As Charlie has been experimenting with timed rites since at least the early seventies (genesis period of the new A.'.A.'. and the I.O.T.) when the Tamworth group was developing its own modus operandi with astrological magick and E.'.Q.'., I recommend this book to all our readers. BUY IT!

JAKE STRATTON-KENT

I've discussed the small presses on the occult end of the market, where is the BIG U.K. press that will match LLewellyn and the other U.S. companies for quantity and quality of occult literature? The writers exist, but whereas the N.Z. and German authors are having a field day, the U.K. lot have a hell of a struggle, especially since the demise of Gerald Yorke and Israel Regardie, who used to give the up and coming types a hand up. I know there's a recession, but British publishers should realise that occultism thrives in such times (Theosophy, Spiritualism etc. during the Depression for example) and books are the cheapest form of entertainment after sex.

JAKE STRATTON-KENT

[That's enough Jake Stratton-Kent. Ed.]

THE DEMON KINGS AND THE LEMEGETON. By Jake Stratton-Kent. 1980.

The first part of the Lemegeton being the Goetia of Solomon the King is perhaps one of the most influential Grimoires of contemporary magickal practice. This notwithstanding, the technical instructions regarding its modus operandi are incomplete. The 72 Demons of the Goetia are said to be under the rulership of "the Four Great Kings ruling in the Four Quarters". The Lemegeton states that the various Demons are to be called through the authority of their respective Kings, and that the Triangle of Art is to face the direction to which both Demon and Infernal Monarch are attributed. But it is nowhere given in the text just which Demon is ruled by whom, or to which direction each Demon belongs, apart from a few references to individuals. We might suppose that the attribution of Zodiakal Signs to Elements and Directions furnished the answer (see 777), but from the occasional references to King and Subject in the text this method is seen to be invalid, e.g. Pisces is generally called a "Northern" Constellation in Astrology but the Piscean Demon Seere is "Under Amaymon, King of the East".

Crowley's 777 gives the attributions of the 72 Evil Spirits to the Diurnal and Nocturnal Decanates of the Zodiakal Signs. From this information and the Lemegeton's references to Bael, Agares, Vassago, Gaap and Seere, all of whom are said to be of the Eastern jurisdiction we have been able to reconstruct the original method of assigning Demons to Quarters and Kings. Bael, Agares and Vassago are Demons of Aries, Seere of the Constellation Pisces, Gaap of Aquarius. These three signs form a quarter of the Zodiakal cycle, and logically constitute the Eastern Quarter of the curious system of the Lemegeton. Thus the other constellations, working "backwards" from Aries are readily allocated to their respective Kings and the mystery of which King holds sway over whom is neatly solved. The following table shows at a glance the information completing the practical data of the Goetia and its method of evokation."

EAST - AMAYMON		SOUTH - GOAP		WEST - CORSON		NORTH - ZIMINIAR	
PHOENIX ♈	BAAL	CIMERIES ♑	FORNEUS	OSE ♎	MARAX	HAGENTI ♋	SITRI
HALPAS ♈	AGARES	ANDREALPHUS ♑	ASTAROTH	GOMORY ♎	PURSON	VUAL ♋	GUSOYN
MALPAS ♈	VASSAGO	HAUROS ♑	BERITH	OROBAS ♎	SALEOS	BIFRONS ♋	BUER
SEERE ♓	FURFUR	ANDRAS ♐	RONOVE	MURMUR ♍	BATHIN	VINE ♊	PAIMON
DANTALIAN ♓	MARCHOSIAS	VALAK ♐	BUNE	CAYM ♍	BOTIS	SHAX ♊	BARBATOS
ANDRAMALIUS ♓	STOLAS	ZAGAN ♐	GLASSYABOLAS	ALLOCER ♍	ZEPAR	SABNACKE ♊	AMON
AMDUSCIAS ♒	FORCAS	VAPULA ♏	CERBERUS	BALAAM ♌	ELIGOS	VEPAR ♉	VALEFOR
BELIAL ♒	ASMODEUS	ORIAS ♏	AYM	FURCAS ♌	ORAY	FOCALOR ♉	MARBAS
DECARABIA ♒	GAAP	AMY ♏	AYPEROS	PROCEL ♌	BELETH	RAUM ♉	GAMYGYN

Anyway, back to the book under review, Mandrake's "Goetia"; if you don't have one, get this one, if you have Laurence's get this one, if you have Shah's (Idries, not Eddie!) "Secret Lore of Magic", get this, if you have Priscilla Schwei's thingy GET THIS ONE! The Goetia system is well worth getting to grips with; and if you have been reading Hine, Sherwin and some of the old Order of the Cubic Stone material on the subject you ought to get back to sources before risking your sanity relying on any of them - however good they may be. My one-time mentor used to recommend invoking all 72 spirits in Via Combusta in order to de-bug your system - since he is regularly going for outings in his yacht with a sizeable harem you might consider it worthwhile having a bash.

Remembering Aleister Crowley by Kenneth Grant ISBN 1-871438-22-5 Skoob Books Publishing Ltd., Southampton Row, London. £25.00, 66pp. This is a well produced hardback, containing a lot of memorabilia including letters and photos from Grant's days as Crowley's amanuensis, which are described candidly in the commentary. Some fascinating glimpses into AC's interpretation of AL, as on pages 38/39 where Crowley writes "It is good that you have now become a "typhoid carrier" for the G.'.W.'. {Great Work}" which Grant glosses "I was disseminating Liber AL and Liber Oz wherever I happened to be". This of course refers to the "centres of pestilence" phrase in the Class A commentary on AL itself. In earlier days AC abused his authority to spite Leah Hirsig, ostracising her for breaking the "study of this book is forbidden" clause, which is so evidently a serpentine invitation to the Eves of the Thelemic Eden. Despite the surplus of Crowleyabilia on the bookshop shelves already and the high price of this book the juxtaposition of "Aossic" and "Therion" is likely to assure rapid sales and rewarding reads.

Jake Stratton-Kent

The Complete Golden Dawn System of Magic edited by Israel Regardie ISBN 0-941404-12-9 Weiser. £39.99. 1060pp. Hundreds of pages, and I mean hundreds, and weighing in at about two kilos this is a very major source work. It combines everything in the old "Golden Dawn" edition, in four, two or one volume depending what year you bought it, plus an amazing amount of additional material including additional mss. and alternative rituals from Waite's "Holy Order of the Golden Dawn". The occult revival in many ways started with Regardie producing the predecessor of this work way back when. This book contains enough material for the long overdue second wind. I should add that in my opinion the GD corpus gives a false appearance of completeness by its very size - there is much esoteric material, within the western tradition as well as outside it, that this book does not touch upon. That said there is an enormous amount of material that it contains within the mighty sweep of its angelic wings. Its great strength is its presentation of the correspondences of the Hebrew Qabalah in a manner appropriate to ritual magic. In this it is in the tradition of Agrippa and Pietro d'Abano - though considerably more contemporary in outlook and more colourful to boot. The Enochian material (deriving from the mss. of Dee but demonstrating in its new shape the energetic genius of Mathers) is something of an extra, and while ably synthesized with the other material there is still something unconvincing about the grafting of Enochian onto Hebrew. My advice to the student of occultism who does not possess the older version of this work is to grab this one, and gradually assimilate the knowledge lectures and from there the rest of the material. It will take time, but the work will be well worth it. If you possess a well stocked internal storehouse of qaballistic correspondences and have several years of ritual experience behind you then maybe you can do without! Whilst I do not entirely endorse the GD methodology that privilege is mine only after obtaining much of my experience and knowledge within their framework - it would be dishonest of me to say otherwise. The well is by no means dry even now.

Jake Stratton-Kent

Liber Aleph vel CXI - The Book of Wisdom or Folly by Aleister Crowley ISBN 0-87728-729-5 Weiser. £12.99. 220pp. Handsome new edition, with a text collated from three sources: the holograph manuscript in the Yorke Collection, a typescript from the Germer Accession of the O.T.O. Archives and the 1962 first edition. The Prolegomenon by Hymenaeus Beta deals with the history of the book, its connection with Frater Achad as Crowley's "Son", and some account of Crowley himself as its author. The design of the book including the typefaces, capitals &c. is also by HB, rather confirming the unofficial interpretation of OTO as "Order of Typesetting Operatives". A great deal of trouble has evidently been taken to present this book; the index has been completely revised and reshaped. Its new shape consists of three sub-indices, one general, one technical (references to qaballistic correspondences &c.) and one specifically dedicated to deal with the references to AL within the text of Aleph. Since many of our readers are perhaps familiar with this work, it suffices to say that this is the most complete and reliable edition to date, and the OTO are to be congratulated on doing their usual good job on presentation. Those readers who are not so familiar may need some brief account of the book's importance in the Crowley "canon". The book is a very controlled form of epistle; it deals with a variety of subjects related to Thelemic Magick, philosophy and psychology in a manner that is extremely concise. The majority of its chapters fit exactly on one side of a page, yet are wonderfully complete. The literary style is quaint at first glance, sounding like a thirteenth century arab sage addressing a favoured disciple, but this has great rhythm and power, and expresses perfectly the sanctity and depth of the feelings and experiences described. As such it is unquestionably one of the major Crowley writings - ranking in importance with "Book 4" and "Magick without Tears". With the latter book it bears some comparison, since Aleph is written as a "letter" to his Son, and MWT is a series of letters on various occult subjects to a disciple. But where MWT has a "personal" tone and deals with matters at some length on a straight-forward level Aleph deals with an equally wide range of ideas on a much more fundamental level, where intuition is as important as paying attention with one's whole intellectual apparatus on max. This is Crowley as almost a discarnate intelligence, shorn of his 19th/20th Century personality, addressing humanity as a whole, rather than people of particular backgrounds whom he had known during his life.

RL

Gold in the Crucible - Teresa of Avila and the Western Mystical Tradition by Deirdre Green ISBN1-85230-070-1 Element Books. £8.95. 215pp. This book was an adventure for me - by which I mean that unexpected and exciting things developed from the process of reading it. Firstly the picture drawn from Crowley and his contemporaries who were my only sources on the subject was widened and altered fundamentally. Crowley and others saw her visions and ecstasies as the result of supressed sexuality - and point to sexual or sensual images and language in her writings. The picture that emerges from this book by no means excludes her emotional life, or her close friendships with equally devout men. But this is by no means all: Teresa emerges as a heroic figure; at odds with the Inquisition, fighting for the Order of which she was head, and writing controversial and important spiritual guides. Writings which to her enemies may have bordered on the heretical - some indeed were circulated secretly during her lifetime - but which the scholarship of Ms. Green shows to be heavily influenced by concepts found within the qaballistic tradition. Here was the adventure for me: in Chapter Three; "'The Interior Castle' and Jewish Mysticism", there are extensive quotations from her works and from "Hekhalot" texts dealing with the Mysteries of the Chariot. The stories regarding the Jewish saints who explored these secrets had a potent effect on me twenty years ago when I first came across them in Graves' "White Goddess" - and here was a mystic - a **female** mystic - of the sixteenth century whose familiarity with them was as great as those saints. This adventure had been stalking me for a long time, and finally caught up with me in the biography of a christian nun. This book is very moving, and confronts issues of importance to all mystics and qaballists, male and female. It also led me, via the bibliography, to the next book in these reviews.

Jake Stratton-Kent

Meditation and Kabbalah by Aryeh Kaplan ISBN 0-87728-616-7 Weiser. $14.95/£11.95. 355pp. A friend laid a copy of this on me when he heard me raving about the Hekhalot - he got it from Temple Press, P.O. Box 227, Brighton, Sussex BN2 3GL, England - and so could you. I have been griping for years that the Qaballa is a desperately misunderstood subject. The G.D., Crowley et al only dealt with the dogmatic qaballa - and almost everybody outside certain select circles has done likewise ever since. Filing cabinet my eye! The Practical Kabbalah is far more than a few grubby recipes from the Sword of Moses, more even than the more polished rituals of Solomon or even the Hermetic Order of the Golden Dawn. This book shows quite what we have been missing. Herein are meditations and rituals which can make your hair stand on end, not with the grotesque gothic tripe of the Lovecraftian mythos (even mentioning them in this context is in questionable taste), but with awe and trembling such as Dee must have experienced in his dealings with the Angels. There are to be sure complexities and some obscurities with the material, due to the reverence and circumspection with which the authors approached their subject. But in this one book are whole slices of a tradition which few of us have suspected even existed. Previously unpublished manuscripts are here laid before us, and the whole subject is transformed before our very eyes, for those of us who have them.

Jake Stratton-Kent

Ω Ω Ω Ω Ω Ω Ω Ω Ω Ω

And now ..... foreign magazines - reviewed by your favourite reviewer and mine, Jaaaaaaayke Stratton-KENT!

Khoronzone Kids - the Journal of Reckless Alchemy. $4.00. Box 579 Station P, Toronto, Ontario M5S 2T1 CANADA. The latest issue I've seen is #3, and it is excellently produced by a fanatic called Lawrence Hobson, who also does some incredible sounds under the name Juicy Pillows (I've got tapes to prove it). Within are fevered rantings and original speculations regarding subjects ranging from traditonal qaballistic cosmology to Fortean phenomenon, mostly from his own overheating pen. Larry is rather uncritical of a certain English Thelemic Journal, even dare we say glowing in his approval. Unlike us he doesn't bitch about bad reviews, probably because he doesn't get them. People who get mildly castigated in his reviews have been known to defend themselves at great length, which is an indication that Larry, if not his victims, has something to say. And say it he does. In some cases he says it in very original ways, which is very rare nowadays, even er, original I guess. I advise all admirers of the cartoon genre to see at least one of Larry's strips - because you will never have seen anything quite like it, although at the same time there is something hauntingly familiar about them.....

Fenris Wolf. Edited by Carl Abrahamsson, Psychick Release PCP, PO Box 26067 A-10041 Stockholm, Sweden. As a complete incompetent it's only fair that I admit that Carl probably did tell me how much it costs but that was then and this is now, and I can only find my treasured copy of the magazine. I found it because I'd looked after it, and I looked after it not because I'm an anal retentive collector because I'm not - if you could only see the state of some of the stuff I haven't burnt yet you'd know! Why did I like it? several reasons, the subject matter is interesting, and it is well dealt with. Carl, we deduce, obviously has some contacts, "you know my methods" - a) he gets to interview Kenneth Anger in person, b) he doesn't write all, or even most of the material himself, but gets other interesting people to contribute from all over the world. The magazine has shifted to paperback format as he has found this is the format given most respect - astute guy. Not only does he have contacts he has brains and resources (important thing that, I've learnt the same lessons but don't have the same resources, think I'll be a Swede in my next life!) Who else do we have in here, flicks page, ah yes Lionel Snell, cogent as ever, and Carl himself, and Anton La Vey, and Genesis P Orridge, some curious photos by Carl's swedish colleagues I assume, Jack Stevenson with some newspaper material relating 15 "God told me to do it" cases and 18 fatal argument cases, then Tim O'Neill on the occult and performance art, Terence Sellers, Stein Jarving, one by NEMA I think, and more besides. Some of it is obviously more Gothic than I usually like, but it is more interesting than I usually find such material. All in all this is good material, well handled and of sufficient interest to occultdom at large to do well. Presuming some of us can forgo the odd gallon of lager that is!

Pamphlet Reviews; also by Jake Stratton-Kent [Who he? Ed.] [You, you fool! Ed.]

Bibliotecha Crowleyana. J.F.C. Fuller. Delectus Books 28pp £5.50/$10.00 inc. postage and packing. The price seems a bit steep. A facsimile (hip talk for photocopies?) of Capt. Fuller's post-infatuation catalogue when he placed his collection in auction, with a memorial essay by the good captain himself - also the author of The Star in the West and a decentish book on Qabalah. His main claim to fame for **practising** magicians is the authorship of the Class B portion of Treasure House of Images - now a decent cheap edition of that would be worth having (the Caliphate edition was mega-bucks, especially as you could do with three or so at any decent astrological rite!) Anyway this is okay for collectors, some interesting details of court cases &c. Available only from Delectus Books. 27 Old Gloucester Street. London. WC1N 3XX. Tel: 081 963 0979. Their catalogue has some interesting stuff, Occult, Gothic &c. I find the "cheap thrills" Gothic-Occultish crossover angle increasingly tedious - although certain JP's might disagree with me on this, but then I'm talking as an occultist! [Aha! I think there is a US edition too. Ed.]

The Lowly Turtle! Or TzB TzNVA'a. With a Consideration of Tzaddi in Liber AL I: 57. appended. by R.C. Enquiries to Pyramid Lodge O.T.O., P.O. Box 219, Buffalo N.Y. 14217. USA. I don't seem to have any price details on this either, still it's about the same size as the prior pamphlet in the same red card cover - but distinctly more esoteric in content. A consideration of qaballistic questions pertaining to the Hebrew Alphabet and AL. One such consideration concerns the final forms of the letters: apparently these are "new letters" historically, the "old letters" in AL on this hypothesis are the better known 22 letters. Some esoteric methods of attribution to paths and worlds of the Tree of Life, all very erudite and of interest to Thelemic Qaballists. Of particular significance to the generality of AL's readers is the info relating to the supposed letter Tzaddi in the Ms. of AL. Take a butcher's at the nearest facsimile of the Ms. and tell me if it was a Tzaddi in Crowley's mind when he started to write. This essay considers the problem of deciding whether it might be a Tzaddi, an Ayin or a Tzaddi final, and thus the question of "Tzaddi is not the star" &c.. Liber Trigrammaton is considered in relation to the Sephiroth, and various details pertaining to the deeper aspects of Hebrew Qabalah are dealt with. Heady stuff, and only 93 copies.

Chaos Servitors - A User Guide. Phil Hine. Pagan News/Chaos International Co-Production. 33pp. £3.00. This startlingly original pamphlet reveals never before published information on the utterly unknown subjects of sigil construction (not reprinted half a dozen times by Ray Sherwin not to mention Pete Carroll, Frater UD &c. &c. &c.) and banishing rituals (not first published in 1907). Other gems include indispensable directions showing how you can bring your Dungeons and Dragons figures to life as shambling monsters to perform your every whim. Hine can do better, as witness his Goetia article in NOX 6 - perhaps next time he'll write something for grown-ups.

The Equinox. Vol.III. No.10. Edited by Hymenaeus Beta X°. S. Weiser Inc. (distributed by Airlift, 26 Eden Grove, London N7). Photos and line drawings. ISBN 0-87728-719-8/ISSN 1050-2904. 209pp. £11.99 As the Editor of an "apocryphal Equinox" - in the quaint terminology of certain Caliphate bibliographers - it is appropriate and amusing to receive for review "The Equinox. Volume III. No. 10", which, being as it is somewhat more than a posthumous fulfilment of Crowley's intended publishing programme, might very well be considered "apocryphal" by those who are less assured of, or remain indifferent to, Caliphate claims to "orthodoxy". Since Crowley's death other numbers of this Volume have been issued by the Caliphate but were essentially part and parcel of Crowley's legacy, and thus entitled to claim canonical status, for what it is worth. This book, as we have said, does not possess the same degree of "historical inevitability"; according to "The" O.T.O. it is the last of Crowley's own, but it might equally be seen as the first of the Caliphate's. As such, Motta's "apocryphal" Volume V, and his rearguards Volume VII (of more recent vintage incidentally than our own VII) are no more "apocryphal" than theirs. Each must be examined on their merits alone - a task to which your humble reviewer will now apply himself.

The introduction insists on the value of "a balanced, wide ranging education [as] a prerequisite to complete initiation" in the course of extolling the literary merits of the Crowleyan Equinox, and by extension, theirs. However, for those of us who are not particularly interested in questionable poetry, who have only a passing interest in the cinematic work of Kenneth Anger, does this "Equinox" give we poor benighted mal-eduquées other evidence of this exalted status? Or is some brand of intellectual snobbery assumed along with the threadbare mantle of To Mega Therion?....There are ONE HELL OF A LOT OF O.T.O. BYLAWS in this book, many of which, furthermore, the editors concede are either inoperable, repealed or not yet in force; there are also accounts of their court cases with Motta. There is some valuable material to be sure - a goodly proportion of which is readily available in "Gems from the Equinox", and thus of course, in Volume I. Numbers 1 to 10, and Volume III. No. 1.I In this it is by no means unique: Crowley's own "Blue Equinox", the first of Vol. III. as this is - allegedly - the last, was extremely tedious in places, and the recent Motta diehards' Volume VII. No. 1 (Bloody Cheek!!) contained plenty of reprints, along with one or two original items - which this book does not, aside from the artistic material. There are also some previously unpublished Crowley items, which I shall come to later; but first, a question. What has this book got going for it - as the first Caliphate Equinox that is not a mere posthumous fulfilment of Crowley's intended publishing programme? What, in a word, do the Caliphate possess in their own right other than a collection of mss. and a membership list? The answer is, surprisingly enough, and I venture this only as my opinion: that they possess a certain dignity, occasional humility and a genuine reverence for the tradition which they have, in their eyes and others', inherited as a sacred trust. This is true, I aver, no matter how worldly and grubby some of us may find the court cases etc.. The Caliph in some of his pronouncements has on occasion ventured to honour Motta's achievements and strengths - and in this very book he makes clear there is no "party line", and recognises without apparent scruple that many of Grant's most enthusiastic readers are Caliphate members.

Okay, so I can live with the Caliphate, but how about this book? Some of the "previously unprinted Crowley" stuff is of dubious value, particularly the association of "Hermit, Lover and man of Earth" Grades with O.T.O. grades. Since the Caliphate make distinctions, correctly, between O.T.O. and A.'.A.'. grades (let us ignore the apparent similarity of say the V° and Minor Adept ceremonies, both inspired by Rosicrucian themes and comparable as such to the 18° of the Ancient and Accepted Rite of Scottish Freemasonry), and the A.'.A.'. Grades have Class A authority (Liber Tau et al) to substantiate the equivalence of the Three Orders of the Tree of Life Grade system with the Three Grades of the Book of the Law, there can be no equivalence between O.T.O. grades and the Three Grades of the Book of the Law. It matters not one whit to me that Crowley himself can be quoted to substantiate the O.T.O. position on this point - so Crowley could be wrong on Thelemic matters, what else is new?

As you may have guessed, I don't urge you to rush out and buy this book, but don't expect the Caliphate to crumble due to my reservations or anyone else's; they are built of sounder stuff than that, though as this book shows, papal infallibility is not part of the New Aeon equation.

Jake Stratton-Kent

Hecate's Fountain. Kenneth Grant. Skoob Books Pub. Ltd. £25.00. This promising young novelist has a fine grasp of the Gothic genre. He employs, for example, the traditional gambit of representing the text as the Journal of a central character. Naturally enough, this character's name is that of the author, but this cannot be really so, since the action (in a supposed magical "Lodge" called Nu Isis Lodge of the O.T.O.) is set in the late 50's and early 60's, about the time the real Ken was born I should think, because otherwise this would be a hack book by a sad old man. But let us suspend disbelief and assume the book is literally true. It shows the signs of having sat on a shelf for about 12 years before being spruced up for publication. Spruced up in this instance means "he" (i.e. the "cult leader" character) has added Starfire magazine and his own recently republished works to the otherwise rather dated bibliography. All things considered, the author could improve the realism of his alleged occultism by learning some astrology from his big brother Russell.

If you are seriously considering imitating the supposed magical techniques of this imaginative series, consider first these two admissions. 1) "Western women who possess the required traits are rare....Even in the East - modern conditions make it almost impossible to find women with the necessary aptitude...As it is we can but preserve the formula, confident that the present magical revival [sic. Ed.] will discover genuine priestesses to serve Our Mass." ("Aleister Crowley and the Hidden God" p. 64.) Okay, so he hasn't the secret of female initiation. 2) In "Hecate's Fountain", we discover that every Priestess he has managed to find was first violated astrally by a qlippothic entity and then killed in an "Elemental" accident. No wonder that Karl Germer (a real person incidentally) rejected the rituals of Nu-Isis Lodge as unsound!

Other works from the same author: The Magical Retrogression; Kenneth Grant and the Obvious Bogey; Fanclubs of the Murk; Downside of Croydon; Into the Grey Area.

Jake Stratton-Kent

The Magick of Thelema: a Handbook of the Rituals of Aleister Crowley. Lon Milo DuQuette. S. Weiser, Inc. ISBN 0-87728-778-3. 271pp. £12.99. Aha! With books like this coming out, the Caliphate's credibility will recover from the universal disappointment with "The Equinox. Vol.III. No.10." It is quite simply the best book we saw in 1993. Most Thelemic rituals are explained in detail, in a manner easy on the head as on the eye. Unpublished and published sources have been liberally consulted to elucidate such contentious puzzles as the inverted Pentagrams of The Mark of the Beast rite. Everything you need to know to perform these rituals is laid out for you here, with scholarship, humour and humility. Omitted, unfortunately, is Liber Pyramidos (personally I would have foregone the Gnostic Mass in its favour, but that's me folks, vide supra!), and the tantric element of the Bornless Rite goes un-noted, but these are trifling omissions in the face of so much excellent information and encouragement. The one bummer of the book is the photographic section on the gestures - could be he got the film back late or something, but some of these are palpably inaccurate, including the captions. Puer has the left hand on the thigh, should be the groin, Mulier the legs should be apart, Mater Triumphans is not Set Triumphant. Again, this is a small matter; one awaits more from this writer in future with interest.

Jake Stratton-Kent

Rhythmagik: Practical Uses of Number, Rhythm and Sound. Z'ev. Temple Press Ltd. ISBN 1-871744-40-7. 207 p.p. £10.95/$17.95. Z'ev, a performance artist/Qabalist, best known for trance-inducing metal percussion, has here attempted to lay out a system of sacred drumming and visualization based upon the Hebrew Qabalah. His essays take up a minute portion of the book, most of which consists of a large index of numbers and correspondences. The idea seems to be that the Qabalistic number is accompanied by an equal number of beats, omitting the zeros, and that the Qabalistically appropriate image be viewed. Although between the various conflicting correspondences and techniques, such as halfing the sum of Jupiter when retrograde, me thinks the Gods would be getting pretty confused when Z'ev starts drumming. The writing style is quite bare bones dry, rather like an essay on Ethnomusicology. If one actually went and built a drum and tried to use the method, it might be fun; otherwise as a resource work it is largely redundant, as the Sepher Sephirothic tables can be found in 777 and elsewhere. There is a problem communicating the core concepts of the system and in sparking the enthusiasm that the percussionist undoubtedly would feel/generate during performance.

BALOSOPHISTRA

Magical Alphabets. Nigel Pennick. S. Weiser, Inc. ISBN 0-87728-747-3. 244 p.p. £10.99. Contains basic information on the evolution and uses of Runes, Hebrew, Greek and Alchemical-Magical alphabets. I was rather disappointed by its easy level of research. Any book that reaches climax with examples such as J.R.R. Tolkien's "magical alphabets" and the trendy but fallow ciphers of inner city graffiti is missing it somewhat. I wanted to learn about the Phoenician alphabet, precursor to all European phonetic alphabets, as well as Greek, Hebrew, and Arabic. One would have supposed that the opening chapter should have exposed the fascinating Phoenix-like Phoenicians - but NO! What we get in Ch.1 instead is little more than re-heated Golden Dawn qabalah - despite existing archeological research. Much of the text is superficial and thoughtlessly edited. The chapter on magic squares contains such items of importance as the Qabalah of the author's name. The Inquisition were such hypocrites as to use a secret alphabet based upon Hebrew; the author here has done much better by writing an index of magical alphabets suitable for crossword puzzle and jumble enthusiasts!

BALOSOPHISTRA

FUTHARK. A Handbook of Rune Magic. Edred Thorsson. S. Weiser, Inc. ISBN 0-87728-548-9. 156PP. £7.99. I mentioned this book before when reviewing "Fire and Ice" - it is basically a compendium of most of the magical theory and practice connected with the Runes. The author is careful to point out that Runes are not to be treated as another set of qaballistic correspondences à la 777, but as the basis of another system entirely. I found myself much in sympathy with his approach, hey folks the supposed synthesis of the Golden Dawn has geographical limitations! May as well concede the so called Western Tradition is really the

Mediterranean Tradition. Thelema, on the other hand, is **not** synonymous with the Western Tradition, but can possibly benefit from the wave of Runic lore sweeping occultdom at large. Thorsson's books are sensible, insofar as occult books ever are, and informative. The roots of English as a magical tongue are to be found in Enochian and in Runic, consequently intelligent books on either subject are to be avidly welcomed.

Mister Ecumenical

RUNELORE. Edred Thorsson. S. Weiser Inc. ISBN 0-87728-677-1. 219pp. £8.99. "Runelore incorporates into a system of living philosophy and practice the latest and best **scientific** scholarship of runologists from all over the world. The method used in the present book is essentially one of intuition firmly based on **scientific** data." Thus speaks the preface of this book; the Acknowledgements follow and include a credit to Michael Aquino of the Temple of Set, an organisation with an interest in the German "Order Fraternitas Saturni" (Fire and Ice), and then we're into the introduction with a kind of Nietzchean pep talk about the failure of previous efforts to construct a "meta-langauge" (including Kabbalah and Sufism among the losers) which the Nordic Rune-Masters are going to accomplish by will and intellect. The scientific credentials are insisted upon several times in the first three pages. I was ready to slay by now if he slipped in the next three! But he didn't; he notes correctly that the word rune is as much Celtic as Teutonic, gets stuck into Proto-Indo-European etymology, brings in the Old Indic cultures, and presents thesis and counterthesis on the origin of the word rune which leave the Celts on level terms with the Teutons. So far, so good. Then more interesting history and artefactual studies, including some fascinating stuff on Old English Runes; apparently the oldest of the variant systems started out as 24, but very rapidly expanded to 26 in about the 6th Century. Well, I'm interested, even if you're not - this is well put together, no cheap runes for Glastafarians. All's well until he gets to the recent past. Here, of course, loonie theories abound, some with rather unwholesome pedigrees attached. Here, unfortunately, the author fails to do his thesis and counterthesis stuff convincingly, if at all. He simply says that Guido von List's unpublished book, "Armanismus und Kabbalah", was intended to show: "the kabbalah was actually Armanen [German runelore] wisdom that had been absorbed into Judeo-Christian thought and esoteric philosophy." There is a whole section on List with absolutely no critical reservations whatsoever! The Jews nicked the Kabbalah from the Germans and made it into a commentary on the Torah - I don't think so. Later on, while discussing the post-war period, he mentions getting excited by Trevor Ravenscroft's "Spear of Destiny", and remarks somewhat obliquely that he "set out to find the original texts on which its edifice was built. Later I found that many had been misused." Not the biggest pile of pseudo-historical nonsense this side of the Book of Mormon then? Just "misused" facts a bit. Then: "Intellectual studies had led me to the realization that in order to know the runes as they truly are, one must work with the ancient archetypal system as it truly was." This is good; at least he can see that runes have their own point of view, maybe we can get on....But not yet, first we revisit historical rune magic; well, okay, I've read Caesar's Gallic War too you know. Then more bits on poetry and codes, and on to Part Two, with a tabulation of the cosmic significance of each rune and some cosmology which seemed rather anthropological, hardly a "meta-language" superior to the Kabbalah. I began to suspect that Thorsson was a cranky old fascist who considered Runes superior to Kabbalah because Krauts are better than Yids. Runic numerology too seemed a little trite; then we were on to Runic psychology with Jung, I mean bloody Jungian archetypes again, come on mate, the whole revival has been there already, some of us have grown out of Jung, and you saved that till last? Well, not quite, next comes Big Daddy Odin, giants and dwarfs, good grief, and tables at the end that teach you to write and pronounce Old Norse. I mean, I like Vikings as much as the next man, but whoever said they had a Kabbalah for anyone to steal was off his chump!

Mister Angry

MEDITATION AND THE BIBLE. Aryeh Kaplan. S. Weiser Inc. ISBN 0-87738-617-5. 179 pp. £10.99. This book contains an excellent explanation of key Hebraic mystical concepts and practices in a manner most inoffensive, unless you get worried by impending messiahs. If only the Golden Dawn was as knowledgeable about the Hebrew Qabalah. For such as myself who has never had much success with the H.Q. it was a relief to read and finally understand these concepts. Kaplan drops some large hints: "...idolatrous and other occult practices often shed light on the prophetic methods." "One thing that we see clearly is that the forbidden idolatrous and occult practices very closely resembled the mystical practices of the philosophers." A muddy zone, to be sure, for who can tell whether someone is using occult practices for spiritual ends or religion with negative motivations? Such hidden practices were extremely occult, i.e., hidden. It is something just to learn that our Biblical ancestors had higher states of consciousness and a vocabulary to describe them.

BALOSOPHISTRA

Mystical Qabalah. Dion Fortune. S.Weiser, Inc. ISBN 0-87728-596-9. 309pp. £7.99. To say that this book is a classic is to state the obvious. As a breakdown of the Mathers/Crowley redaction of the Qabalah, it is unsurpassed, and despite one or two flaws (like her reference to the Lord's Prayer, where she atttributes "Power and Glory" to Hod & Netzach instead of Geburah and Gedulah/Chesed), the book carries substantial authority. It is a far more original effort than Mather's "Introduction" to "The Kabbalah Unveiled", which did not deal with G.'.D.'. style Qabalah. It is left then to Ms.Fortune to expound Mather's system for him. In her opening chapters, she goes to great lengths to place this system in context; her argument is essentially sound, if somewhat unfashionable. "It is not necessarily incumbent upon us to do certain things or hold certain ideas because the Rabbis **who lived before Christ** had certain views. The world has moved on since those days and **we are under a new dispensation."** [Editor's emphasis.] This new dispensation is, of course the Christian "Aeon". In this Ms.Fortune is utterly correct, historically speaking, whatever the readers views on Christianity. The "Western Tradition" is based on the "Christian Qabalah" of Pico della Mirandola et al, of which the G.'.D.'. system is a lineal descendant. To adhere to the pattern and plan of the G.'.D.'. or any other "Western" school is to work within the context of the Christian Dispensation. From here one must decide whether or no Thelema is "Western", and if so to determine what relation it bears to the Christian Dispensation. If Thelema has superseded Christianity (as Christ did Moses) then the New Dispensation is that of Aiwass and has a relationship with the Christian Qabalists similar to that of Fortune et al with the Hebrews. It is significant to note that Ms.Fortune omits a survey of the Paths from her book, a task she left - on his testimony - to W.G.Gray. He, of course, substituted English for Hebrew in his exposition, some details of which emerge in our next title for review.

Jake Stratton-Kent

Magical Ritual Methods. William G.Gray. S.Weiser, Inc. ISBN 0-87728-498-9. 301pp. £10.99. The late W.G.Gray was in every sense a Radical Traditionalist. His books deal with the ideas behind magick & religion without cluttering the landscape with outworn forms. This book is in many ways his greatest. As a former pupil of Dion Fortune, he had inherited an obligation to complete her work by dealing with the Paths, a subject dealt with here more than adequately: "Scholars of Hebrew have a perfectly good system of letter-attributions on the existent Tree of Life Plan, but such is not very helpful to those accustomed to thinking in English. On Inner levels...consciousness is not expressed by...'language' but by direct exchanges of energy...In this Outerworld we need a linkage system between pure consciousness & the conventional terminologies of our standardised speech & types of thinking. Hence the connection between Concepts, typified consciousness and...letters. Since our particular language is English, the letter attributions to the Tree-Plan will have to be an English instead of a Hebrew alphabet." This he proceeds to do in a manner unashamedly new, "synthetic" and purpose built. Whilst his scheme is eminently workable, the present writer of course prefers the "organic" system provided by E.'.Q.'.. This reservation apart, Grey's books are a very worthwhile study for the serious occultist, and this one in particular has many merits. The no-nonsense approach to the whole subject of ritual magick is infinitely more radical than any Chaos manual. Grey has been vilified posthumously as a racist; however, it would seem far more likely that he was a separatist in religion. He believed - like Dion Fortune, the G.'.D.'. and the Theosophical Society - in racial dharmas peculiar to distinct races, and thought black people were better off with their own traditions - and whites with theirs. This attitude is present in the above work by Fortune, but while she is the darling of the revival, Grey's works, often of a higher standard than hers, have been overlooked by the shallow herd. Grey's unfashionable and supposedly "old-fashioned" magick is that of the last of a generation of occultists whose accomplishments eclipse those of most moderns.

Jake Stratton-Kent

The Bahir. Translated, Introduced and with a Commentary by Aryeh Kaplan. S.Weiser Inc. ISBN 0-87728-618-3. 244pp. £10.99. The Bahir is almost certainly the first of the ancient Kabbalistic texts, older even than the Sepher Yetzirah. As such, it is a major source work for students of the Hebrew Kabbalah. These students must be very hardy fellows, since even the vowel points of the Torah are kabbalistically significant - a clear distinction from the "Christian" or G.'.D.'. redactions. The actual text, given here in translation and in Hebrew, is too complex to deal with in a review; the introduction and commentary, however, are perhaps of more general interest. Therein, Kaplan expounds some very important elements of Kabbalism with striking clarity, of which some at least are of great use in other contexts. For example: "The proper way to study any Kabbalistic text is to take it as a whole, using every part to explain every other one. The student must find threads of ideas running through the text, and follow them back and forth, until the full meaning is ascertained." This advice is extremely sound not only with such books as The Bahir but in the reading of AL as a Qaballistic Holy Book.

Tau Magnus

The Book of Black Magic. Arthur Edward Waite. S.Weiser, Inc. ISBN 0-87728-207-2. 326pp. £14.99. Waite has had somewhat of a bad press from Crowley & others, but has something to say regardless. In some respects, his reputation for wordy obscurity is well earned, but behind the black-letter lies an original thinker. Original, that is, in the modern sense, of having well developed but unfashionable views. Waite's estimation of the grimoires is shown in the preface: "It would be unbecoming in a professed transcendentalist to deny that there is a Magic which is behind Magic, or that the occult sanctuaries possess their secrets and mysteries; of these the written ceremonial is either a debased and scandalous travesty or a trivial and misconstrued application." And this: "It is permissible to bring forth from the obscurity of centuries a variety of processes which would be abominable if it could be supposed that they were to be seriously understood." This is well said in advance of a bumper compilation of medieval grimoires, including Honorius, the Grimoirium Verum & the Black Pullet among many others. There is much of wisdom & insight in Waite's observations, reducible to the statement that the grimoires are ludicrous and vile travesties of genuine Mysticism, the source of "real magic". However, the case is complicated by omission - the Hermetically inspired "Picatrix", with its sophisticated modus operandi, is not mentioned - and by simplification - the "Goetia", for example, shows signs of a concealed "Memory Theatre" M.O. which would imply a deeper meaning via the Shemhamphorasch etc.. Nevertheless Waite's thesis is essentially sound and worthy of study. A further point of consequence to our readers is his estimation of the Kabbalistic elements in the grimoires: "Ceremonial Magic which at a long distance draws from the Kabbalah, [only] reproduces its absurdities..." and "...an exaggerated importance [is] attributed to the processes in question on the ground of their exalted connections." With these sentiments I heartily concur.

This is essentially the same book as "The Book of Black Magic and of Pacts" and "Book of Ceremonial Magic".

Jake Stratton-Kent

Milton Keynes UK
Ingram Content Group UK Ltd.
UKHW051128040424
440588UK00001B/2